Studying the Media Se

General Editor: Tim O'Sull.

D0533745

Studying Radio

ΓON PEVERIL C⌐

SERIES EDITOR'S PREFACE

Although radio was the first truly *broadcast* medium to emerge and to make its mark in the homes of the twentieth century, it has received relatively little attention by comparison with cinema and television. In modern cultures and modern times, with the premium placed on sound *and* vision, if not interactivity, radio has tended to be regarded as an increasingly obsolete or anachronistic medium – the 'secondary', the 'blind' or 'background' medium; the 'Cinderella' of Media Studies.

In the face of such conventional wisdom, this book in fact provides evidence of the continued, perhaps confounding, resilience and relevance of radio in the early years of the twenty-first century and of its worldwide, local and domestic presence and significance as a public and private mediator *par excellence*. It also attests to the recent resurgence of interest in both radio's traditional and evolving place in modern cultural life.

Stephen Barnard has researched and written a timely and valuable volume for this series which responds to the need for an up-to-date, useful book on radio which is in touch with both historical and modern radio times and forms. The result is an impressive resource for media students and syllabuses; carefully organised, well illustrated, accessible and above all, written with an ear to the radio.

Tim O'Sullivan
January 2000

Studying Radio

STEPHEN BARNARD

A member of the Hodder Headline Group
LONDON
Co-published in the United States of America by
Oxford University Press Inc., New York

First published in Great Britain in 2000 by
Arnold, a member of the Hodder Headline Group,
338 Euston Road, London NW1 3BH

http://www.arnoldpublishers.com

Co-published in the United States of America by
Oxford University Press Inc.,
198 Madison Avenue, New York, NY10016

British Library Cataloguing in Publication Data
A catalogue record for this book is available from the British Library

Library of Congress Cataloguing-in-Publication Data
A catalog record for this book is available from the Library of Congress

ISBN 0 340 71965 6
ISBN 0 340 71966 4

1 2 3 4 5 6 7 8 9 10

Production Editor: Julie Delf
Production Controller: Priya Gohil
Cover Design: Mouse Mat Design

Typeset in 10 on 12.5 Sabon by Phoenix Photosetting, Chatham, Kent
Printed in Great Britain by JW Arrowsmith Ltd, Bristol.
Bound in Great Britain by MPG Books, Bodmin, Cornwall

What do you think about this book? Or any other Arnold title?
Please send your comments to feedback.arnold@hodder.co.uk

Contents

Acknowledgements

My thanks go to the many people who have assisted, either directly or indirectly, in the researching, writing and production of this book – not least Eril, my wife, son James and daughters Anna and Sara, who put up with such a lot during its two year gestation period. Particular thanks are due to Tim O'Sullivan for first suggesting the book and guiding me through the various stages from proposal to final draft; to Lesley Riddle, Julie Delf and the team at Arnold; to Liz Hornby and William Sims for their copy editing and proof reading input; and to Rachel Towner, who not only undertook some of the interviewing but brought an invaluable media student's perspective to the book. The enthusiasm with which managers at various radio stations across the country gave their time and opinions was much appreciated, especially John Ryan (CTFM), Stephen Mitchell (BBC News), Richard Park (Capital), Jerry Scott (Yorkshire Coast Radio), Tony Dodd (Radio Verulam) and the press office team at Heart 106.2. Anna Thomas at BBC Radio 4 was enormously helpful in providing the research graphs reproduced in Chapter 5. Finally, a warm note of thanks to Ingrid Bardua, PR/Promotions Manager at Essex Radio Group, who supplied excellent visual material – including some specially taken photographs – at almost a moment's notice.

The author and publisher wish to acknowledge the following for permission to use copyright material in the book:

BBC Broadcast for figures 2.6 and 2.7; Radio Times/BBC Worldwide Limited for figures 2.8, 6.1 and 11.1; Roger Baird and Marketing Week for figure 3.4; Ingrid Bardua and Essex Radio Group for figures 5.11, 10.1, 10.3, 12.1 and 12.5; Music Control UK for data reproduced in figure 7.2; Heart 106.2 FM for figures 10.2 and 12.6; Classic FM Magazine for figure 12.4; Atlantic 252 for figure 12.8; Kirsty Cockburn and BBC On Air Magazine (BBC World Service) for figures 14.1 and 14.2; Haymarket Business Publications Ltd./Campaign for figure 15.1.

Every effort has been made to trace copyright holders of material reproduced in this book. Any rights not acknowledged here will be acknowledged in subsequent editions if notice is given to the publisher.

Introduction

[Radio] is a composite of opposites: speaking to everyone abstractly and no one in particular; ubiquitous, but fading without a trace; forever crossing boundaries but with uncertain destination; capable of the most intimate communion and the most sudden destruction. Radio is a medium voiced by multiple personalities, perfect for pillow talk, useful as an anti-depressant, but also deployable as a guiding beam for missile systems.

Gregory Whitehead, *Out of the Dark*

How do you regard radio? As a portable pal, an ever-ready source of information and news, a means of blocking out boredom or melancholy, a means of keeping in touch with the world beyond the front door? More to the point, how do you *use* radio? Activity I.1 will help you focus on your use of the medium and assess how far your listening habits are tied to your daily routine, at which times you are most likely to have the radio on, and whether you would characterize your listening as concentrated (primary) or passive (secondary).

Thinking through one's own use of a mass communications medium such as radio is a good point of departure for a study of how the media operate and wield whatever power they have. Until you appreciate your own viewing, listening or reading habits, trying to understand the habits and predilections of audiences – and the way the media perceive their audiences, respond to, adapt to, and cater for them – is almost impossible. In any discussion of broadcasting media, it can be very easy to neglect the role of the individual listener, viewer or consumer. Some classic analyses of broadcasting assume a paralysing impact on viewers and listeners, or at best a pacifying effect, as if listeners and viewers are robbed of the process of discriminating or thinking for themselves by the very act of switching on a TV set or turning a radio dial. It is undeniably true that the media, *all* media, re-present the world to us, selecting and drawing from it, often sensationalizing and trivializing. But the fact is that listeners *do* make choices, that no two people's listening patterns are exactly the same, that the individual's tastes and interests are not always (if ever) dictated by fashion or fad.

In media as in life, individual choices – what music to listen to, what food to eat on a particular day, what programmes to watch, what friends to make contact with – do not always make rational sense. They may be dictated by experience, whim or mood, but they nevertheless inform our lives and reflect on the way we like to see the outside world re-presented to us. In short, we bring part of ourselves to the way we experience, regard and use all media. Radio's characteristic accessibility and intimacy – its presence in private or solitary moments, its subtle incursion into parts of our lives that other media do not reach – give this 'composite of opposites' a very particular and fascinating role to play in the life of each listener.

THE UNIVERSAL MEDIUM

For most of us, life without radio is difficult to imagine. Of all the major mass communications media, radio is perhaps the most ubiquitous and most easily available. It's also the hardest from which to escape. Unless you stay at home with the radio switched off, negotiating a normal day without hearing the radio in shops, workplace, passing cars, restaurants or places of leisure is close to unachievable. Even supermarkets and football clubs 'broadcast' information, music and advertising to customers and spectators in a manner that imitates the formats, conventions and language of radio.

Another sign of radio's omnipresence is the way its output accompanies human activity round the clock. The portability and small size of radio sets enables listening in bedroom, bathroom, kitchen and beyond the home. The car radio, once a luxury addition to motor vehicles, is now a universal feature of vehicle production in virtually every country in the world, and in-car listening accounts for over 25 per cent of all radio listening in Britain alone. The cheapness of radio sets is such that most households in western countries own several.

Radio's universality is demonstrated in other ways. In mid 1999, there were 257 radio stations – local, regional and national – operating within Britain, and the list grows by the month. And these are just the officially sanctioned stations, either run by the BBC or operating under licence from the Radio Authority. There are also innumerable 'pirate' stations, broadcasting illegally in mainly urban areas; hospital radio stations and student-run stations affiliated to universities and colleges; stations broadcasting to Britain from other countries and from offshore sites; and stations available only through cable, satellite or the Internet. Collectively, radio stations offer widely differing services to different audiences, from pop music to 24-hour news, from round-the-clock traffic reports to programming aimed at ethnic minorities or listeners with particular musical tastes. The political impetus behind the legislation that created many of these stations – the Broadcasting Act of 1990 – was to encourage radio to develop a new universality, both as a matter of public policy (radio being seen to be serving the whole community, including minorities of taste and ethnic background) and as a boost to commercial expansion (widening the choice of the radio consumer). A similar impetus lies behind the drive for digital radio, which, when fully operational, will further expand the number of radio stations available to listeners.

RADIO AND MEDIA STUDIES

Radio, then, is a universal soundtrack to life at the start of the 21st century, punctuating, enlivening and infiltrating the lives of its listeners, and offering a regular flow of information and entertainment. What makes radio the particular kind of mass medium that it is – in broad terms, what characterizes its output and the context in which it operates – is the main concern of *Studying Radio*. The book is an attempt to draw together many of the strands of interest in relation to radio – programming, ownership, regulation, audiences and so on – and provide an introduction to the medium as a subject for serious academic study. It is neither a complete history of the medium nor a fully comprehensive analysis of each of these relevant strands; it should, however, give the student of radio a grounding in the basics of the subject and some direction about how to pursue it further.

Radio has been a neglected field within Media Studies over the years, but there is a growing literature. Academic approaches to radio have drawn on many disciplines – cultural studies, linguistic analysis, political and economic history, sociology, psychology, business studies and marketing, even literary criticism – and this multi-disciplinary approach is echoed in *Studying Radio*, both in the way the book is structured and in the design of activities that pull the various themes together in a practical way.

The five main parts of the book look at the medium from specific perspectives, which are interrelated. Part One considers the current institutions of radio, their historical roots and their grounding in particular philosophies of broadcasting: broadcasting as a public service (a term that, as we will see, is rife with dilemmas and shifting meaning), as a commercially supported (and owned) enterprise, and as an expression of community solidarity or support. All such philosophies carry preconceptions, regarding audiences as either passive assimilators or potential participators, and the function of audience in programming and policy-making is explored in Part Two, together with the especially problematic question of just how listeners do use the medium and how that usage can be assessed both quantitatively and qualitatively.

In Parts Three and Four, the focus turns to the specifics of programming – the preponderance of particular programme forms (music radio, for example) and the editorial processes at work in each, and the placing and timing of programming within the broad context of day-to-day programme provision. The emphasis here is on the ultimate 'meaning' of radio programming and particularly the way in which it represents its consumers – in other words, the ideology that radio articulates (consciously or otherwise) through its content; through the style and manner in which programmes are broadcast; and through the extension of that sense of style, personality or attitude to the branding of radio stations.

Finally, in Part Five, *Studying Radio* looks beyond radio's customary parochialism to consider the global implications of the changes brought (or about to be brought) by new technology. If one of the persistent themes of radio history – and this book – is the medium's adherence to a safety blanket of traditionalism, what kind of challenges do the Internet and digital broadcasting pose? Can we expect a mere adaptation of programming to fit new means of dissemination, or something more fundamental, a basic redefinition of broadcasting as something much more intimate and enabling?

PRACTICE AND INVOLVEMENT

Studying Radio is neither a guide to radio practice and technique nor a manual: there are several excellent texts available which cover this ground, with a view to encouraging a basic level of production competence and developing technical experience (see the section on technical and training guides in the Bibliography). However, in studying any subject theory and practice go hand in hand, with practical work giving students an opportunity to test out, reinforce or even contradict what is taught. Practical exercises can help the student to develop his or her own skills of expression, analysis and creativity and the activities in this book have the further function of encouraging the reader towards a practical understanding of the programming and policy questions explored in the text. 'Gatekeeping', for example, is a process (at the heart of all media) that can be informed by all manner of professional conventions, behaviours, expectations and assumptions regarding the medium's audience: only when students take on a 'professional' editorial role – that is, making selections on content and style according to an objectively defined policy – do the nuances, ambivalences and dilemmas of the process come to the surface. A number of the activities are designed as experiments in gatekeeping to help demonstrate this point from different perspectives.

The activities have another function: to encourage the student towards a personal viewpoint on the issues raised and the particular subjects covered. The media student of the early 21st century will have spent his or her childhood and/or teens living through one of the most intense periods of change in the history of mass media. The perspective of personal experience each reader brings to the study of radio will not only illuminate and clarify the subject, but will also serve as a reminder that the power of radio stems from its ability to touch lives in small and sometimes very ordinary ways.

Activity I.1

Keep a diary of your own listening habits over a seven-day period, listing all stations that you tune to and the amount of time spent tuned in to each. Differentiate between those programmes that provide you with background music or talk and those that you make an active attempt to listen to. Are your listening needs different at particular times of day? How typical do you think you are of those of similar age and social background?

Activity I.2

List the changes in your listening habits since you were a child and the circumstances that prompted them. Note particularly the time in your life at which you started finding your own programmes to listen to, and assess the times and moments when radio had the most value and meaning for you.

Part One

Institutions and Systems

There are many possible points of entry to the study of radio. We could begin with the *content* of the programmes themselves, whether considered individually or as part of a daily sequence; with the *institutions*, stations or individuals producing those programmes, and an analysis of the processes and perspectives that shape them; or with the *audience* itself and the way that radio content is received and the environment in which it is heard.

In this book, the starting point is the history of the radio medium and the organizations, companies and regulatory bodies that have shaped it and continue to shape it. There are two main reasons for this. First, the message/content of radio broadcasting (and the manner or style in which that content is broadcast) is filtered through a whole battery of editorial conventions, listener expectations, external pressures and internal institutional priorities invariably related to who owns, funds or controls the means of media production. All help determine the 'message' of radio in both its specific and more general, ideological sense.

Second, radio's history *is* overwhelmingly the story of institutions. The technological development of radio as a mass communications medium has been overseen, directed and at times stifled by institutions. In Britain, the BBC came into being with a fairly well-defined perspective of who and what the medium should be for, and those considerations have informed its development ever since. Since the subsequent introduction of commercially funded radio, the medium's history has been the story of managed change – influenced by external factors, certainly, and not least by changing listening patterns and a changing media context, yet still regulated and determined by established institutional cores (BBC management, the Independent Broadcasting Authority and its successor the Radio Authority, and the government). This was the case even during the deregulatory years of the 1990s. Out of the BBC's paternalism sprang a huge investment in cultural production – orchestral performance, drama, light entertainment – which still provides the basis of its claim on the licence fee. When commercial radio was introduced in Britain, it was informed by many of the paternalistic traditions of public service established by the BBC, while pay scales and copyright fees were for a long time disproportionately based on what the BBC itself paid.

While the style, manner and nature of what we hear on the radio are not wholly determined by institutional considerations, those considerations are the bases for radio output. Studying radio content means exploring, at the outset, what these are and where they came from. And this means looking not only at the institutions as distinct functional bodies – stations, networks, corporations, commercial companies – but as embodiments of broadcasting philosophies as old as radio broadcasting itself.

1

Chronology and Themes

So much relating to radio's content, organisation, structure of ownership and relationship with its audience is a matter of precedent and tradition. Many of the contemporary radio industry's conventions, practices, perceptions of its audience and assumptions about consumption have their antecedents in the pre-World War Two era. But, as Michele Hilmes suggests in *Radio Voices*, the history of radio is neither a neat chronology of finely weighed programming decisions leading seamlessly from one era to another, nor the story of technological developments alone. Rather, it is the story of how broadcasting institutions have negotiated around and through periods of volatile social and cultural change by a process of re-presentation and incorporation.

The timelines on pages 19–28 give a sense of the chronology, but it is useful to consider the history of radio as a mass medium by studying the creation and evolution of institutional and regulatory *structures*; the development of production cultures within those institutions, in which contexts programmes were created and new forms of programming were evolved; and in the context of *social history* – how the medium responded to the growth and contraction of the radio audience, and who precisely that audience represented.

BEGINNINGS

The first question to consider is how technological developments have been utilized and exploited (and by whom and to what end) at different points. The late-19th-century pioneers of radio (the 'wireless') saw it not as a mass medium but as a means of one-to-one communication – this at the same time that the telephone was being developed as a quasi-broadcasting medium capable of relaying information and entertainment from one central point to a multiplicity of reception points. The early history of radio was partly that of a battle between the two technologies for application and acceptance, and of their adoption by particular commercial, military and political interests.

One of the advantages of the telephone was assumed to be that it could bring 'programmes' of entertainment direct into the home: public demonstrations of the telephone during the 1870s stressed how music or lectures could be received down the wire from distant places. But the potential went unfulfilled, partly because of problems with the quality of reproduction, mostly because the cost of sustaining such services was prohibitive for the level of public interest. Meanwhile, wireless technology – so called because it sent messages (initially codes but eventually the human voice and music) via radio waves – was developed in disparate forms in different countries. It eventually superseded wired telegraphy – which used Morse code – as the principal means of sending messages from one place to another.

Wireless technology underwent intensive development in the period up to World War One not because of consumer interest (though there was a growing body of amateur wireless enthusiasts and a nascent industry in wireless equipment for domestic purposes) but because of commercial and government-sponsored military involvement. Marconi's Wireless Telephone and Signal Company Ltd manufactured and leased transmitters and receivers to merchant fleets. At a time of growing international tension, the ability of radio waves to cross thousands of miles alerted the British government to a new means of maintaining and defending links with its colonial territories.

It was after the war, with military co-option of the airwaves relaxed in 1919, that consumer interest began to build, centred mainly on amateur operators. In the US, an employee of the Marconi Company named David Sarnoff was the first to conceptualize a mass-produced radio receiver – what he called a 'radio music box' – that would have a place in the home alongside the phonograph and the telephone. This was a crucial leap of imagination, taking wireless beyond the world of the amateur and into the realm of mass availability. It was also marketed cheaply, as a household utility (Sarnoff's own words) rather than an expensive novelty.

It was a limitation of the technology – the scarcity of spectrum – that gave governments and, in the US, increasingly powerful commercial concerns a reason for institutionalizing the radio medium. That the wireless medium should attract government involvement in Britain was inevitable, as telegraphy and the telephone were already controlled by the Post Office, a self-financing branch of the state under nominal royal patronage, that charged users for carriage of letters. The telegraph (or 'wire') was seen as an extension of the letter, and the telephone message as an extension of the telegraph, so there was logic in keeping wireless broadcasting in the control of the Postmaster-General, under procedures established by successive Acts of Parliament. In the US, governmental involvement was minimal and concentrated mainly on ensuring that operating companies did not offend anti-trust legislation.

INSTITUTIONALIZING RADIO

In spite of the proliferation of amateur operators, it was the equipment manufacturers who were best placed to establish broadcasting services, and in both the UK and the US they saw their future in some kind of institutionalized monopoly. In Britain, competing manufacturers were encouraged, with the tacit approval of the Postmaster-General, to form what was in effect a cartel, a British Broadcasting Company, to offer a service of national coverage centred on London and eight specified regional centres. In the US, attempts after the war by the country's leading wireless manufacturers, cable providers and electrical companies to create a monopoly of station ownership through merger led directly to the creation of the Radio Corporation of America (RCA), which incorporated the American division of the Marconi Company and which in time led to the setting up of America's first national network, the National Broadcasting Company (NBC) in 1926. The amateur sector was pushed out of the equation by intense lobbying by RCA, on the grounds that (echoing the BBC in Britain) only culturally 'responsible' institutions could be trusted with such a powerful medium. In both countries, the aim was to create a broadcasting system that would encourage a rapid expansion in sales of radio sets, and there were debates in both territories about the most appropriate means of funding the services themselves. General Electric, for example, at one point favoured the adoption of a tax or levy on radio sales which was not so far from what was adopted in Britain in the form of the licence fee.

Government stood back from taking much of a role in the establishment of broadcasting in the US. The Republican administration, sympathetic to the corporate business culture (indeed, funded by it) and to an 'honest broker' approach to settling trading conflicts, did not act until 1927, when the Federal Radio Commission was created to reassign wavelengths and end years of chaos on the airwaves. It had no censorial role: its real power lay in removing licences, and then only at renewal time. The FRC's main impact was to cement the pattern of radio station ownership and takeover that had by then become established – a pattern increasingly dominated by operators with designs on national coverage. The chaos in American radio at the start of the 1920s, meanwhile, convinced British manufacturers and politicians of the need to avoid the American experience.

Intimately connected with the issue of funding was the question of control – control and management of a scarce resource (wavelength capacity), the physical establishment of a broadcasting infrastructure (transmitters, studios, relay stations), the selection and supervision of broadcasting content – and, in each case, the question of who should do the controlling. There were no ready-made solutions, especially while the BBC remained a private company operating under government licence. As the BBC's first Director-General, John Reith, put it, there were 'no precedents to cite, no stores of wisdom to be tapped, no experienced staff to hand' (Reith, p. 99). The Company's appointees, led by Reith, to some extent followed their noses, making the broad assumption that the audience shared their tastes, basing programmes on traditional English middle-class entertainment forms. Gradually the *ad hoc* nature of programmes gave way to careful planning, simultaneous programming between regional stations, and increasing centralization of output and policy-making from the BBC's London base, so that by 1925 Reith was setting out his own blueprint for the Company's reinvention, by Royal

Charter, as the British Broadcasting Corporation. Under this banner, and guided by a well-articulated vision of broadcasting's cultural importance, Reith sought to harness what he described as 'the brute force of monopoly' for the public good.

With government funding by tax or licence ruled out, stations in America found their own means of raising money through sponsorship of programmes by individual companies such as hotel chains, restaurants or food manufacturers, or by 'toll broadcasting', the renting of airtime to advertisers.

Out of these two institutional responses to technological change grew the principles, priorities and mechanics of public service radio on the one hand and commercial radio on the other. Both systems enabled mass ownership of the means of *reception* while limiting access to the means of *dissemination*. In turn, this enabled an intense concentration and centralization of cultural production within the institutions and, in the US, a quick diminution of local control via network-diffused programme syndication and aggressive purchasing policies.

VERSIONS OF CULTURE

The contribution of these nationally based radio institutions to the creation of a national culture – that is, re-presenting a 'nation' to itself in a coherent, unifying form – is unquestionable, but the great issue pursued by radio historians like Scannell and Cardiff in Britain and Hilmes in the US is precisely how and to what effect this national 'picture' was shaped, pursued and legitimized. Hilmes, for example, finds a core undercurrent in American broadcasting history that historians and commentators have long ignored – the consistent representation of racial, ethnic and gender difference according to a pre-assumed yet constantly renegotiated hierarchy of social groups (Hilmes, ch. 3 *passim*).

This is not to say that, in either Britain or the US, the radio institutions remained aloof from social or cultural tensions or rigidly imposed their own rules upon their representation. The major programming changes of the World War Two years and after, and the reworking of radio as a medium once another technology (television) became shaped for mass consumption, were attempts at accommodating profound changes within the social structure. For all the apparent rigidity of control, and its policing by means of 'professionally' driven gatekeeping cultures in commissioning and production, radio ultimately survived as a medium by keeping pace with its audience and creating in its programming – through music and comedy as much as political discussion – some temporary resolution to the anxieties and dilemmas prompted by change itself.

The growth of the post-war consumer culture not only fuelled television's expansion at the expense of radio listening, it altered the economics of leisure and fanned demand for goods and services from newly buoyant sections of the marketplace, notably young people. This was apparent by the late 1940s in the

US, but took longer to take effect in Britain because of the delay in emerging from post-war austerity. The BBC's perceived success at uniting and speaking for the country during the war, coupled with the fixed level of finances that this helped secure, led to a certain amount of laurel-sitting and a continuing preoccupation with making programmes with a domestic, insular stance. This was most evident in protectionist entertainment policies explicitly framed to combat the 'Americanization' of British culture. How to protect the nation's youth in particular from the effects of supposed American economic and cultural imperialism was a preoccupation not just of the BBC but of both right- and left-wing opinion formers throughout the 1950s. Behind all this lay a sense of national economic inferiority exacerbated by Britain's dependence on American finance for post-war reconstruction and a feeling that Britain's cultural 'superiority' over the US was under threat.

BBC radio had long produced programmes for adolescents, but the emergence of rock'n'roll as a distinct form of teen-oriented music in the mid 1950s represented a particular challenge. Part of its response was to encourage interest in the more 'acceptable', 'authentic' and less commercially tainted American folk music. In programmes like *Saturday Skiffle Club* on the Light Programme and *Six Five Special* on television, the BBC gave prominence to 'skiffle' music as a style (basically American folk songs played to makeshift guitar and washboard accompaniment) and actively encouraged teenagers to form their own skiffle groups. This flowering of music-making was the genesis of the beat music boom of the early to mid 1960s, during which ex-skifflers, having switched to electric guitars when the relaxation of hire purchase restrictions brought them within reach, began taking American rock'n'roll styles as their models. BBC radio was therefore an often uncredited and quite unthinking contributor to Britain's creative supremacy in global pop music, which began with the Beatles. (This was a far more important role than that played by Radio Luxembourg, which embraced the teenage audience wholeheartedly but gave over most of its English-language airtime to programmes created and paid for by British record companies.)

The 1950s tends to be portrayed as the era in which American radio went over to rock'n'roll, but the switch was not wholesale. Improvements in recording technology, the introduction of the long-playing stereo record and the steady introduction of FM favoured not the relative aural crudity of rock'n'roll but the orchestral mood music albums of Mantovani and others. There was also intense debate within the radio industry regarding whether the professional and cultural standards of radio were threatened by rock; as in the 1920s, race was at the heart of much of it, specifically the presence of black artists on white radio stations and the emergence of white singers (most influentially, Elvis Presley) who sang in an explicitly black style. The subsequent development of rock'n'roll as a recording style and as a form of radio output was a process of accommodation and dilution, with radio stations switching to pop music formats that utilized and promoted record company products that in themselves crystallized the more 'acceptable' or traditional strands of the music – the simple dance rhythms, lyrics centring around high-school culture, wholesome boy-next-door performers. Many pop music historians claim that rock'n'roll was already 'tamed' (and certainly de-ethnicized) by the time the Top 40 format had become dominant in American radio.

CONTRACTION AND REPOSITIONING

The newly emerging forms of radio from the 1950s onwards represented a confluence of different influences and effects. Loss of investment, advertising and sponsorship to television – and the crucial switch to television of the family-based night-time audience – radically altered ownership patterns in American radio, encouraged the kind of specialization in output and audience-targeting that led to rock'n'roll radio, and focused attention on more cost-effective formats such as Top 40, which used inexpensive material (commercially available records) as the primary station resource.

BBC radio attempted to adapt to the loss of evening audiences to television through major programming revisions in 1957 and again in 1964, but its increasing accommodation of pop music from 1964 onwards was not enough to ward off the appeal of non-stop, Top 40-formatted music from a clutch of pirate radio stations operating from the North Sea. Although their coverage was mostly restricted to the Midlands and south east of England, the pirates had a high enough profile to warrant legislation and the dusting down of one of the Light Programme's frequencies, 247 metres, for a part-time BBC pop music service. The inauguration of Radio 1 and the renaming of the other networks in September 1967 had the air of a radio revolution but was essentially cosmetic. The real impact of the pirates lay in the shaping of a strong pro-commercial radio lobby in Britain and in the BBC's seizure of the opportunity to create a fledgling system of local radio. In programming terms, the pirates' legacy was to focus the daytime output of Radios 1 and 2 on music, and to move both networks away from the production of programmes on a discrete basis towards stripped programming – records and speech in two- or three-hour sequences. This was the basis on which the new commercial stations developed their programming – an adaptation of American Top 40 radio for a local but (in age terms) homogenous market, by the circuitous route of pirate radio and the BBC.

The other main driver for change in radio from the 1950s onwards was mass marketing of new technology. On a hardware level, transistorization took radio out of the domestic environment into the worlds of leisure and work. In transmission technology, FM (frequency modulation) came into its own in the US from the mid 50s onwards, when a new context was found for the waveband as a vehicle for specialized programming and subsequently as a superior audio medium for music. The new dualism of AM (amplitude modulation) and FM created massive new expansion opportunities and encouraged investors and entrepreneurs back into the medium. In Britain, where it was originally known as VHF (very high frequency), the development of FM as a separate waveband gave the BBC the means by which to launch an entirely new stream of local radio programming without impacting on frequencies allocated to its existing services.

One of the lessons of media history, however, is that technology *in itself* rarely drives change, nor does consumer demand for new means of technically superior dissemination. The driver is the level of commitment to technological change on the part of radio's institutions and their paymasters – a level usually determined by political, commercial or economic considerations. In spite of its obviously superior technical quality to AM, FM's development in the US was put back years because of the attitude of RCA, to whom its progenitor Edwin Armstrong was contracted; he committed suicide after a protracted legal case which, if he had won, would have enabled him to take his work elsewhere. Just as it took enforcement measures by the Federal Communications Commisson (the reconstituted FRC) to drive FM's expansion in the US, Britain's regulator, the Independent Broadcasting Authority (IBA), kick-started commercial radio's half-hearted embrace of FM in the late 1980s by insisting that franchisers provide separate services on AM and FM. The BBC, instructed to free Radio 1's AM service for national commercial radio, moved all its networks to FM only in the late 80s (though Radio 4 did retain a Long Wave outlet). This required a major publicity effort to promote FM's virtues over those of AM. A similar process was started by the BBC in late 1998 to prepare viewers and listeners for digital TV and radio.

The emergence of digital as a new technical means of broadcasting is tied in with a new era of 'convergence' in communications – literally, the potential converging of personal and mass communications means (telephone, computing, broadcasting) under a single system. In historical terms, a clear line can be traced of political and economic change that both facilitated the move to convergence and altered the ecology of broadcasting in almost all the world's major radio markets. The marker for this change in Britain was set down during the Thatcher administration (1979–1990), in the liberalization of the broadcasting market through a process of deregulation.

■ DEREGULATION AND SOCIAL CHANGE

Timeline III on pages 26–28 lists the key staging posts in the deregulation process, including the 1990 Broadcasting Act which created the Radio Authority and precipitated a massive expansion in commercial radio, locally and regionally. But there were other aspects to it, including the increasing politicization of the BBC at governor level: by making appointments on a political basis, the government broke with the principle of consensual management and began a process of reshaping the Corporation into a leaner, more commercially minded and pragmatic organization. The production of BBC programmes was opened up to independents, weakening the collective power of trade unions at the BBC, and the role of each network reassessed according to its fit with the rest of the radio marketplace.

The overriding point is that the philosophical basis under which radio was institutionalized in the 1920s – the paternalistic notion of a service provided by an appointed class of professionals, to appeal to an assumed consensus of taste and interest – was undermined in the pursuit of a quasi free-market model. This was neither wholesale nor unchallenged, and neither were the panoply of paternalistic assumptions and regulations that informed both BBC programming and that of the commercial stations (which were set up on an ITV-modelled basis) thrown overboard overnight; the deregulatory process has itself been a *negotiated* process, with the existing institutions manoeuvring according to the shifting political climate. The economic reality of radio's low share of national advertising in comparison to other media and an acceptance that localities would be unlikely to be able to support directly competing services led to expansion of the commercial radio sector on a schedule as tightly managed and as politically sensitive as anything that the IBA had effected.

Timelines take no account of the changing audience – either how changes in attitudes or simple demographics impact upon programming and even regulatory decisions, or how the audience's uses and perception of the medium change over time. Neither can they fully reflect the circumstances through which community radio, for example, emerged as a viable broadcasting precept (and a working alternative to the BBC/commercial radio duopoly) in the 1970s. Paralleling the breakdown in broadcasting consensus that the Thatcher years catalysed came an increasing social fragmentation, a questioning of established social attitudes, and a rising sense of divorcement from the political centre.

Technology's contribution to this sense of isolation has been a paradoxical one, giving us quicker, clearer, cheaper and more accessible means of communication with other people (mobile phone, fax, e-mail) while simultaneously reducing the need for actual human contact. Radio embodies a similar paradox in its biggest generic growth area of the post-1970s period, the phone-in, which – like chat groups on the Internet – encourages a free-flow of opinion and conversation within the safety of an artificially created community. Music and talk radio, like other forms of technologically generated entertainment such as video, CD-ROM and computer games, have flourished partly because of their cocooning effect in offering access to a community of sorts while maintaining the listener's sense of preferred isolation.

In the 1950s, radio seemed a victim of changing lifestyles – a casualty of a television-led consumer culture. The medium survived by becoming more audience-aware, to the point of offering listeners a neatly packaged soundtrack running parallel to their own lives. Over 40 years on, in a much more competitive media environment, patterns of usage – not to mention cultural preferences – have again changed. The increase in the number of women working part-time or full-time, rising unemployment and increased leisure time have challenged (though not eradicated) the common radio perception of the daytime audience as housebound and female. Work schedules are no longer necessarily nine-to-five; the availability of other media makes it less vital to tune in for items like news bulletins at fixed times; the switch from commuting by train or bus to car gives more opportunity for radio listening (and also participation: mobile phones have prompted a startling increase in the number of people contacting talk shows from their cars). More people live alone than ever before: could increasing divorce rates and greater instability in relationships contribute to the popularity of solitary media such as radio and the Internet? Historically, radio's ability to survive in a competitive media environment has always depended on how well broadcasters tap into social, cultural and technological change – but within political and regulatory constraints that are both surprisingly stable and subject to sudden transformation.

Further Reading

Barnouw, Erik (1968): *Tube of Plenty: The Evolution of American Television.* Oxford University Press.

Briggs, Asa (1965–79): *The History of Broadcasting in the United Kingdom*, vols 1–5. Oxford University Press.

Briggs, Susan (1981): *Those Radio Times.* Weidenfeld & Nicolson.

Crisell, Andrew (1997): *An Introductory History of British Broadcasting.* Routledge.

Hilmes, Michele (1997): *Radio Voices: American Broadcasting, 1922–1952.* University of Minnesota Press.

MacDonald, J. Fred (1979): *Don't Touch That Dial! Radio Programming in American Life from 1920 to 1960.* Nelson-Hall.

Reith, J.C.W. (1949): *Into the Wind.* Hodder & Stoughton.

Scannell, Paddy, and Cardiff, David (1991): *A Social History of British Broadcasting*, vol. 1. Blackwell.

Waller, Judith C. (1946): *Radio – The Fifth Estate.* Houghton Mifflin.

Activity 1.1

Using the relevant texts listed at the end of this chapter, research the 'pre-history' of radio during the late 19th and early 20th centuries, with particular emphasis on how the key technological developments were advanced (and by which interests) in the US and Britain. Account for the telephone's development as a medium of one-to-one communication, while radio developed as a medium for broadcasting to the mass.

Activity 1.2

From your own research, prepare a timeline covering the period 1870–1930 to detail the history of radio in a country other than Britain or the US. Assess which sectors were of most importance – commerce, government, wireless manufacturers, the military, the public at large – in determining how the broadcasting institutions in your chosen territory took shape.

Activity 1.3

In their study *On Air* (Arnold, 1997), Shingler and Wieringa stress the importance of the 'vision' of particular individuals in shaping radio broadcasting. From your reading about radio in the 1920s, summarize the achievements of John Reith in Britain and David Sarnoff in the US and assess how different the development of broadcasting in each country might have been without them. Do they deserve a status as 'visionaries'?

Activity 1.4

Draw on discussion and interviews with parents, grandparents and older acquaintances to build a picture of what listening to the radio was like during the 1930s, 40s or 50s. In your conversations, concentrate particularly on your interviewees' recall of particular entertainment programmes and news events, and radio's place in daily life. To which radio network or station did they listen most often, and why? How was their pattern of listening changed by the acquisition of a television set, and in what way would they characterize the differences between radio programming in the past and today? How did their home life as a whole change with the advent of television?

Activity 1.5

A common view of pop music history is that American radio 'tamed' rock'n'roll by promoting records that de-emphasised its basic raucousness and salaciousness. Investigate the history of pop music over the last 25 years or so for comparable instances of how rebellious or disruptive musical styles became part of the mainstream – for example, punk rock in the 70s or rap or dance in the 90s. How much was this incorporation into the mainstream a direct result of radio's support or otherwise of the emerging form, and how did the music itself change in response to the requirements of radio? Was the reaction of radio stations uniform, and did established radio institutions and independent stations differ in their attitude to the new music?

Fig. 1.1   Radio timeline I: Establishment and expansion, 1880–1944

YEAR	TECHNOLOGICAL DEVELOPMENTS	WORLD EVENTS	UK RADIO	PROGRAMMING (programme titles in italics)	US RADIO
1887	Rudolf Hertz (Germany) transmits electro-magnetic waves.				
1894	Guglielmo Marconi (Italy) experiments with transmitting Morse code via Hertzian waves.				
1897	Marconi patents wireless telegraphy in UK and sets up Wireless Signal and Telegraph Company.				
1899					Marconi sets up Wireless Company of America.
1901	Marconi receives first transatlantic wireless signal. Reginald Fessenden (US) superimposes voice over radio waves.				
1902					Fessenden forms National Electric Signalling Company.

Fig. 1.1 *continued*

YEAR	TECHNOLOGICAL DEVELOPMENTS	WORLD EVENTS	UK RADIO	PROGRAMMING (programme titles in italics	US RADIO
1904			Postmaster-General takes over control of wireless telegraphy.		
1906	Lee De Forest (US) patents 'Audion' vacuum tube.				Fessenden makes ground-breaking broadcast heard over several hundred miles.
1910					De Forest broadcasts Enrico Caruso live for New York's Metropolitan Opera House.
1912		Titanic disaster: rescue operation aided by Marconi-led wireless telegraphy.			Radio Law gives Department of Commerce with responsibility for issuing licences and wavelengths.
1917		US enters World War One.		First US university station, 9XM (Wisconsin), on air.	Marconi's US arm taken over by US military. Amateur broadcasters banned from the airwaves for duration of war.
1919					Radio stations returned to former owners. American Marconi, General Electric, Western Electric and American Telegraph and Telephone Company (AT&T) merge to form Radio Corporation of America.
1920			Marconi Company begins broadcasts from Writtle (Essex) headquarters. Broadcast by Dame Nellie Melba (July) sparks interest.		America's first radio station, KDKA, launched by Westinghouse Electric and Manufacturing Company.

Fig. 1.1 *continued*

YEAR	TECHNOLOGICAL DEVELOPMENTS	WORLD EVENTS	UK RADIO ·	PROGRAMMING (programme titles in italics)	US RADIO
1922			10 shilling licence introduced. British Broadcasting Company founded on merger of major wireless manufacturers.		Westinghouse joins RCA. AT&T establish first station funded by on-air advertising.
1923			*Radio Times* first published. Sykes Committee inquiry rejects advertising as funding for BBC.	First complete BBC drama broadcast: *Twelfth Night*. BBC begins broadcasts for schools.	
1925			Crawford Committee confirms BBC's position as monopoly broadcaster, funded by licence fees.		
1926		General Strike, UK.	International Broadcasting Union produces Geneva Plan, reducing BBC's allocation of wavelengths.		RCA takes over toll stations owned by AT&T and forms twin-network National Broadcasting Company (NBC).
1927			British Broadcasting Corporation started under Royal Charter.	BBC takes over Henry Wood Promenade Concerts. BBC outside broadcast 'firsts' include commentaries on rugby, football, Grand National, Boat Race and Trooping the Colour.	Radio Act creates the Federal Radio Commission (FRC). Columbia Broadcasting System (CBS) launches.
1928			Ban lifted on broadcasting of controversial material.	*Daily Service*. First BBC Dance Orchestra broadcast.	
1929	Regional broadcasting in UK begins with opening of Brookmans Park transmitter.				

Fig. 1.1 *continued*

YEAR	TECHNOLOGICAL DEVELOPMENTS	WORLD EVENTS	UK RADIO	PROGRAMMING (programme titles in italics)	US RADIO
1930				BBC begins own news service. Regional broadcasting officially begins (March).	
1931			Radio Normandie opens.	First broadcast by BBC Symphony Orchestra.	
1932	First experimental TV broadcasts by BBC.		BBC Empire Service launched (December), forerunner of the World Service. Broadcasting House opens.	First Christmas Day message by reigning monarch, George V.	
1933	Edwin Armstrong (US) demonstrates frequency modulation (FM).			Debut of *Scrapbook* series. *In Town Tonight.*	
1934			Radio Luxembourg begins broadcasting commercially sponsored English-language programmes to UK.	Royal Wedding ceremony broadcast for first time.	Mutual Broadcasting Company becomes fourth national network. FRC reconstituted as Federal Communications Commission (FCC).
1936	BBC inaugurates world's first television service.	Abdication crisis, UK.	Ullswater Committee.	BBC Listener Research division formed.	
1937			BBC's Charter renewed for ten years. Reith resigns. Welsh Region inaugurated.	Coronation of George VI broadcast live on national and Empire Services.	Live commentary on *Hindenburg* disaster.
1938		Munich crisis.	BBC begins first foreign language services.		*The War of the Worlds.*
1940		German *blitzkrieg* across Europe.	Forces Programme begins.	J.B. Priestley's *Postscripts.* *Music While You Work* begins.	
1941		Russia and US enter World War Two.		*Workers' Playtime, Sincerely Yours, Brains Trust.*	

Fig. 1.1 *continued*

YEAR	TECHNOLOGICAL DEVELOPMENTS	WORLD EVENTS	UK RADIO	PROGRAMMING (programme titles in italics)	US RADIO
1942					Voice of America launched.
1943			General Overseas Service supersedes Overseas Forces Programme.	*Saturday Night Theatre.*	American Forces Network established. NBC forced to sell one of its two networks. NBC Blue becomes American Broadcasting Company (ABC).
1944		Allied invasion of Europe.	General Forces Programme begins.	Government instructs BBC to introduce 14-day delay between debates in Parliament and their coverage on radio (the '14-day rule'). *War Report.*	

Fig. 1.2 Radio timelime II: Contraction and repositioning, 1945–78

YEAR	TECHNOLOGICAL DEVELOPMENTS	WORLD EVENTS	UK RADIO	PROGRAMMING	US RADIO
1945		World War Two ends. UK General Election: Labour landslide.	BBC Home Service and Light Programme introduced.	*Family Favourites.*	FCC reserves 20 channels exclusively for non-commercial FM broadcasting.
1946			BBC Television resumes. Third Programme launched (September).	*Housewives Choice, Have A Go, Letter From America, Woman's Hour, Down Your Way, Dick Barton.*	
1947			BBC Royal Charter renewed for five years.	*Much Binding In The Marsh, Twenty Questions.*	
1948		Berlin airlift.			

Fig. 1.2 *continued*

YEAR	TECHNOLOGICAL DEVELOPMENTS	WORLD EVENTS	UK RADIO	PROGRAMMING	US RADIO
1949					Pacifica Foundation starts KPFA, California, as first station run by non-profit-making group. 'Top 40' format introduced.
1950			Beveridge Committee.	*Listen With Mother.*	
1951				*The Archers, The Goon Show.*	
1952	Stockholm agreement on use of VHF (FM) in Europe.		Fourth BBC Charter.		
1953		Coronation of Queen Elizabeth II.		*Journey Into Space.*	Voice of America brought under control of US Information Agency.
1954				*Under Milk Wood, Hancock's Half Hour, Children's Favourites.*	
1955	First BBC VHF service opened.		BBC's broadcasting monopoly broken by launch of commercially driven Independent Television (ITV).	*Pick Of The Pops, From Our Own Correspondent.*	
1956		Suez Crisis. Soviet intervention in Hungary.			
1957			Suspension of 14-day rule.	*Today, Saturday Club.*	
1959					Congressional inquiry into payment for airplay ('payola') in US radio.
1960			Pye Ltd publish Plan for Local Broadcasting, suggesting commercial radio on local basis.	*Nine o'clock News* ended.	

Fig. 1.2 *continued*

YEAR	TECHNOLOGICAL DEVELOPMENTS	WORLD EVENTS	UK RADIO	PROGRAMMING	US RADIO
1962		Cuban Missile Crisis.	Pilkington Committee report published, supporting BBC plan for 250 stations.		
1963		Assassination of President Kennedy.	Northern Ireland Home Service launched.		
1964			BBC 2 TV launched. Radio Caroline begins broadcasting to UK from North Sea.	*Children's Hour* ends.	FCC instructs stations to provide distinct programming on AM and FM frequencies.
1965		Vietnam War escalates.		*The World At One.*	
1967			Outlawing of broadcasting from offshore. BBC Radio restructured as Radios 1, 2, 3 and 4. BBC local radio launched on VHF with Radio Leicester.	Radio 1 launched as a national pop music service.	Corporation for Public Broadcasting formed.
1969		Moon landing.	Publication of *Broadcasting in the Seventies* by BBC.		
1970		Conservative government elected, UK.		*The World Tonight.*	National Public Radio (NPR) formed by CPB.
1972			Sound Broadcasting Act on statute book, making commercial radio possible on local basis under Independent Broadcasting Authority (IBA).	*I'm Sorry I Haven't A Clue.*	
1973		Israel–Egypt six-day war.	LBC is first Independent Local Radio station in UK.		

Fig. 1.2 *continued*

YEAR	TECHNOLOGICAL DEVELOPMENTS	WORLD EVENTS	UK RADIO	PROGRAMMING	US RADIO
1974		Minority Labour government elected, UK.	Second wave of BBC local stations given government go-ahead.		
1977			COMCOM group formed. Annan Committee reports, recommending local radio transfer to Local Broadcasting Authority.		
1978	FM listening surpasses that of AM in US.		BBC Radio Wales launched.	Broadcasting of Parliament begins.	FCC refuses to license stations at less than 100 watts.

Fig. 1.3 Radio Timeline III: Deregulation and convergence, 1979–99

YEAR	TECHNOLOGICAL DEVELOPMENTS	WORLD EVENTS	UK RADIO	PROGRAMMING	US RADIO
1979		Election of Conservative Thatcher government, UK.	BBC Radio Cymru launched.	Radio 2 becomes first BBC network to go 24-hour.	
1980		Election of Ronald Reagan as President.			
1981			Citizen's Band radio legalized, UK. BBC Charter renewed until 1996.	*In the Psychiatrist's Chair.*	
1983			Community Radio Association formed. Channel 4 Television opens.		
1984			Increased land-based piracy prompts anti-piracy action by government.		

Fig. 1.3 *continued*

YEAR	TECHNOLOGICAL DEVELOPMENTS	WORLD EVENTS	UK RADIO	PROGRAMMING	US RADIO
1986			Experiment in community radio aborted. Peacock Committee. IBA encourages ILR stations to provide separate services on AM and FM.		
1989		Fall of communist governments in Eastern Europe.	Atlantic 252 launched.		
1990			A new Broadcasting Act disbands IBA and creates Radio Authority and Independent Television Commission. BBC launches Radio 5 – first new national network since 1967.		Local Marketing Agreements (LMAs) introduced for simulcasting of programming, prompting new wave of syndication.
1991		Gulf War. Collapse of Soviet Union.	Radio Luxembourg closes. Radio 4 provides temporary war information service on FM.		
1992			Classic FM is first national commercial station in UK.		
1994			'Producer choice' underway at BBC. Radio 5 relaunched as Radio 5 Live.		International Broadcasting Bureau created.
1995	BBC begins development of digital services.		Talk Radio launched. Radio 1 repositioned.	Total audiences for commercial radio exceed those for BBC radio for first time.	

Fig. 1.3 *continued*

YEAR	TECHNOLOGICAL DEVELOPMENTS	WORLD EVENTS	UK RADIO	PROGRAMMING	US RADIO
1996			A further Broadcasting Act introduces auctioning of TV franchises. BBC restructures into five directorates and combines radio news and TV news.		Telecommunications Act.
1998			First digital multiplex licence awarded to Digital One consortium.		
1999		NATO–Yugoslavian conflict.	Applications invited for digital radio service for London.		FCC considers licensing microradio stations.

2

Public Service Radio

Histories of the radio medium often refer to the BBC as the first great working example of the 'public service model' in broadcasting. This can be misleading, as it implies a conscious attempt to create a blueprint for others to follow, and suggests that in structure and programming the concept was fully conceived. In fact, 'public service' is an elusive concept – one that, as Lewis and Booth point out in *The Invisible Medium*, has been continually redefined throughout the BBC's history to suit the political climate of the time.

John Reith, who as first Director-General of the BBC is credited with defining the philosophical basis of public service broadcasting, set out four underlying principles in his book *Broadcast Over Britain* (1924) – a *public service motive*, equivalent to that guiding the Civil Service; a sense of *moral obligation*; *assured finance* from public sources; and *monopoly of operation*. The latter two were enabling devices, to ensure that the BBC would have the time and resources to expand, free of commercial pressures. Only as the BBC developed and its programming took on a momentum of its own did 'public service' become synonymous with non-profit-making, universal availability, centralized control and cultural enhancement. These notions were rooted in the paternalistic perception of the public as being capable of development rather than an audience to be exploited or pandered to.

Serving the public meant giving listeners programming deemed to have cultural, intellectual or educational merit; it meant setting cultural priorities (what the BBC should concern itself with in the public interest, and what it should not) and policing them according to standards laid down by the policy committees; it meant adhering to an assumed consensus of attitudes that reflected the basically middle-class values of the ruling elite. Like public education and basic health care, the BBC was a form of dispensed public service, provided to do good to a passive and unquestioning public. This meant entering areas in which government itself had the primary role, such as education. The BBC began broadcasting to schools as early as 1923; by 1927, it was working with the Workers' Educational Association to provide programmes of adult education.

What made the BBC unique was its status as a national broadcasting service *distanced* from the machinery of the state – and the extraordinary trust placed

by the government in those appointed to run it. The BBC's means of income –
not a direct tax but an annual payment for use of a receiver, which the Post
Office collected on the BBC's behalf – embodied the arm's-length relationship
of state and broadcaster. Almost alone in Europe, the BBC was conceived with
virtually no political direction informing its programming or internal
structure. It was Reith who masterminded the BBC's evolution from a
commercial company into a Corporation operating under Royal Charter and
created the architecture of control – overseen by a Board of Governors
appointed by the government – which is still largely in place nearly 80 years
later. The Governors' role was to act as a collective guardian of the airwaves
on behalf of the nation. Over the years, Conservative and Labour governments
adhered to the principle of making appointments to reflect the prime aspects of
the political, social and cultural life of Britain, from peers of the realm to trade
union leaders – though that consensual spirit has come under serious pressure
since the 1980s.

ORIGINS OF PUBLIC SERVICE RADIO

There was nothing new about a public corporation run by a board answerable
to Parliament, nor about royal patronage of an institution: the Royal Academy
and the Royal College of Music offered precedents. The notion of public
service was ingrained into national life through the tradition of *noblesse
oblige*, the centrality of public school, regiment, church and Civil Service
within British upper-class life, and the programmes of building works that
transformed the centres of Birmingham, Manchester, Cardiff and other cities.
Devotion to public service in the cause of one nation – drawing together all
classes in a common national goal – was at the philosophical heart of the post-
Disraeli Conservative party. If all were to some extent under threat in the
1920s, Reith's great skill was to shape the BBC's constitution in the nostalgic
self-image of the country itself *and* in a way that embraced modernity,
technological progress and a commitment to culture and literacy.

A 'public service' ethos of broadcasting was a product of the social and
political environment of the 1920s. Newspapers had wider national
distribution than ever before, provision of welfare, education and libraries was
improving, together with general standards of literacy. Rising phonograph
sales illustrated a growing demand for music in both classical and popular
forms, the relative merits of which were debated long and hard in publications
such as *Melody Maker* at the very time the BBC was coming into being.
Concerns about the disintegration of culture in the face of socialism, mass
enfranchisement, creeping Americanization (especially the cinema) and
consumerism were matched by fears – articulated in the novels of H.G. Wells
and Aldous Huxley – of a new cultural barbarism and political breakdown.
World War One left a particular imprint, offering recent memories of the
power of the press to manipulate public opinion by confusing news with
propaganda. How could the new medium – the awesome novelty of which was

that the same message could be received *simultaneously* by the masses – be protected from becoming a propaganda vehicle?

Unlike newspapers, which theoretically any company or individual could produce in any volume or variety, radio was a limited resource. Controlling who had access to the limited wavelengths and on what terms demanded a particular kind of responsibility: 'broadcasting began as an advanced technology of mass communication but with a series of doubts hanging over it concerning the manner of entertainment and education of a mass society; all the uncertainties were made the responsibility of a single organisation' (Smith, pp. 59–60).

CULTURAL PRODUCTION

The security of fixed finance enabled the BBC to transform itself quickly from a *relayer* of information, education and entertainment into a *producer* of all three. From a dependence on external sources for programme content, the BBC used its financial clout to form new relationships with key parties in the entertainment industry – copyright owners, trade unions (notably the Musicians Union), West End theatres and variety agencies – and in areas such as music and drama, the departments concerned moved rapidly to a position of near-complete self-sufficiency in production. It was the BBC's proactive role in cultural production that cemented its pre-eminence at all levels of British life and culture from the 1930s onward, its mission characterized by a commitment to excellence in the arts, a dedication to intellectual betterment of the mass audience, and a sense of moral leadership.

With self-sufficiency came a growing bureaucracy of organization which fed from and perpetuated a kind of high-minded self-confidence, exemplified in policy diktats and the prioritization of resources for cultural projects. At times, the BBC appeared to be assuming responsibility for cultural excellence in areas to which other, more established institutions laid claim – the creation of a symphony orchestra, for example, creaming off the best talents from existing British orchestras. The purpose was to improve standards of musical performance, but, as Paddy Scannell has pointed out, the BBC's policies on the arts and on music in particular were riddled with contradictions and conflicts from the start. Having set out with the stated aim of educating the mass audience in musical appreciation – what the then controller Basil Nicolls called 'the great missionary element of broadcasting' – policy became so sidetracked that, by the mid 1930s, the Music Department was using its vast resources to cater for one particular section of musically well-versed listeners (Scannell, pp. 243–60).

DEFINING PUBLIC SERVICE

Throughout its long history, the BBC's version of public service has been articulated within political and financial restraints imposed by government.

Under the BBC's constitution, the government can set, distribute and limit the proportion of the licence fee that the BBC receives; it also has the ultimate sanction of discontinuing the BBC. The parameters of this relationship have been tested at various points in BBC history – notably during the General Strike of 1926, when Reith stage-managed the BBC's reporting of events to suit the government position (acting 'responsibly', as he put it) in order to secure the BBC's subsequent independence from government control.

The major preoccupation of BBC Governors and management has always been that the Corporation should be seen to consistently deliver on matters of coverage, cost and quality – especially at times of charter renewal and periodic committees of inquiry (there were seven between 1923 and 1986) into how the BBC is run and whether alternative methods of funding are appropriate. Coverage means 'the universal right to the signal' – every licence holder's right to receive the full range of BBC services; cost traditionally meant keeping within budget, though in recent years it has come to encompass cost-effectiveness in terms of delivering audience satisfaction and a general leanness of organization; quality was once thought to be self-explanatory but has, as the BBC has expanded, become the most contentious area of all. Which areas of programming the BBC should concern itself with, how resources are allocated to these designated areas of programming, how responsive the BBC should be to the tastes and demands of the audience – these are basic cultural dilemmas that the BBC has grappled with for over seven decades, and which the weight of precedent and tradition makes no less complex.

The core dilemma lies in the phrase 'serving the public'. For Reith and his policy committees, this meant providing the public with access to excellence and knowledge and finding the right strategies to do so. It also meant defining what exactly constituted excellence – selecting certain musics for broadcasting over others, categorizing content according to its educational value or its entertainment value and framing it accordingly, and in practice generally siding with the views of the existing cultural elite (indeed, the respective policy committees were drawn from these elites). The problem for the BBC in the 1930s was how to maintain this basically elitist approach while its audience was not only growing but also reflecting a broader social profile and showing a marked preference (especially on Sundays, when dance music and variety disappeared from the BBC schedule) for the light, populist fare of Radio Luxembourg. How could the BBC justify its level of funding if large sections of the public were so obviously not satisfied?

The coming of war crystallized the issue and prompted a shift in definition. The creation of an entertainment-based Forces Programme alongside the National Programme gave the BBC the opportunity to pull in both directions, massively boosting its variety and dance music output on the one hand while maintaining its cultural commitments on the other. Paradoxically, the wartime necessity to speak to and for the whole community of classes, regions and tastes – to *unify* – led immediately after the war to a programming strategy based on a kind of cultural apartheid, with the Forces becoming the Light Programme, the National revamped slightly as the Home

Service, and the Third Programme launching as an exclusively arts- and music-based network, aimed unequivocally at a minority highbrow audience. The BBC was now a public utility that consciously tried to cater for the available audience, but this was to be achieved by separating the highbrow from the popular, the light from the serious, the relaxing from the challenging. Again, this was a source of much debate within the BBC and in political circles: was the BBC simply acknowledging the reality of listener preferences, or was it absolving itself of its original public service aim of educating the listener out of the fripperies of escapism – of leading taste rather than following it?

Right through a post-war era in which attention switched to television and the BBC reorganized its priorities accordingly, this generic model of broadcasting – catering for separate listenerships with different expectations and tastes by distinct channels or networks – proved enormously resilient. The introduction of Radio 1 as a pop service and, later, Radio 5 Live as a news and sport station were extensions of the model – both allowing BBC radio to expand into new modes of broadcasting and focus on increasingly fragmenting audiences without impacting on the existing services. The one curiosity – though on paper it represented 'public service' at grass-roots level and as such seemed a natural development for the BBC to undertake – was local radio, which the BBC entered in 1967. Its early difficulties hinted at larger problems to come: it was politically unloved, funding was minimal, stations were scattered and local awareness poor, programming was limited to a few hours each day, reception was initially on VHF only, and 'needle-time' restrictions on playing commercial records forced reliance on phone-ins and recordings from the BBC library. The BBC's perception of public service broadcasting as something provided *for* a listening community – dispensed to it by a team sent from head office – flew in the face of the experience of local radio abroad, where local broadcasting generally meant communities talking to themselves and a major level of community involvement. By the time BBC local radio did begin to establish itself, commercial radio at local level had been introduced and the BBC's hegemony across radio was disrupted forever.

FROM COMPETITION TO COMPLEMENTARITY

Local radio was criticized as another example of BBC empire-building, but the reality was that, by the 1970s, the BBC was already in contraction and having to evaluate once again the scope of its activities and its purpose as a publicly funded body. Competition from ITV from the mid 1950s onwards refocused the BBC's television service towards providing audience-winning entertainment: the pursuit of ratings for their own sake became a political necessity in order to justify the level of funding (subsidization, in effect) for programmes which were not necessarily audience grabbers yet continued the BBC commitment to education, culture and the arts. Competition from commercial radio – and progressive deregulation of the commercial sector, which freed it of many of the BBC-like public service obligations originally placed upon it – brought the same pressures to bear on BBC radio.

The difference was that the generic pattern of BBC networks laid bare the contradictions and anomalies behind the 'ratings and reputation' arguments that were made on the BBC's behalf. When, for instance, there were complaints that the BBC had no business spending licence payers' money on a network for a music of purely popular rather than cultural value – pop music – the BBC could point to the popularity of Radio 1 and the comparative cheapness of its operation as justification in itself. On a straight comparison of running costs, Radio 1 has, since its inception, been by far the least expensive and most cost-effective BBC network in terms of cost-per-listener (see Figure 2.1). Yet as audience figures declined as more commercial operators arrived, the argument changed: what made Radio 1 distinctive was *precisely* its basis in the public service ethos of cultural production – its encouragement of new music, which commercial radio was neither equipped for nor interested in undertaking – together with its centring on the youth audience via social issue campaigns (drugs, AIDS awareness, unemployment) that commercial radio ignored. In other words, the justification for Radio 1's continuance was surprisingly close to the arguments for Radio 3, that here was a service of unparalleled value to the country's cultural welfare, which – if it were to be abandoned – could not be recreated elsewhere. (Radio 3's running costs are so high because they include the major part of the BBC's investment in orchestras and events such as the annual Promenade concerts.)

To some, this was a rewriting of history. Radio 1 had started as a pop music network *per se*, not as a youth station; at its mid-80s peak, its audience

Network	Cost (£m)	Cost per hour (£k)*	% share BBC radio listening	% share all radio listening
Radio 1	38	2.7	21.9	10.6
Radio 2	43	3.4	27.0	13.1
Radio 3	63	5.2	2.6	1.3
Radio 4	90	10.2	21.6	10.5
Radio 5 Live	54	5.3	7.3	3.6
Regional and local**	148	5.3	19.3	9.3
Total	436	32.1	100.0	48.4

* programming costs only – does not include administration costs
** includes Radio Scotland, Radio Wales, Radio Cymru, Radio Ulster

Sources: BBC Annual Report, 1997–98; RAJAR Sept–Dec 1998

Fig. 2.1 Comparative running costs, BBC radio, 1997–98

BBC radio listening: price to listener per hour	2.5p
BBC television viewing: price to viewer per hour	5.5p

Source: BBC Annual Report, 1997–98

Fig. 2.2 Television/radio price comparison

Television	1345.0
Radio	436.1
BBC Online	18.7
News 24	26.5
Digital start-up costs	18.3
Licence fee	109.5
(collection and enforcement)	
Corporate centre and restructuring	90.2
Total:	2044.3

Source: BBC Annual Report 1997–98

Fig. 2.3 BBC operating expenditure (£m), 1997–98

spanned an age range from teens to pop fans in their forties. Radio 1's espousal of 'new music' (progressive rock in the early 70s, punk later that decade, indie music in the 80s, dance in the 90s) was down to the activities of a handful of producers and presenters (notably John Peel) working outside the daytime mainstream, who were given a largely free rein but could never count wholly on backing from the station's management. In the 90s, however, this rewriting underscored the reinvention of Radio 1 as a quasi-cultural, youth-appeal network – and the consequent loss of a large slice of Radio 1's traditional audience base. The makeover was achieved by a ditching of established daytime presenters, a change in music policy that precluded playing virtually anything recorded before 1990, and a more selective playlisting policy tilted towards 'Britpop', indie and dance. What Radio 1 lost in numerical terms, it gained in terms of a renewed credibility among its newly defined target audience and an acceptance of the political argument for its existence on the part of the BBC's paymasters, for whom the privatization of Radio 1 has at times seemed an attractive proposition.

Radio 1's high-profile problems in the 1990s were a paradigm for the BBC's root-and-branch rethink of its role and identity at a time when the old public service certainties (not least funding by the licence fee) were under threat as never before. These were partly to do with fundamental technological changes that impacted heavily on the cost and means of producing and delivering programming, and with the Thatcher government's dismantling of the public utilities and commitment to privatization and industrial deregulation, which was accompanied by an unprecedented exercise in political patronage in appointing new Governors and a remoulding of management to inject free-market thinking (via cutbacks, job losses and an opening up of programme-making to the independent sector) into all aspects of the BBC's operations (O'Malley, pp. 136–65).

Under Director-General John Birt, the BBC has, since 1989, brought in a series of major changes including the creation of an internal market within the BBC for resources (called 'producer choice'); building new relationships with programme suppliers and rights holders (such as Sky TV and the FA Premier League); a new emphasis on 'branding' the BBC and marketing its products, especially overseas; and restructuring the Corporation into five directorates with responsibilities across both television and radio. The latter has enabled combinations of roles – for example, the appointment of a head of music coverage across both media, to whom the Controller of Radio 1 reports, so that Radio 1 and BBC 1's *Top of the Pops* work in tandem and cross-promote each other. The post-1996 structure is shown in Figure 2.4.

Radio 1's repositioning also points to a new complementarity of approach within BBC radio, grounded in the three-way post-1945 network structure but

BBC EXECUTIVE COMMITTEE

Chief Executive, BBC Broadcast
Chief Executive, BBC Production
Chief Executive, BBC News
Chief Executive, BBC Resources
Director of Personnel
Director of Finance

BOARD OF MANAGEMENT

BROADCAST	PRODUCTION	NEWS	WORLDWIDE	WORLD SERVICE	RESOURCES
Commissioning and scheduling (except News)	*In-house production of TV and radio programmes*	*Radio, TV and online news including Radio 5 Live*	*Commercial and international activities*	*International radio broadcasting*	*Broadcast facilities to internal and independent programme-makers*
BBC 1 BBC 2 Radios 1 to 4 Education Services BBC Prime Digital Services Local radio Regional radio					

Fig. 2.4 BBC internal structure (introduced 1996)

modified to take into account present and future commercial competition. Complementarity in radio services means the provision of programming which dovetails, rather than directly competes, with that of other stations. Radio 1's programming changes were enacted in tandem with changes at Radio 2, which was simultaneously refashioned to attract Radio 1's lost listeners. So while the audience profiles of networks change – or can be *engineered* to change – BBC radio can act corporately, by cross-promotion and targeted marketing, to make sure that listeners stay within its family.

We can also see complementarity at work in the way the BBC has positioned itself against commercial rivals. Whereas the focus when Independent (i.e. commercial) Local Radio started in 1973 was to make Radio 1 the brand leader in pop radio and beat the ILR stations at their own game, the priority when Virgin started in 1994 was to ensure that Radio 1 was as distinct as possible. As Virgin's heartland was to be the 25+ age group, with a strong bias towards listeners aged 30–40, Radio 1 pitched itself towards the 15–25 age range and changed its music policy accordingly. While Radio 3 experimented with supposedly more accessible ways of presenting classical music after the launch of the populist Classic FM, it too returned to stressing its uniqueness as a network committed to recording and presenting complete works. Similarly, BBC local stations switched in the early 1990s from a mixed output of music and speech to an all-talk format focused on the over-45s, in an attempt to fill the gap left by ILR's increasing concentration on formatted music for people aged 25–45.

The new BBC radio is not (officially) in competition with commercial radio: what the commercial stations will not or cannot provide, the argument goes, the BBC will fulfil out of public duty. Yet apart from programmes such as those for schools (now pushed to the night-time hours, for teachers to record for later classroom use), precisely what a BBC station can provide that commercial radio cannot is problematic. Radio 1 initially replaced its Top 40 bias with a policy built on a loose definition of alternative music – and listeners left in droves. For some, the new Radio 1 had an arrogance every bit as galling as that which once dictated airplay choices according to chart positions and dubious notions of 'acceptability' to mass audiences. It depended, still, on programme-makers making music choices in line with the self-image of presenters and the 'professional' assessment of producers as to what its target audience would prefer.

In John Birt's perception, providing a complement or alternative to an increasingly one-dimensional, format-led commercial medium gives public service broadcasting its unique selling point. Again, there is pragmatism here: it supposedly places BBC radio outside the ratings circus and makes audience appreciation rather than listening numbers the central issue, and it enables a focusing of resources on BBC radio's perceived strengths. In theory, it is possible to see radio in Britain as a patchwork of complementary services, BBC and Radio Authority-franchised, publicly funded and commercially based, national and local, neatly dovetailing with each other to offer real choice in listening to the consumer. Where this argument falls down is in the policing of

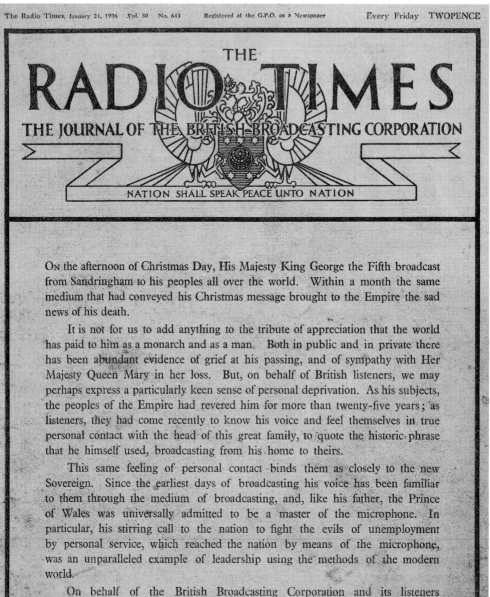

The Radio Times, January 24, 1936   Vol. 50   No. 643   Registered at the G.P.O. as a Newspaper   Every Friday   TWOPENCE

THE
RADIO TIMES
THE JOURNAL OF THE BRITISH BROADCASTING CORPORATION

NATION SHALL SPEAK PEACE UNTO NATION

On the afternoon of Christmas Day, His Majesty King George the Fifth broadcast from Sandringham to his peoples all over the world. Within a month the same medium that had conveyed his Christmas message brought to the Empire the sad news of his death.

It is not for us to add anything to the tribute of appreciation that the world has paid to him as a monarch and as a man. Both in public and in private there has been abundant evidence of grief at his passing, and of sympathy with Her Majesty Queen Mary in her loss. But, on behalf of British listeners, we may perhaps express a particularly keen sense of personal deprivation. As his subjects, the peoples of the Empire had revered him for more than twenty-five years; as listeners, they had come recently to know his voice and feel themselves in true personal contact with the head of this great family, to quote the historic phrase that he himself used, broadcasting from his home to theirs.

This same feeling of personal contact binds them as closely to the new Sovereign. Since the earliest days of broadcasting his voice has been familiar to them through the medium of broadcasting, and, like his father, the Prince of Wales was universally admitted to be a master of the microphone. In particular, his stirring call to the nation to fight the evils of unemployment by personal service, which reached the nation by means of the microphone, was an unparalleled example of leadership using the methods of the modern world.

On behalf of the British Broadcasting Corporation and its listeners throughout the Empire, we offer our loyal greetings to the new King.

Source: *Radio Times*

Fig. 2.5 Created by John Reith prior to the BBC's establishment as a Corporation under Royal Charter, *Radio Times* not only gave listeners information regarding timings of programmes but acted as a vehicle for expounding BBC policy on programming matters. In editions such as this, on the occasion of the king's death in 1936, its editorial approach was to cement a bond between monarchy and populace

such a system – in ensuring that stations stay within their original remit. The less regulated the market, the freer commercial stations become to expand and reinvent themselves – and pursue different audiences. This inevitably impacts on the BBC's own policies, though the commercial sector counters that the BBC is itself a completely free agent in programming matters, that nowhere in the BBC Charter is it stated what any of its networks should consist of, and that it enjoys an independence of operation, a fixity of finance and a general lack of accountability unmatched by any commercially run organization.

In fact, the BBC *is* subject to a whole bureaucracy of accountability, both internally and in a battery of external committees and advisory boards at national and local level. The Birt era has been characterized by an almost obsessive concern with making the BBC at least *appear* responsive and accessible, whether through its vast web site or an ongoing project called 'The BBC Listens' comprising special programmes, public meetings and audience research. The BBC's 1998 Statement of Promises uses the language of customer service to articulate 'core promises' which include a stated commitment to consultation and accountability as well as the customary litany of quality, distinctiveness and efficiency. Though some have described the 1980s and 90s as marking the beginning of the end of the BBC's independence in a political sense, the concern with customer service pointed to a loss of something more general – 'an erosion of the relative autonomy of broadcasting from capitalist economic pressures . . . which [has] tied the broadcasters more closely to the economic system which the state exists to guarantee' (O'Malley, p. 179).

As a mission statement, the 'core promises' (see Figure 2.6) can be read as a succinct summary of how the BBC now interprets its public service role – not as one of challenge or cultural leadership but as a tightly run, efficiently managed provider of broadly acceptable programming. Even the mention of producing programmes 'which commercial broadcasters are unlikely to undertake' is equivocal, as it does not preclude the BBC from creating programmes that the commercial sector *does* make. It is a limited but pragmatic vision that defines the listener and viewer primarily as a customer and programming as something arrived at by research and consensus and delivered with professionalism. Paradoxically, it represents the BBC as a market-led organization for which exposure to, and admiration of, its products by its audience is enough. It's as if customer satisfaction is, finally, the BBC's reason for existing.

A PUBLIC LIBRARY OF THE AIR?

The efforts of Birt and his team secured the BBC's short- to middle-term future, though how the BBC continues to be funded is a political question outside its control. By the time of the next review of the BBC's Charter, the licence fee will be approaching a century old. Alternatives have been broached and investigated over many decades – direct government grant, advertising, subscription – but the system of taxing receiving equipment still has the

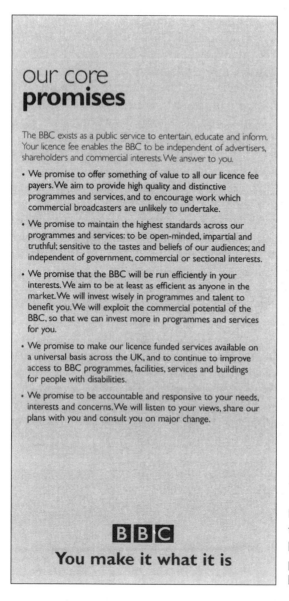

our core
promises

The BBC exists as a public service to entertain, educate and inform. Your licence fee enables the BBC to be independent of advertisers, shareholders and commercial interests. We answer to you.

- We promise to offer something of value to all our licence fee payers. We aim to provide high quality and distinctive programmes and services, and to encourage work which commercial broadcasters are unlikely to undertake.

- We promise to maintain the highest standards across our programmes and services: to be open-minded, impartial and truthful; sensitive to the tastes and beliefs of our audiences; and independent of government, commercial or sectional interests.

- We promise that the BBC will be run efficiently in your interests. We aim to be at least as efficient as anyone in the market. We will invest wisely in programmes and talent to benefit you. We will exploit the commercial potential of the BBC, so that we can invest more in programmes and services for you.

- We promise to make our licence funded services available on a universal basis across the UK, and to continue to improve access to BBC programmes, facilities, services and buildings for people with disabilities.

- We promise to be accountable and responsive to your needs, interests and concerns. We will listen to your views, share our plans with you and consult you on major change.

BBC
You make it what it is

Source: BBC

Fig. 2.6 In 1998, leaflets issued to every licence-holding household set out the BBC's priorities for the coming year and beyond

advantage of maintaining the BBC's independence from government and commercial pressures, and avoiding bias in favour of sectional interests. Antiquated and anomalous it may be, but then the BBC is itself a product of a particular time, political climate and mindset. As Radio 4 Controller James Boyle put it when introducing major changes to the network's schedules, no one setting up a broadcasting operation from scratch in 1998 would ever consider a Radio 4 as part of its remit or strategy – but, like much of the BBC's activities and ethos, it is so rooted in tradition, reputation and public sentiment that to dispense with it altogether would be politically unacceptable.

Whatever the discussion at home, the BBC continues to be revered overseas

Source: BBC

Fig. 2.7 The BBC's involvement in cultural production is ongoing and includes investment and sponsorship of concerts by national and regional orchestras

as a model for harnessing media for the public good, especially by broadcasters idealizing the middle ground between direct state involvement and the economic rationalism of the free market. Historically, its influence has been greatest within the British Commonwealth, with both Australia and Canada evolving multi-tier systems with publicly funded, nationally managed broadcasting organizations at their heart. In the US, where non-commercial broadcasting was pushed to the margins in the 1920s yet never quite died, the efforts of individual stations and private foundations like Pacifica paved the way for formal government recognition of the need for broadcasting run solely as a public service. This took shape with the creation of the Corporation for Public Broadcasting in 1967 and its offshoot, National Public Radio, three

YOUR WEEKLY LISTENING GUIDE STARTS HERE

BBC RADIO WALES

SATURDAY 23
NEWS: 6.00am, 9.00, 1.00pm, 5.00, 6.00
WEATHER: after most news bulletins plus 12.59pm, 5.59
NE WALES NEWS: (657kHz only) 9.00am, 10.00, 12 noon
HILL FORECASTS: 8.59am

6.00am Chris Needs
Early morning entertainment.

6.00 657kHz only
Alan Daulby
The breakfast show for north-east Wales.

7.30 Good Morning Wales
With Mark Hutchings and Peter Johnson.

8.30 The Back Page
Eddie Butler looks back at the week's sporting issues.

9.05 Money for Nothing
The best music from the sixties and seventies. Phone 01222 552121 or 01248 370870.

11.00 The Weekenders
With Gareth Jones and Andrea Lewis.
E-MAIL: theweekenders@bbc.co.uk

12.30pm True Lives
Gunfight in the Ad-lands. A week in the life of voice-over artist Peter Page.
Repeated from yesterday

1.05 Box Your Ears
Ruth Terrett and captains Brian Hibbard and Shelley Rees test their knowledge of TV and film trivia.
Repeated on Monday at 6.30pm

1.35 Sportstime
Chris Stuart presents FA Cup fourth round action, rugby, and other news.

6.00 The Glass Onion
Alan Thompson's unsubtle mix of music, triva and chat.

8.00 House Party
DJ Precious delivers the best in house and garage direct to your radio.

10.00 The Club
John Lenny Jnr with a mix of house music, rap and R 'n' B.

12.00–6.00am
as World Service

SUNDAY 24
NEWS: hourly 7.00–10.00am, noon, 1.00pm, 4.00, 6.00, 8.00
WEATHER: after news bulletins plus 8.59am, 12.59pm, 5.59pm
HILL FORECASTS: 7.29am, 11.59

6.00am Chris Needs

7.30 Country Focus
A spotlight on rural issues, with Gaina Morgan.

8.05 Celebration
A service of worship from the Presbyterian Chapel at Garndiffaith, near Pontypool, led by the Rev Mary Turnock.

8.30 In the Papers
A live review of the Sunday papers, hosted by Eddie Butler.

9.05 A String of Pearls
More musical nostalgia presented by Dewi Griffiths.

10.00 Station Road
Omnibus. Ossie causes problems and tensions spill over. Meanwhile, Griff botches another simple job.

11.00 Sunday Best
With Sioned Wiliam.

12.00 Sunday Edition
Presented by Steve Evans.

12.30pm Eye on Wales

1.00 All Things Considered
Roy Jenkins examines the religious scene today.
Repeated tomorrow 1.30pm

1.30 First Hand
The best of the arts in Wales.
Repeated on Tuesday 1.30pm

2.00 Mollie's Place

4.00 Play It Again, Frank
With Frank Hennessy.

5.00 In Living Memory
Anita Morgan meets coal miners and their families who share memories of work, leisure and family life from the early days of the century.
Rpt

5.30 Patriots' Tour
Brian Harries reaches the end of his grand tour of Wales.
Day 4. The lessons of two millennia are put into present-day context.
Repeated on Thursday, 6.30pm

6.00 With Melody in Mind
With Beverley Humphreys.

7.00 Skidmore

7.30 Caniadaeth y Cysegr
Welsh hymn-singing.
Repeated from Radio Cymru 4.30pm

8.00 Nocturne
With Alan Christopher.

9.00 Movers and Shakers
Repeated on Wednesday, 1.30pm

9.30 Jeff Hooper's Songbook

10.30 Short Story
Beginning of Something by Catherine Merriman. Alex and his mother contemplate their changing lives as Alex prepares to leave home and go to university. Read by Rhian Morgan.

10.45 All The Best Tunes

11.15 Catchphrase Colour Supplement
The week's Welsh lessons.

12.00–6.30am
as World Service

MONDAY 25
WEEKDAY NEWS: half-hourly 6.30am to 8.30, hourly 9.00 to 4.00pm, 4.30, 4.45, 5.00, 5.30, then hourly 6.00 to 10.00
WEEKDAY WEATHER: 7.58am, 12.59pm, 5.34, plus after most news bulletins
WEEKDAY NE WALES NEWS: (657kHz only) 7.05, 7.30, 8.05, 1.00pm
WEEKDAY HILL FORECASTS: 6.58am, 6.29pm

6.30am Good Morning Wales
News and sport roundup

presented by Peter Johnson and Mark Hutchings. Call in on 01222 322142, or fax 01222 555960.
WRITE TO: Newsline, BBC Radio Wales, Cardiff CF5 2YQ
E-MAIL: newsline@wales.bbc.co.uk

8.30 Roy Noble

10.20 Station Road
Sandy comes up with something special for Spanish Night.

10.35 Elimination

11.00 Livetime
Topical talk and information with Charlotte Evans and Steve James.
E-MAIL: Livetime@bbc.co.uk

1.00pm Wales at One
The latest news.

1.30 All Things Considered
Repeated from Sunday 1pm

2.00 Chris Needs PM

4.00 Four Star
Lisa Barsi with entertainment news, and the Screen Test competition.
To take part call 01222 578928 or 01248 370870.

5.00 Good Evening Wales
The day's news with Phil Parry and Patrick Hannan.

6.30 Box Your Ears
Repeated from Saturday 1.05pm

7.00 Adam Walton

8.00 Kevin Hughes

10.05 Catchphrase

10.30 Steve Dewitt's Late Show

12.00–6.30am
as World Service

TUESDAY 26
6.30am Good Morning Wales

8.30 Roy Noble

10.20 Station Road
Some things are worth more than money.

10.35 Elimination

11.00 Livetime
The topical magazine with Charlotte Evans and Oliver Hides. Including computer news and the daily diary.

1.00pm Wales at One

1.30 First Hand
Repeated from Sunday 1.30pm

2.00 Owen Money

4.00 Four Star

5.00 Good Evening Wales

6.30 Landscape
Gareth Heulfryn unearths the secret history of the Welsh landscape.

7.00–12 midnight
as Monday

12.00–6.30am
as World Service

WEDNESDAY 27
6.30am Good Morning Wales
Presented by Peter Johnson and Vaughan Roderick.

8.30 Roy Noble

10.20 Station Road
Griff makes Bob an offer he can't refuse.

10.35 Elimination

11.00 Livetime

1.00pm Wales at One

1.30 Movers and Shakers
Repeated from Sunday 9pm

2.00 Chris Needs PM

4.00 Four Star

5.00 Good Evening Wales

6.30 Scope

7.00–12 midnight
as Monday

12.00–6.30am
as World Service

THURSDAY 28
6.30am Good Morning Wales
With Mark Hutchings and Vaughan Roderick.

8.30 Roy Noble

10.20 Station Road
If you ask nicely, it's amazing what you can get.

10.35 Elimination

11.00 Livetime

1.00pm Wales at One

1.30 Kane
Vincent Kane continues his investigation into the farming crisis. This week's spotlight falls on the unions.

2.00 Owen Money

4.00 Four Star
Film, theatre and arts review.

5.00 Good Evening Wales

6.30 Patriots' Tour
Repeated from Sunday, 5.30pm

7.00–12 midnight
as Monday

12.00–6.30am
as World Service

FRIDAY 29
6.30am Good Morning Wales
A roundup of news and sport.

8.30 Good Morning Wales – the Friday Phone-in
To take part call 01222 552121 or 01248 370870
E-Mail: newsline.wales@bbc.c.uk

9.05 Roy Noble

10.20 Station Road
Sian dances to her own tune. Where does that leave Mike?

10.35 Elimination

11.00 Livetime
Charlotte Evans and Steve James talk to people in Wales with a story to tell, plus a visit to the Livetime allotment.

1.00pm Wales at One

1.30 This Way Up
An alternative view of the week's events.

2.00 That Friday Feeling
With Hywel Gwynfryn.

4.00 Four Star
Entertainment, film and sports news with Lisa Barsi.

5.00 Good Evening Wales

6.00 People's Assembly

6.30 True Lives: Another Day at the Office
Behind the scenes with the Welsh MPs and the Welsh Office.
Repeated tomorrow, 12.30pm

7.00–10.30 as Monday

10.30 Voice for All

12.00–6.00am
as World Service

■ **BBC Wales**
Broadcasting House
Llandaff, Cardiff CF5 2YQ
Tel: 01222 322000

BBC RADIO CYMRU

SADWRN 23
NEWYDDION/TYWYDD:
bob awr 7.00am–1.00pm, 5.00, 6.00

6.00am Galwad Cynnar
Gyda Gerallt Pennant.

7.30 Byd Amaeth

7.55 Dros Fy Sbectol
Ail-ddarlledir Sul 8.25pm

8.00 Ar y Marc

8.30 Eifion Jones A'r Boi Clên
A oes gennych ffrind yn dathlu penblwydd neu'n priodi?
Ffoniwch (01248) 361361.

10.00 Ram Jam Sadwrn

12.00 Bydy Bel
John Hardy fydd yn bwrw golwg dros bynciau llosg yr wythnos ar y mesydd chwarae.

12.30pm Y Stori Tu Ol I'r Gan
Cyfansoddwyr a pherffformwyr amryddawn Cymru yn datgelu'r gwirionedd am eu caneuon.
Darlledwyd Llun

1.00 Y Sioe Fawr
Mae Dudley Newbery wedi gadael ei gegin eto'r wythnos hon a theithio i Westy Llanina Llanarth. Cynhwysion cerddorol y "Sioe Fawr" heddiw yw Grenda Owen a'r Band, Brychan Llyr, John Rodge a Caryl Caffrey. Fe gawn ni gyfarfod ag ambell gymeriad yn y gynulleidfa hefyd.

1.30 Jonathan

2.00 Chwaraeon
John Ifans, Bryn Tomos a Mike Davies fydd yn cadw golwg ar y mesydd chwarae–sylw i bedwaredd rownd Cwpan Lloegr a'r gorau o'r Gynghrair Genedlaethol. O'r caeau rygbi, gemau Caerdydd ag Abertawe yn y Gynghrair Eingl-Gymreig answyddogol yn ogystal a'r gemau o'r Cwpan Her.

6.05 Wythnos i'w Chofio
Ail-ddarlledir Sul 12.30pm

6.30 Clonc
Clonc, Yr Adran Addysg, BBC Llandaf, Caerdydd CF5 2YQ.
Rhif ffôn: 012222 322973.

7.00 Gwyndaf Roberts

8.30 Beth Angell

10.00 Y Boi Clen
Y Boi Clen ar nos Sadwrn.
Digon o hywl a chystadleuthau
Ffoniwch Dylan Wyn ar 01248 361361 rwan.

12.00–6.00am gweler Radio 5

SUL 24
NEWYDDION/TYWYDD:
bob awr 7.00–9.00am, 11.00–1.00pm, 4.00–6.00, 10.00

6.00am Clasuron

7.30 Taro Nodyn

8.30 Bwrw Golwg
John Roberts yn trin a thrafod materion crefyddol yr wythnos.

9.00 Llinyn Mesur

9.35 Beti a'i Phobol
Darlledwyd Iau

10.15 Alun Thomas
"Ymunwch a Alun Thomas am ysbaid hamddenol o gerddoriaeth ysgafn, cyfarchion, sgwrs a chystadlu."

11.30 Oedfa'r Bore
Capel Ebeneser, Clynnog Fawr.

12.00 Parod Arlan

12.30pm Wythnos i'w Chofio
Darlledwyd Sadwrn 6.05pm

1.00 Llinyn Mesur
Rhaglen materion cyfoes yn bwrw golwg fanwl ar bynciau'r dydd yng Nghymru a thu hwnt.

1.30 Manylu

2.00 Geraint Lloyd

3.45 Ponty
Cyfle i wrando ar holl helyntion yr wythnos a aeth heibio ym mywydau brodorion Ponty.

4.30 Caniadaeth y Cysegr
Cymanfa Annibynwyr/Bedyddwyr Ceredigion (2).

5.00 Bwrw Sul
Vaughan Hughes a'i westeion. Sgwrsio. Cerddoriaeth. A'r ymfflamychol Jean Hefina.

6.00 Elinor

6.50 Y Talwrn
Ail-ddarlledir Mawrth 1.20pm

7.30 Ar Eich Cais

8.45 Dros Fy Sbectol
John Roberts Williams unwaith eto'n bwrw golwg ar y byd a'i bethau.
Darlledwyd Sadwrn 7.55am

8.50 Dal i Gredu
Ond credu beth yn nhymor yr Adfent?

9.00 John ac Alun

11.00 Haf Wyn
Haf Wyn yn cyflwyno cerddoriaeth i'ch swyno a'ch cyfareddu.

12.00–6.00am
gweler Radio 5

LLUN 25
NEWYDDION/TYWYDD:
6.00am, 6.30, 7.00, 7.30, bob awr 8.00–5.00pm, 5.30, 5.50, bob awr 6.00–10.00

6.00am Post Cyntaf

8.20 Jonsi

9.30 Jonsi a Nia

10.00 Nia Roberts

11.00 Hywel Gwynfryn

12.20pm Ponty
Cyfres ddrama dyddiol. Hynt a helyntion dyddiol trigolion y dref fach yng Ngorllewin Cymru.

12.30 Stondin Sulwyn

1.20 Wythnos Gwilym Owen
Gwilym Owen yn mynd dan groen rhai o sefydliadau pwysicaf Cymru.

2.00 Kevin a Nia
Does dim dal beth fydd yn digwydd gyda'r ddau yma!
Ond yn sicr, mi fydd y rhaglen

Source: Radio Times

Fig. 2.8 *Radio Times* programme schedule for Wales, 23 January 1999

years later. Both were non-profit-making bodies with an enabling function, to encourage 'the use of radio and television for instructional, educational and cultural purposes'; NPR's 700 affiliated radio stations (most independently owned and run) currently benefit from a $57.3 million budget drawn from federal, state and local government funds, which accounts for 47 per cent of its total funding; the remainder comes from private and business sources.

As Figure 2.9 shows, over half of NPR-affiliated stations are university-owned and fall into the category of 'college radio'; these were an important source of, and vehicle for, strands of 'alternative' rock music in America from the early 1980s onwards. The bands REM and Nirvana were among college radio's most famous graduates. Mostly, however, NPR tends to be likened to BBC Radio 4 in programming terms, with an emphasis on national news (provided from central NPR resources), discussion, documentary, drama, education and self-help. Like Radio 4 in Britain, NPR is one of the last bastions in the US for the traditional individually produced radio programme; like the BBC in general, NPR has not avoided criticism for being middlebrow in nature and elitist in tone.

Especially through their educational programmes, many of which feed directly into the curriculum, NPR and its television counterpart PBS have established publicly funded broadcasting as a national asset, but with this has come a sense of institutionalization. The development of another tier of radio in the US, community radio, was in part a reaction against institutional funding of radio and a move towards more grass-roots involvement at both a funding and operational level. In early 1999, the CPB made clear its opposition to FCC plans to allow limited development of low-power 'microradio' stations, citing the same arguments about interference and a crowding of the airwaves that the commercial operators made.

Owners	Stations	Grantees	Licensees
Non-profit community organizations	236	151	133
University	362	218	194
Local government	33	28	27
State government	63	11	8
Total	694	408	362

Notes: 'Grantees' are FCC-licensed stations or groups of co-licensed stations to which the CPB makes grants. 'Licensees' are organizations holding FCC licences for CPB-supported stations.

Source: Corporation for Public Broadcasting

Fig. 2.9 Public radio in the US: numbers and ownership

The American version of public service radio, then, falls into the same paternalistic pattern as the BBC's – a service created 'from above' and dispensed down (albeit with a strong local base) and facing some of the same issues of funding, direction and accountability that have so preoccupied the BBC in recent years. When NPR president Delano Lewis made his representations to the House of Representatives in January 1995 regarding future funding, his arguments were remarkably close to those of John Birt in arguing the BBC's case to government:

> Public radio provides high-quality programming and services that are not available anywhere else on the radio dial. Public radio is a good investment of taxpayer dollars. Public radio is an integral part of the informational, educational and cultural lives of American communities. The public radio audience is a broad and diverse cross-section of Americans – not merely the culturally elite . . . It is the public library of the air, free, and universally accessible.
>
> *The Herald-Sun* at www.herald-sun.com/listen/magz/295/69.html

CASE STUDY: TWO KINDS OF NATIONHOOD

Deeply embedded in John Reith's vision of a public service BBC was the intention that it should unite and emblematize the nation. At no time was there a more conscious and pragmatic attempt to do this than during World War Two (ironically, after Reith's departure). It was during the war and its aftermath that the chimes of Big Ben, the Greenwich Mean Time 'pips' on the hour, the music of composer Eric Coates (including the themes of *In Town Tonight*, *Desert Island Discs* and *Music While You Work*), and the theme tune to *The Archers* all became established as great aural signifiers of Britishness.

Significantly, a huge number of wartime and post-war programmes lingered right through to the mid 1960s and well beyond, clustering on Radio 4 and symbolizing a radio service (and a nation?) at ease with an image of itself rooted in wartime certainties but ill at ease with progress. The issue of how far to accept the march of time, and particularly technological progress, was a recurrent theme in *The Archers* throughout the 50s and 60s. If the picture conveyed was a selective one in which youth, changing racial patterns and industrial conflict hardly figured, it concurred with a conservative-minded audience for whom the war remained an overwhelming reference point. In its attempts to revitalize and revamp Radio 4 (and, most of all, attract a young audience to replace its ageing core), BBC management runs the risk of trampling on the qualities of almost mythic middle-class Englishness that make the network unique.

BBC radio's representation of Britain, then, is not an artificial construction. It is rooted in established traditions and class relationships, and in notions of nationhood that crystallized most forcefully in the early Victorian era of the 1840s. But one of the key policy dilemmas of the BBC's early years was how to represent claims to nationhood from *within* Britain – particularly how to reflect regional diversity while at the same time keeping in check the forces that might undermine national cohesiveness. In the case of Wales, this was made yet more problematic by the issue of language and its centrality or otherwise to the Welsh identity.

There was a fierce strain of centralization in planning and programme-making which the creation of the Regional Programme as an alternative to the National Programme only partly lifted. Until 1937, when the Welsh Region was opened, Wales shared its programmes with the west of England. In Wales, the BBC echoed its national efforts in cultural production by funding a National Orchestra for Wales and subsequently establishing the BBC Welsh Orchestra, by launching internal policy discussions to standardize how broadcast Welsh should sound, and at one point by attempting to take over management of the National Eisteddfod.

The Welsh Region came into being against a background of relentless campaigning from the Welsh Language Society, whose members saw the BBC as a means of rescuing the Welsh language from terminal decline. Bilingualism was accepted policy from the start, but the difficulty for the BBC (as for later governments) was that a language that could be a force for cultural unity was also divisive: large parts of Wales, particularly the south and west, were and remain mainly English-speaking, while Welsh was traditionally identified as the language of both the rural north and the middle-class intelligentsia based particularly at the University of Wales in Aberystwyth. This reflected a deeper disunity based on geography and recent industrial history that tended to make the very concept of Wales as a nation an elusive and perhaps even illusory one. Audience research noted how, when programmes in Welsh came on, English speakers switched in droves to services from Bristol or Birmingham.

Welsh-language activism and the parallel rise of the nationalist party Plaid Cymru polarised opinion in Wales during the 1960s but succeeded in its aim of establishing, with the Welsh Language Act, equal status for Welsh and English in local government business and in official communications. This officially recognized equality enabled the BBC in Wales to press for the separation of its English and Welsh services, which was formalized with the creation of Radio Wales in 1978 and Radio Cymru in 1979. All commercial stations operating in Wales were obliged, under the terms of their IBA franchise, to produce a minimum number of Welsh-language programmes each week; most opted to run them in the evening, on their secondary frequencies.

One major significance of the Radio Wales/Radio Cymru split – and the creation of the heavily subsidized Welsh-language television channel S4C in 1982 – was that it enabled the BBC in Wales to remove all its Welsh programmes to one outlet. So while it empowered Welsh speakers, it also freed Welsh-born English speakers from their main sources of exposure to the language. It allowed the two nations of Wales to co-exist – and, by removing the language issue from the centre of Welsh politics, it helped focus the political agenda on different definitions of Welshness – and particularly the need or otherwise for political devolution. Patrick Hannan suggests, in *The*

Welsh Illusion, that without the influence of broadcasting there would have been no Welsh Assembly, and points to the comparatively meagre availability of newspapers in Wales to provide a comparable 'uniting' function.

The outcome is that Wales is, on the basis of cost per capita, the best resourced of all the BBC's awkwardly named 'national regions', with two national radio stations and two television stations on top of the ITV service, HTV. (Although S4C is an independent channel, BBC TV has a statutory requirement to provide a large percentage of its Welsh-language programming.) This massive concentration of resources has led the BBC to a major employer status within Wales, besides encouraging a growing independent production industry and creating vocational opportunities for Welsh speakers that were non-existent before the 1980s. The resourcing that BBC Wales receives is a real anomaly in the deregulatory, cost-trimming atmosphere of the late 1990s, and as such it represents perhaps the last gasp of public service broadcasting in Britain in its traditional, consensus-driven guise.

In *The Welsh Illusion*, Hannan comes close to describing modern Wales as a creation of the BBC – as owing its sense of national cohesion to the BBC's representation of it. He also points out the role that the media has played in the almost Blairite relaunching of Wales as 'cool Cymru', epitomized by the studios and production workshops of regenerated Cardiff and the idiosyncratic music and stance of Catatonia and Gorky's Zygotic Mynci (both of whom have made a point of recording in Welsh). The irony is that this new sense of national identity, like the earlier BBC-shaped one and like political devolution itself, has its origins in the enabling investment policies of an administration based in London.

Further reading

Briggs, Asa (1965–79): *The History of Broadcasting in the United Kingdom*, vols 1–5. Oxford University Press.

Davies, John (1994): *Broadcasting and the BBC in Wales*. University of Wales Press.

Hannan, Patrick (1999): *The Welsh Illusion*. Seren.

Lewis, Peter M. and Booth, Jerry (1989): *The Invisible Medium: Public, Commercial and Community Radio*. Macmillan.

Madge, Tim (1989): *Beyond the BBC: Broadcasters and the Public in the 1980s*. Macmillan.

O'Malley, Tom (1994): *Closedown? The BBC and Government Broadcasting Policy, 1979–92*. Pluto Press.

Reith, J.C.W. (1924): *Broadcast Over Britain*. Hodder & Stoughton.

Reith, J.C.W. (1949): *Into the Wind*. Hodder & Stoughton.

Scannell, Paddy (1981): 'Music for the multitude? The dilemmas of the BBC's music policy, 1923–1946' in *Media, Culture and Society*, July 1981. Sage.

Smith, Anthony (1976): *The Shadow in the Cave: The Broadcaster, the Audience and the State*. Quartet.

Activity 2.1

Figure 2.1 lists the annual running costs of each of the BBC's principal domestic radio services, and the audience figures for each in terms of reach and share.

1. What would be the arguments for, and the arguments against, continuing to fund Radio 1 at the same level?
2. Make a case for the continuation of Radio 3 on the same cost basis as shown here, with the same level of listenership.
3. Account for why Radio 4 is the most cost-intensive of the BBC networks.

Activity 2.2

Investigate the provision of local radio in your home town or place of residence, both publicly funded and commercially run. What makes the public service version of local broadcasting distinct in terms of programme output and presentation? Are there differences in the way in which the publicly funded station relates to the life of the locality and its audience, compared to the commercially run station? Find out how much funding the public station receives and from what principal source(s). What rules govern the accountability under which the station operates?

Activity 2.3

'The BBC isn't serving the public by providing teenagers, through Radio 1, with a diet of non-stop pop music that they can find elsewhere. It's doing a disservice to the public because they're having to pay for it.'

1. What are the assumptions made in this statement about 'teenagers' and 'the public'?
2. What perception does the person making this statement have of Radio 1? Is it a fair one?
3. What arguments would the BBC be likely to use to respond to such a criticism?

Activity 2.4

Compare the BBC's level of funding of radio services in Wales with that of services in Scotland and Northern Ireland. What makes BBC Wales a special case in broadcasting terms? How differently might a commercial station approach the task of broadcasting to the whole of Wales? What arguments might there be for and against a national radio service for England?

Activity 2.5

Consider the analogy of public service radio to a public library made in the quotation on page 44. It might suggest an indispensable public resource or an outdated institution protected and preserved at excessive public expense. Is either description appropriate to the BBC today?

3

Commercial Radio

Commercial radio – meaning radio run for profit-making purposes, usually through the sale of airtime to advertisers – is by far the most dominant form of sound broadcasting in the world. American radio was developed on commercial principles, chiefly because of the absence of government involvement in its regulation; British broadcasting, though traditionally public service-based, has had a system of commercial stations since 1973 which now collectively outnumber the local and national stations operated by the BBC (and which, according to 1999 RAJAR figures, now take over 50 per cent of listening). In many other countries, commercial stations run alongside public and community-based stations in a pluralistic system with varying degrees of governmental regulation.

The focus in this chapter is on how commercial radio operates – its sources of income and profit, who owns what, how it is regulated, and its place in the wider context of national and even global mass communications media. Out of this we can begin to assess what makes commercial radio distinct in terms of content and presentation, how it differs from its public service and community counterparts, and whose interests it best serves.

THE DYNAMICS OF COMMERCIAL RADIO

Commercial radio stations are businesses, established and maintained to provide income to those who hold shares in the station or its controlling company. The chief means of raising income is the sale of a commodity – airtime – to advertisers, the *value* of which is determined by the volume and 'quality' of a station's audience. Advertising rates vary according to the time of day, the numbers listening and the degree of competition with other stations for advertising space. The 'quality' of an audience refers to how well the listening profile matches the specific *consumer* profile sought by particular advertisers. A station aimed at the business or financial sector, for example, may – because of its high penetration into a lucrative target market – attract a lower volume of listeners yet charge a higher rate for advertising than a mainstream music station in the same locality. (A good analogy here is with national newspapers: the *Financial Times* has a far lower circulation than the *Daily Express* but achieves a higher level of advertising revenue because of its reach among the business community.) Successful targeting of readers/listeners creates greater demand for advertising space, enabling the newspaper/station to charge higher rates.

The primary dynamic in commercial radio is therefore the effectiveness with which a station delivers potential customers to its advertisers. The aim of programming strategy is to attract listeners and keep them tuned in, in order to ensure that they are exposed to the advertising message. Advertisers (and agencies acting on their behalf) have had varying levels of involvement in this strategy over the years. In the early days of commercial radio in the US, advertising generally took the form of programme sponsorship: a company would buy segments of airtime, provide a dance band or vocal group to fill it and intersperse the selections with product endorsements. By the 1930s, the networks had conceded the production of much of their prime-time evening programming directly to the sponsors themselves, on whose behalf advertising agencies fashioned shows and daily melodramas ('soap operas', so-called because they were sponsored by detergent companies). It was from the advertising sector, rather than from within radio itself, that US radio derived many of its most familiar and most popular programmes during the decade prior to World War Two. Audience research, too, was developed to new levels of sophistication at the behest of the agencies. In Europe, this operating model was adopted by Radio Luxembourg and Radio Normandie, which broadcast variety and dance music shows that were conceived and produced by London agencies on behalf of British companies. (During the 1950s, Radio Luxembourg took the principle further by selling blocks of airtime to British record companies, who provided programmes that were elongated advertisements for their latest products.)

The 1940s saw the US networks reassume control of programme content, as sponsors switched to television and station ownership became much more localized. Stations found that they could maximize revenue by offering spot advertising – 30-second or longer advertisements, either pre-recorded (on disc or magnetic tape) or delivered live on air – in tandem with sponsorship. This brought more advertisers into radio and became the funding model used by Britain's offshore pirate stations in the 1960s. One of the principles of the legislation that created legal commercial radio in Britain was that there should be a distinct, appreciable separation between editorial content and advertising content, which the spot advertising model made possible.

Selling airtime to advertisers is the lifeblood of commercial radio. A huge amount of corporate investment (managed by the Radio Advertising Bureau in Britain) goes into research designed to strengthen the medium's credibility as an advertising platform in the face of competitive media such as the press and television. Stations usually control their own local sales but entrust national sales of advertising space (which is by far the biggest source of advertising revenue) to any one of a number of national sales houses, most of which are run as profit centres in their own right by the bigger station groups. The creative aspects of radio advertising are usually handled by specialist agencies, though increasingly stations (and groups) have taken on copywriters and production teams to act as in-house suppliers. Historically, radio in Britain has had a Cinderella image as an advertising medium, attracting a low share of national advertising revenue compared to the press and television and failing to attract the same calibre of creativity found in television advertising; since the post-1990 expansion of stations, its share has risen to 5.3 per cent, reflecting a growth rate of 184 per cent (source: Advertising Association).

Traditionally, radio has tended to be used as a *tactical* medium, to reinforce a television campaign, becoming most viable as an advertising medium in its own right when the cost of television airtime increases. The biggest users of radio on a national scale are financial services, public utilities and office equipment sectors, while the adaptability and relative cheapness of radio have made it an ideal medium for fundraising advertisements in response to famine or disaster. Classic FM is a favourite for charities, according to one agency's creative director, 'because it reaches the elderly retired middle-class people who listen in the daytime'. Radio is of most use and value to local advertisers, to advertise locally available services or products, but here the stations are competing directly with freesheets (free local newspapers), which have guaranteed circulations and have the advantage of being read primarily for their advertising. In other words, freesheet readers actively *pursue* consumer information, while in radio it is accepted and perhaps more freely ignored.

What impact does a reliance on advertising as a source of revenue have on the content and character of what is broadcast? The classic critical argument against the commercialization of mass communications media is that pursuit of advertising revenues encourages programming assumed to appeal to the greatest number, thereby marginalizing less popular tastes and interests. It creates an environment most conducive to reception of the advertising message, leading to programming that is undemanding, unchallenging and pacifying. But how much influence *individual* advertisers have over programming on radio is debatable. Advertisers compete among themselves for a commodity (airtime) that is limited by regulation – nine minutes per hour is the limit on British radio – and by the stations' awareness that listeners will tune out if advertisements are too prevalent. Collectively, the picture is different: there have been points in radio's history when the interests of advertisers in particular markets and the radio stations themselves have coincided. In the US during the late 1950s, the switch from family-oriented programming to that aimed at teenagers was fuelled by the growing demand among cosmetics and fashion manufacturers for an advertising outlet aimed specifically at young consumers. Certain types of programming are precluded from prime-time commercial radio – drama and documentaries, for example – because the advertising support they would engender would not be of sufficient scale to justify the cost of production when other, cheaper and more proven forms of programming could fill the space.

More pernicious is the impact of sponsorship on programming. Sponsorship brings extra revenue to the radio station or the production company responsible for the programme and relieves them of some of the cost of production. The sponsoring company is not so much buying airtime as underwriting it, for which it receives in return far greater (and more cost-effective) coverage than it would if it invested in spot advertising alone. Sponsorship is a powerful branding aid, as it allows companies with interests in particular markets to align themselves directly with the lifestyle or self-image of that market. Pepsi-Cola, for example, not only sponsors the nationally syndicated chart show on UK commercial radio but also the tours and promotional activities of pop music acts which have included Michael Jackson, the Spice Girls and B*witched. Financial companies sponsor programmes dispensing financial or consumer advice, thereby enhancing their image within their prime market. Critics of this development suggest that editorial independence is compromised by the blurring of content and advertising.

One of the tasks of programme controllers, producers and presenters is to create an on-air environment in which advertising or a sponsor's name-check is accepted as an integral, non-intrusive part of programming. Their gatekeeping function – deciding what music is played, which presenter is hired, even the news policy of a station – is marketing-led, based on the market targeted by the station and its advertisers, and on a professional appreciation of that market's tastes, interests and foibles. The cheery, bright, upbeat tone of commercial radio provides the ideal setting for advertising that is also mainly cheerful, bright and positive. It is a tone that is conducive to a general, if temporary, sense of emotional well-being – and also conducive to consumption.

CONTROLLING COMMERCIAL RADIO

Even in a much deregulated era, commercial radio does not operate in a totally free market. The issue of regulation is important because *it defines the environment in which, and the rules by which, the broadcasting institutions operate.* How extensive or limited broadcasting is allowed to become is a political decision. This is especially true in Britain, where commercial radio arrived late – in 1973, nearly 50 years after BBC radio – and in a localised rather than national form, which restricted the medium's 'saliency' (perceived effectiveness) as an advertising medium. The ownership structures of stations, their remits with regard to content and even the extent of their profits (on which a levy was initially imposed) were determined quite specifically by the Sound Broadcasting Act of 1972, which applied to a radio context many of the features of Independent Television, launched by an earlier Conservative government in 1955. It allowed for the establishment of stations on a franchise basis under the aegis of the Independent Broadcasting Authority (a revamped Independent Television Authority, now with extra responsibility for radio), whose tasks were to select suitable contractors to run services in designated areas, to supervise planning across the new network, and to undertake the actual transmission of the output of each station. A network news service was envisaged in the manner of Independent Television News, to be funded by an annual subsidy from all the ILR stations. Stations were expected to provide a service to appeal across all age groups and create programmes that reflected the diversity within the community.

All this placed commercial radio in Britain, like ITV, in the paternalistic public service tradition of the BBC. Because the airwaves were deemed to be national property, ownership of the transmitters was vested not in the stations themselves but within the IBA, from which the contracting companies effectively rented airtime; investors were denied a major role in more than one station; investment by other media interests such as newspapers was strictly limited; foreign investment was barred; a system of cross-subsidy ensured that stations in more profitable (usually metropolitan) areas would support those in districts which could not attract the same level or type of advertising; strict rules on the volume of advertising per hour were introduced, together with a complete ban on sponsorship. At heart, ILR (like ITV) was an exercise in regulated, interventionist capitalism entirely in keeping with post-war 'one nation' Conservatism.

After the election of a far more *laissez-faire* Conservative administration in 1979, the principles of giving priority to local programming and ownership, of broad programme schedules, cross-subsidization and a strict division between editorial and advertising content became progressively undermined. The ILR stations saw their profits and audiences decline in the face of breakfast television and an upsurge in land-based piracy; the IBA responded to demands by deregulating by stealth – allowing existing stations to expand into neighbouring areas and take controlling interests in other stations, and also giving the nod to syndication and programme sponsorship for the first time. In 1990, Britain's commercial radio map was effectively redrawn as the IBA was disbanded and the Radio Authority set up in its place to oversee a massive expansion in commercial radio at regional, local and national level, and to police the airwaves with 'a lighter touch'.

The process of deregulating radio needs to be seen as part of a broader, politically generated deregulation of media that encompassed the coming of cable and satellite, Channel 4 (creating a new market for independently produced television programming), the relaxation of rules over overseas investment in British media, the privatization of British Telecom, and a neutralizing of the power of the broadcasting unions. Equally, radio has seen – because of the enabling effect of the 1990 and 1996 Broadcasting Acts – a greater concentration of media ownership as media groups diversify and take advantage of new opportunities to acquire and expand. Most of all, broadcasting has seen a marked shift away from the concept of a publicly owned spectrum, best exemplified by the relatively unreported sale of Britain's network of transmitters to a US company, Castle Tower Communications, in April 1997 at a cost of £210 million.

Ironically, however, deregulation has to be managed politically – it has to be regulated *for*. The mark II version of commercial radio in Britain was not simply the outcome of a policy of encouraging commercial expansion. The Conservative government tried to manage the opening up of media with new priorities that were not paternalistic in the old public service sense but (1) encouraged an even spread of investment and (2) created a new ecology of sound broadcasting, with every niche and market segment catered for and stations dovetailing with one another in terms of their content. (This is also the principle on which the development of cable television and digital television has been based.)

'LISTENER CHOICE'

The government-appointed nine-member Radio Authority licenses and regulates all non-BBC radio services according to procedures and criteria broadly laid out in the Broadcasting Acts of 1990 and 1996. Up to 1999, the Authority had issued over 90 new licences, had re-awarded 116 pre-existing licences as a result of re-advertisement, and had awarded over 2,000 Restricted Service Licences (RSLs), which allow experimental or event-related services to broadcast for 28-day periods. The Authority is funded entirely by the fees paid by would-be stations when applying for licences and the subsequent annual fees paid by licensees. Its main tasks are to plan frequencies (which geographical areas can sustain radio services on which frequencies); to regulate programming and advertising across all licensees, with the power to impose financial penalties or revoke licences if its various codes of practice are violated; to enforce ownership rules; and to appoint licensees *'with a view to broadening listener choice'* (Radio Authority fact sheet No. 1).

The method of awarding licences varies according to the geographical spread of the proposed service. National licences are awarded according to cash bid: the company or consortium with the highest bid wins the licence, while another would-be operator applying for the licence when it comes up for renewal should, in theory, be awarded it automatically if its bid is higher than that of the existing provider. For regional and local services, the method is what is known in radio circles as 'the beauty parade', where the Radio Authority chooses the most 'beautiful' proposal of those matching its criteria for distinctiveness. RSLs are the most widely available (at a cost) and most regularly awarded of all licences in the Radio Authority's gift.

'Listener choice' is the key to broadcasting policy on radio in the 90s (which the Labour government has shown no inclination to waver from): an applicant for a national, regional or local licence must offer its potential audience a radio service that is distinctly different from what is already available in that area – and it must demonstrate a demand for that service in its application and a financial commitment to it in bidding for the licence. The Authority does not set down what form the new service should take, but expects the applicants to research the proposed catchment area and tailor their programming plans to what the existing operators are not providing.

Creating a complementarity between services is a pragmatic solution to the problem of over-demand for frequencies, but it is *not* the free market in action: the policy positively *discourages* outright competition between stations for the same broadcasting markets. This reflects economic realities: radio's share of the total UK advertising spend, though growing year on year, is still too small and the availability of frequencies too limited to support a radio industry based on competition for the same mass audience. The three national commercial stations that exist at the time of writing – Talk Radio, Virgin and Classic FM – do compete for sponsorship and advertising sales, but the terms of their licences prevent them from diverging from their chosen programming in pursuit of other, perhaps more lucrative audiences. Rather than create a rash of directly competing services, therefore, what the deregulatory era has produced is a plurality of services that dovetail in a haphazard way.

Any number of policy dilemmas and contradictions have emerged during the ten years or so since the legislation was enacted. One is that the Radio Authority's selection process demands a choice, ultimately, between communities of taste or interest – say, between a jazz station or a service aimed at Asian listeners, between children or over-35s, between classical music or a phone-in format. Communities effectively compete for attention and priority, leaving some feeling marginalized. The atmosphere of grievance was compounded until mid 1998 by the Authority's refusal to explain their particular licensing decisions. Also, applying for a licence is an expensive undertaking, the heavy investment required inhibiting access to the airwaves by community groups. This hasn't necessarily favoured expansionist radio groups such as GWR, Capital, EMAP and Scottish Radio Holdings – prior to a change of management at the Authority in 1996, not a single licence had been awarded directly to any of the big four radio groups. Ralph Bernard, Chief Executive of GWR, complained bitterly in 1999 of the Authority's policy on this matter: 'It is unbelievable that no large commercial radio broadcaster has been offered a virgin area licence because the application wasn't good enough. You cannot tell me that Capital or EMAP or GWR – with a combined market capitalization of £1.5 billion – haven't come up with a successful format to run a local licence. You tell me the Authority hasn't got an agenda' (*Broadcast*, 18 June 1999).

The dominance that the groups named by Bernard now enjoy has been built on investing heavily (and taking holdings) in would-be licensees, and on an aggressive and competitive policy of buying up stations once they were up and running. On this, the Authority's attitude has been ambivalent. Even the most committed stations can find difficulty achieving their commercial targets, and poor performance (measured by low revenues) can prompt not only management and ownership changes but changes to the programming promised in the original application.

The real winners of the deregulatory era were not the new operators but the existing ILR owners, and especially Capital and GWR. In 1990, they found themselves freed of all IBA-imposed programming requirements and able to operate in the newly deregulated environment from a position of entrenched strength. They were then able to expand, merge, take over their neighbours and remould their programming – and in some cases expand into foreign markets – with remarkably little interference. They have become national operators by stealth (GWR, for example, eventually bought its controlling stake in Classic FM in 1996).

▉ OWNERSHIP AND CENTRALIZATION

Whatever the prescriptions and programming promises demanded of commercial radio operators in the public interest, there are comparatively fewer restrictions in relation to ownership and investment. Very few of the larger stations are privately owned; most of the station groups are listed on the stock market. Figure 3.1 lists the breakdown of ownership of one group, the Independent Radio Group. In Britain as in the US, commercial radio stations remain commodities to be bought, sold and integrated into the grand plans of multimedia (and sometimes global) operators. However, to guard against too great a concentration of ownership by one group, the Radio Authority has, since 1996, maintained a ceiling of 15 per cent on the total ownership points that an individual radio group can claim. Here again we see a form of interventionism in action, much disliked by the radio groups as it inhibits the kind of expansion that would be unquestioned and even encouraged in most other fields of capitalist enterprise. In these circumstances, the most dominant groups have to constantly balance the quest for new acquisitions with the requirement to sell off other holdings (often to direct competitors) in order to make room for them. Even within these limits, a merger, sale or takeover may not be straightforward: Capital's bid for Virgin in 1998, for example, was overruled not by the Radio Authority's automatic public interest test (in which the Authority investigates objections) but by its referral to the Monopolies and Mergers Commission, which decided that Capital would enjoy an unfair domination of the radio advertising market in London if the deal went ahead. In spite of this, it is still possible for a company with virtually no experience in radio ownership to take a controlling stake in a national commercial station – for example, Kelvin MacKenzie's consortium purchase of Talk Radio and Chris Evans' Ginger Productions purchase of Virgin, both in 1998.

Figure 3.2 shows the breakdown of ownership across the UK as it stood in

	%
Trinity plc	20.00
Mercury Asset Management plc	10.92
Robert Fleming Nominees Ltd	9.52
UKRD Group Ltd	9.24
Scottish Amicable Investment Ltd	6.16
AXA Equity & Law Investment Managers	5.6
Equitable Life Assurance Society	4.87
Mercury Alpha Investment Fund	3.92
Other directors	0.71
Figures correct as at 14 May 1999	

Source: Hemmington Scott, 1998

Fig. 3.1 Major shareholders: Independent Radio Group

Fig. 3.2 Station ownership, UK commercial radio

COMPANY	WHOLLY-OWNED LICENCES	OTHER HOLDINGS
3i plc		CFM (25%), The Radio Partnership (27.5%), Marcher Sound (6.6%), Radio Tay (4.7%), Scottish Radio Holdings (1%), UKRD (7.4%)
Border Media Holdings	Century Radio (Teesside/Tyne & Wear), Century 105 (NW England), Century 106 (East Midlands), Sun FM (Sunderland)	A1FM (49.9%), CFM (Carlisle/Cumbria) (20%), Radio Borders (16.7%), South West Sound (Dumfries) (15%)
Bucks Broadcasting (see UKRD)		Mix 96 (Aylesbury) (30%), The Bear (Stratford) (30%), The Wolf (Wolverhampton) (30%), Arrow FM (Hastings), (32.5%), Surf 107 (Brighton) (40%), Centre Broadcasting (Staffs) (35%)
Capital Radio	Capital Gold, Capital FM (London), BRMB FM (Birmingham), Xtra AM, Invicta FM (Kent), Invicta Supergold (Kent), Ocean FM (Portsmouth), Power FM (Southampton), Southern FM (Brighton), Red Dragon (Cardiff), Touch (Cardiff)	Fox FM (Oxford) (57.3%).
CLT-UFA	Atlantic 252, * Country 1035 (London)	Talk Radio (63.19%), Thames FM (SW London) (19.3%), Xfm (15%), South East Radio (20%)
Chrysalis	Heart FM (London), Heart FM (West Midlands), Galaxy 101 (Bristol), Galaxy 102 (Manchester), Galaxy 105 (Yorkshire)	
Daily Mail and General Trust	Essex FM (Essex), Fame 1521 (Reigate/Crawley), KFM (Tonbridge/Sevenoaks), Mercury FM (Horsham), Oasis FM (St Albans), Ten 17 (Harlow), The Breeze (Essex), Vibe FM (East Anglia)	Radio Trust (39.8%), London News Radio (25%), GWR Group (19.2%)
Dawe Media	KLFM (Kings Lynn), Oxygen 107.9 FM (Oxford)	

COMPANY	WHOLLY-OWNED LICENCES	OTHER HOLDINGS
EMAP	Aire FM (Leeds), City FM (Liverpool), Hallam FM (Sheffield), Kiss FM (London), Magic 828 (Leeds), Magic 1161 (Hull), Magic 1548 (Liverpool), Magic AM (South Yorkshire), Metro FM (Tyne & Wear), Piccadilly 1152 AM (Manchester), Key 103 (Manchester), Red Dragon FM (Cardiff), Red Rose 999 (Preston/Blackpool), TFM (Teesside), Touch Radio (Newport/Cardiff), Viking FM (Hull)	Radio Investments (5.9%), The Radio Partnership (5%)
First Oxfordshire Broadcasting Ltd	Fox FM (Oxford)	ElevenSeventy (High Wycombe) (63%), The Bear (Stratford) (30%)
Guardian Media Group		Radio Investments (8%), Golden Rose Communications (15.1%)
Ginger Media	Virgin Radio (National/London)	
Golden Rose Communications	Jazz FM (North West), Jazz FM (London)	
GWR Group	Classic FM (national), Mercia FM (Coventry), 2CR FM (Bournemouth), Classic Gold 828 (Bournemouth), 2 Ten FM (Reading), Classic Gold 1431 (Reading), GWR FM (Swindon/Bristol), Beacon Radio (Wolverhampton/Shrewsbury), Leicester Sound (Leicester), Classic Gold 1359 (Coventry), Trent FM (Nottingham), Ram FM (Derby), Q103 (Newmarket/Cambridge), Hereward FM (Peterborough), B97 (Bedford), Chiltern FM (Luton/Bedford), Horizon 103 (Milton Keynes), Northants FM (Northampton), Orchard FM (Somerset), Severn Sound FM (Cheltenham), Classic Gold 792 (Luton/Bedford), Classic Gold Amber (Suffolk), Broadland 102	News Direct (London) (20%), LBC (London) (20%), Stray FM (Harrogate) (19.9%), Kestrel FM (Basingstoke) (20%), Local Radio Company (20%)

	(Norfolk), SGR (Colchester/Bury St Edmunds), Lantern FM (Barnstaple), Gemini AM/FM (Exeter/Torbay), Wyvern FM (Hereford/Worcester)	Oxygen FM (Oxford) (49%), Surf 107 (Brighton) (40%), Spirit FM (Chichester) (43%)
Independent Radio Group	1458 Lite AM (Manchester), Scot FM (Glasgow/Edinburgh), QFM (Paisley), Wish FM (Wigan), Discovery 102 (Dundee), Wire FM (Warrington)	
Liberty Publishing	96.3 Liberty AM (London)	
Lincs FM	Lincs FM (Lincoln), Trax FM (Worksop), Rutland Radio, Fosseway Radio (Hinckley)	
Local Radio Company	Connect 97.2 (Wellingborough), Gold Radio (Shaftesbury), Isle of Wight Radio, KCBC (Kettering), Spire FM (Salisbury), Wessex FM (West Dorset), Plymouth Sound FM/AM, Cheltenham Radio	
London News Radio	LBC 1152, News Direct (London)	
Marcher Radio Group	MFM 97.1, MFM 103.4, Marcher Gold, Marcher Coast FM (all Deeside)	
Minster Sound	Minster FM (York), Yorkshire Coast Radio	
Orchard Media Ltd	Orchard FM, Lantern FM, Gemini FM, Gemini AM	
Radio Investments Ltd		Island FM (Guernsey/Alderney) (55%), Central FM (Falkirk) (60%), Local Radio Company (75%), Minster Sound (York) (28%), East Sussex (24.1%), Capital Radio (8.83%), GWR (1%), Radio Trust (1%), Scottish Radio Holdings (0.6%), The Bay (Morecambe) (10.7%), Lantern FM (North Devon) (14.5%), Orchard Media (19.5%), Sunshine 855 (Ludlow) (17.5%), Stray FM (Harrogate) (7%), Yorkshire Dales Radio (20%)

Fig. 3.2 *continued*

COMPANY	WHOLLY-OWNED LICENCES	OTHER HOLDINGS
The Radio Partnership	Pulse FM (Bradford/Huddersfield), Swansea Sound Ltd (Swansea/Neath), Valleys Radio (South Wales), The Wave (Swansea), The Wave (Blackpool), Signal One (Stoke), Signal FM (Stockport)	Solent Regional Radio (24%)
Radio Services		South East Radio (41%), Thames FM (23%)
Scottish Radio Holdings	Clyde 1, Clyde 2 (Glasgow), Forth FM (Edinburgh), Northsound One/Two (Aberdeen),Tay AM, Tay FM (Dundee/Perth) West Sound AM/FM (Ayr), Downtown (Northern Ireland), Cool FM (Belfast), Moray Firth Radio (Inverness/Caithness)	South West Sound Ltd (85%), Radio Borders Ltd (62%), CFM (40%), West Sound AM (20%), Central Holdings (17%), Today FM (Ireland) (22%)
Sunrise Radio	Sunrise Radio – London, Sunrise Radio – Yorkshire	
Talk Co.	Talk Radio (national)	
Tindle Radio	Channel 103 (Jersey), Dream 100 (Tendring), Island FM (Guernsey/Alderney), The Beach (Lowestoft)	
UKRD (UK Radio Developments)	Pirate FM (Cornwall), Delta FM (Haslemere)	The Eagle (Guildford) (55%), Star FM (Windsor) (93%), Wey Valley Radio, First Love (59%), Active FM (East London) (30%), County Sound (Guildford) (85.5%), The Falcon (Stroud) (40%), Oldham FM (45%)

Note: Ownership of radio stations in the UK is constantly changing. This list is correct as far as it has been possible to ascertain on 18 May 1999. The list does not include single stations, nor the full level of investment in them by the larger station groups.

* Atlantic 252 broadcasts from Ireland and is not a Radio Authority-licensed station.

Fig. 3.2 *continued*

June 1999, though such is the volatility in the market for radio holdings that the pattern of ownership tends to change from month to month. The chart indicates the concentration of ownership within commercial radio (to the extent that some outwardly competing groups have stakes in the same station) and shows that 'local' radio is anything but: GWR's portfolio of stations embraces localities as distant as Bournemouth and Coventry, Norwich and Gloucester, while EMAP and Capital each have a brand of stations (Magic and Gold respectively) that do not even identify their locality in their name. This suggests a centralizing of formats and a pooling of resources that acts against the spirit of diversity supposedly enshrined in the original legislation – but then, many of these stations started life under different ownership and different remits. Figure 3.3 traces the evolution of GWR from being a single

1982	Wiltshire Radio established under IBA franchise, serving audience of 630,000 from studios in Wootton Bassett, Wiltshire.
1985	Merged with Radio West (Bristol) to form Great Western Radio – first corporate merger in history of commercial radio in Britain.
1988	Flotation on stock market.
1989	Merged with Consolidated Radio Holdings, which includes Radio 210 (Reading) and Two Counties Radio (Bournemouth).
1992	Classic FM launched with minority GWR holding.
1994	Acquisitions include stations in Wolverhampton, Nottingham, Derby, Leceister, Coventry, Peterborough, Cambridge, Kings Lynn.
1995	Number of licences increased to 28 with acquisition of Chiltern Group, incorporating stations in Gloucester, Luton/Bedford, Milton Keynes and Northampton. Sale of Galaxy Radio to Chrysalis Group for £4.1m.
1996	Full takeover of Classic FM (national). Purchase of 31% stake in London News Radio. Purchase of 12-station New Zealand radio company Prospect for £11.6m, followed by sale of said company to Radio Network of New Zealand for £17m six months later. Purchase of 60% stake in Radio Edelweiss, Innsbruck, and 33% stake in Polish station Inforadio. Acquisition of East Anglian Radio for £24.3m. Pre-tax profits: £7.2m.
1997	Acquisition of Radio Wyvern (Hereford and Worcester) for £3.9m.
1998	Formation of consortium (Digital One) with NTL and Talk Radio to apply for national digital radio licence (subsequently awarded). Acquisition of 90% stake in Austrian station Radio Melody for £3.2m. Pre-tax profits: £14.1m.
1999	Acquisition of four-station Devon/Somerset-based Orchard Media for £26m, giving GWR 'network' continuous broadcast coverage along length of M5 motorway.

Fig. 3.3 GWR: expansion, 1982–99

station operator within the ILR system to becoming one of the largest players in British radio.

The dominance of a handful of radio groups over commercial radio in Britain was not planned; it happened because of an ambivalence within the regulatory system. Unless it is ring-fenced or protected in a planned and consistent way, any broadcast medium will inevitably become subject to market pressures that lead inexorably to ownership concentrations and the very undermining of the diversity that the legislation was supposed to encourage:

> The award of a licence has all too often been followed by a sell-out to an established radio operator. Established radio companies don't like the system, as they end up paying over the odds for the licence. Listeners, especially those who campaigned for or listened to the new station, feel that they have been sold out and watch with dismay as the new licence-holder changes and brands the station with its existing identity. The only winners are those awarded the original licence who walk away with a tidy profit.
>
> Woodyear, *Radio Listener's Guide*, p. 4

In some ways, the tensions between the regulatory and commercial dynamics in radio offer a paradigm of commercial involvement in communications as a whole: if there is no political will to curb the expansionism or overt commercialism of the industry's most powerful operators, the regulatory system itself becomes weakened (as happened with the IBA in the 1980s) and the operators negotiate their way around it. Yet the function of a regulatory body like the Radio Authority is not to be restrictive or inhibiting but *enabling*: it acts as a kind of 'honest broker' between competing commercial interests, managing the system to allow as fair and equal a degree of access and opportunity as possible. But that access is automatically limited, by the policy of auctioning licences to the highest bidder, to the major players. The chief means of access into the industry by other would-be operators remains that of circumventing the application system and buying existing stations.

The concentration of ownership and control favours economies of scale that reduce administration and production costs, and centralize advertising sales. This process leads to what Murdock and Golding have described as a movement in media ownership from 'concentration to conglomeration', in which the merging of media companies and the reduction in numbers of owners works hand in hand with commercial diversification, which in turn expands the media owners' sphere of influence. The classic example of this is Rupert Murdoch's News International, which through acquisitions and aggressive cross-media diversification (notably into satellite TV) has secured a massive position of commercial and possibly cultural and political advantage on a global scale. Having only flirted with radio ownership during the 80s and 90s, Murdoch has turned his organization's attention to the medium in aggressive fashion in recent years, notably by backing former *Sun* editor Kelvin MacKenzie's purchase of Talk Radio in 1998. The article reproduced in Figure 3.4, from a leading British marketing magazine, speculates on the motives behind this belated conversion. Here, too, is another example of how the strategic control of a major part of

MEDIA ANALYSIS

Murdoch muscles in on radio world

News International's expansion into radio is causing nervous industry reaction as Murdoch's reputation for dominating markets precedes him. **By Roger Baird**

MacKenzie: The chairman and chief executive of Talk Radio is under pressure to turn the station around

A year ago, Rupert Murdoch's News International had no interest in the UK radio market. Today, it has a programming agreement with Virgin Radio, which is owned by the UK's most renowned DJ, Chris Evans. Murdoch also has a 20 per cent stake in Talk Co, the company which owns Talk Radio.

That adds up to a powerful influence in two of the country's three national commercial stations built up in less than 12 months, a measure of the speed at which NI moves.

The development is part of a Europe-wide pattern. NI has a stake in two radio stations in the Netherlands: a 71 per cent interest in Sky Radio and a 42 per cent in Radio 538.

In February this year it also acquired a 28 per cent interest in a Swedish station, now also renamed Sky Radio.

These continental stations are what the industry calls "juke box" stations, which means they play 24-hour contemporary popular music with no DJs.

NI has also taken a 40 per cent stake in Music Choice Europe, an audio-only music channel which takes up 44 channels of Sky Digital's system but can easily be transmitted on radio networks. Meanwhile, radio advertising rev-

Murdoch: Looking for opportunities

enue in the UK has risen from £141m in 1992 to over £400m this year.

A rival radio group chief executive says: "Murdoch feels he has missed the boat on radio expansion in the US, and he does not want to do the same in Europe. He has brought in some new staff over the past year or so and asked them to take a look at where he can go with radio."

One of two key people Murdoch has brought into News International is Capital Radio's former business development manager Tom Turcan, who is now head of business development for the group. The other is Frederic Thurad, hired from European radio group Europe One, and now the group's radio development business manager. They are said to

Evans: Being helped out by Sky

have given the go-ahead to NI's latest acquisitions in the UK and on the continent.

Simon Cole, managing director of Unique, the UK's largest independent radio production company, says: "The only surprise is that it has taken so long. Look at radio news for instance. There are only two providers of any size: the BBC and Independent Radio News (IRN). Someone like Murdoch is liable to look at that monopoly and see it as an opportunity."

Last week, it emerged that Sky News is hatching a bid to take over Talk Radio's news service from IRN (*MW* December 10).

IRN is a profitable, well-run organisation. Last year it was under-

stood to have made a profit of £10m on revenues of only £20m.

IRN has warded off challenges from larger players before. Four years ago, Reuters tried to break into the UK radio market as a news supplier, but failed to make much of an impact.

Cole comments: "Reuters is a bit of an oil tanker compared with IRN's speedboat; it was simply outmanoeuvred at every turn. All the same, it should be remembered that the last time somebody challenged IRN, they came away with a bloody nose."

NI, through Sky in the UK, has a strong sports broadcasting arm, which last month secured a contract to supply programming to Talk Radio.

Many radio pundits are already suggesting that when radio goes digital at the end of next year, Sky will be best placed to supply sports coverage across the whole of the digital network. As a national broadcaster, Talk automatically has a place on the digital network.

However, others believe that the Murdoch family is acting from personal motives. Panmure Gordon analyst Lorna Tilbian says: "The move into radio is personality-led. Murdoch wanted to find a place for Kelvin MacKenzie in his organisation, and his daughter Elizabeth has a good relationship with Chris Evans. It's a move to back talent."

Whatever NI's motives, it will have a significant influence, partly because of the sheer amount of money it is able to put into radio. So far, NI has invested £8m in Talk Radio and Sky will foot the £4m bill to transmit Chris Evans' breakfast radio show for an hour each weekday for the next two years.

This investment in programming is the sort of thing the BBC can afford, but would leave even the biggest commercial radio groups such as Capital or GWR gasping.

Compared to the billion-pound European pay TV market, where NI's primary focus is to be found, these figures are small. But it's enough to consistently outspend the rest of the commercial radio sector.

Many in the market believe that what happens at Talk will colour NI's view on radio. Zenith head of radio Yvonne Scullion comments: "The test is what happens with Talk over the next year. If MacKenzie can make it work, then Murdoch may go further with radio."

Sources close to the station say NI has given the new management a year to turn around its programming, and a further year to put it into profit.

The sudden entry of NI into radio concerns both the large radio groups and specialist suppliers, because – as Murdoch has shown with TV, newspapers and film – his instinct is not merely to participate in a market, but to dominate it. ●

Fig. 3.4 *Source: Marketing Week*

the commercial radio spectrum may *potentially* be enjoyed by operators with priorities in other media.

The deregulatory thrust in broadcasting has consequences, as the experience of American radio has shown. US radio was based on the commercial ethos from the start, but until the 1980s there was strong political resistance to media conglomeration, on the grounds that it limited consumer choice and undermined competition. The dropping of the 'three-year regulation', which required that any owner of a station had to hold the licence for at least three years before selling on, produced a frenzy of station trading. The Telecommunications Act of 1996 further changed the landscape by removing the previous 40-station limit on ownership to allow companies to own an unlimited number of stations nationwide and up to eight in a main urban market (defined as one with 45 or more stations, such as Chicago or Los Angeles). Even faltering radio stations became marketable overnight, and around 40 per cent of the country's 10,000 stations had changed hands by the end of 1998, at an estimated cost of over $32 billion. Of these, 1,695 changed ownership during 1998 alone. Just four months after the Act became law, CBS Radio's owner Westinghouse Electric bought the Infinity Broadcasting chain of stations for $3.9 billion; three months later, it bid for the ARS chain for $2.6 billion. In 1998, the merger of Jacor Broadcasting and Clear Channel Communications was valued at a radio industry record of $4.4 billion, while that of Chancellor Media with Capstar Broadcasting gave the new company 463 stations in 105 markets in a reported $4.1 billion deal.

One effect of all this has been that independently run stations have been squeezed out (nationally, the number of owners fell by 14 per cent between 1996 and 1998) and that the big players have claimed the lion's share of advertising revenues in particular localities. The main casualties of this appear to have been those stations (especially those with strong FM signals) owned by and aimed at particular communities: according to US Commerce Department figures quoted in *USA Today*, Hispanic-owned stations fell by 9 per cent during 1997 and black-owned stations by 26 per cent. This trend was exacerbated by the dropping of tax advantages for minority stations in 1995 and the sheer scale of the offers made to independents to sell out – for many, the attraction was simply too great.

COMMERCIAL PROGRAMMING

What kind of implications does ownership concentration – and the potential reduction of radio to a minor role within multimedia strategies – have for programming? Multi-ownership enables networking of shows across stations and customization of programme elements such as weather or traffic reports from a central point, which reduces running costs and offers advertisers wider reach. Local content becomes minimized in the process. Corporate owners impose successfully tested formats on new acquisitions: Capital Radio's 'Gold' format of records from the 60s and 70s, for example, is carried by all its affiliated AM stations, with airtime divided between locally produced 'oldies' sequences and those provided from London.

Formats enable stations to target their programming to particular audiences according to their age profiles, so multi-ownership can have the effect of marginalizing those audiences outside the required profile. Traditionally, radio companies counter this argument by pointing out that those owners with several stations in a locality target each to a separate demographic profile – a process called 'flanking' – so that the *total* listening audience is catered for. In practice, however, there tend to be yawning gaps in the audience profiles targeted by commercial radio as a whole, and an overwhelming bias towards the 'economically active' (i.e. the employed). To date, school-age children and the over-60s have virtually no representation on commercial radio in Britain, though there is plenty of evidence that these are market segments with a great deal of buying power: the over-60s, for example, have greater disposable income than any other age group.

Concentration of ownership enables corporate owners to limit competition – not just directly, by buying into it, but also by using their muscle to cement their supremacy within their markets. In the US during 1998 it was reported that radio groups and record companies were making mutually assisting deals to give exclusive access to live concerts and on-air interviews in return for favourable airplay, to the detriment of smaller stations unable to compete financially on the same level.

Commercial radio programming is driven by the pursuit of higher listening figures, better penetration into particular markets, and greater saliency in the advertising marketplace; it is led by focus-group research and the input of high-salaried consultants whose prime objective is to minimize risk. This does not mean that commercial radio must necessarily be devoid of a public service motive or commitment, nor that programming to 'minorities' in the demographically segmented manner practised in the US is not sustainable in a commercial context. But the current state of commercial radio in the US and the UK shows that it is no longer enough for a radio station to simply provide a service and make healthy profits: deregulation has turned radio into an almost uniquely predatory market.

Further reading

Barnard, Stephen (1989): *On the Radio: Music Radio in Britain*. Open University Press.

Crisell, Andrew (1997): *An Introductory History of British Broadcasting*. Routledge.

Keith, Michael C. (1987): *Radio Programming: Consultancy and Formatics*. Focal Press.

Murdock, Graham, and Golding, Peter (1973): 'For a political economy of mass communications' in O. Boyd-Barrett and C. Newbold (1995), *Approaches to Media: A Reader*. Arnold.

Shingler, Martin, and Wieringa, Cindy (1998): *On Air: Methods and Meanings of Radio*. Arnold.

Wilby, Pete, and Conroy, Andy (1994): *The Radio Handbook*. Routledge.

Woodyear, Clive (1999): *Radio Listener's Guide*. PAQ Publishing.

Activity 3.1

Research the history and management structure of your local commercial station, noting key changes in ownership and programme policy since its opening. To what extent can it be described as locally owned? How much, if any, of the programming is shared with other stations – and on what basis? How far is its programming directed at the whole community in its catchment area?

Activity 3.2

Put yourself in the place of a marketing director of a local commercial radio station seeking sponsorship for a Saturday afternoon sports programme.

1. Research and assess the market for such a programme among listeners in terms of age profile, gender bias, social groups. How would you define the likely target audience?
2. With this target audience in mind, outline the main sports that the programme would cover and its main elements (phone-in, live football commentary, results round-up, etc.), and make a list of the companies that would be most likely to place advertising within it and why.
3. Bearing in mind the form of the programme and the nature of the audience, what companies would you approach for sponsorship? What would be the mutual benefit to station and company of a sponsorship deal?
4. What would be the implications of a sponsorship arrangement – for example, Nike's sponsorship of athletics coverage, or Carling Lager's sponsorship of football commentary – for the programme content?

Activity 3.3

Using Figure 3.3 depicting GWR's growth as one of Britain's biggest commercial radio operators, analyse the strategies that have informed it. Has there been a geographical cohesion to GWR's expansion, and can you account for any gaps in the company's portfolio of stations – for example, a lack of presence in regional radio when compared to local and national radio? Undertake your own research into the type of programming offered by GWR stations and the degree to which policy is centrally defined or imposed. What would you expect GWR's next move to be?

Activity 3.4

Choose a commercial station and log all the advertisements heard during the drive-time period of 4pm to 6pm. Summarize which sector of the listening audience each is aimed at, and give reasons why. Write a brief critique of any one of the commercials in terms of the creativity of its content, the effectiveness of its message and its placing within the time slot. Is the aim of the advertisement to encourage you to buy, to increase brand recognition or provide consumer information? How is radio particularly suited to promoting this product or service?

Activity 3.5

Read the article on Rupert Murdoch's involvement in Talk Radio (Figure 3.4). Summarize the benefits to Murdoch's News International of taking a stake in the station and the particular role that Kelvin MacKenzie is playing in it. Bearing in mind News International's existing involvement in print journalism and television news, what might be the motive behind taking part-ownership of a station that is speech- and news-based rather than music-oriented?

4

Alternativism and Community Radio

In a broadcasting system as long established and as highly structured and regulated as Britain's, it is perhaps not surprising that there is only a limited tradition or culture of alternativism within radio. Other countries have, albeit within institutionalized parameters, encouraged the growth of alternative modes of ownership, funding and programming and with it a different kind of relationship between audience and broadcaster. Such alternativism as there is in British radio has tended to operate and occasionally thrive on the fringes of legalized broadcasting, often taking the form of straightforward piracy (the unauthorized purloining of frequencies for broadcasting) but sometimes operating under the umbrella of officially sanctioned community radio.

Whether legal or not, what such stations represent is a degree of dissent from established broadcasting norms and traditions and a reaction against some of the ideological assumptions discussed in previous chapters. One of the key arguments of supporters of community radio is that it is a response to mainstream radio's tendency to either ignore or fail to adequately reflect the needs of minority audiences, however the term 'minority' may be defined. In this chapter, we will explore this and other arguments and look at the impact of fringe radio on the mainstream.

First, it helps to clarify what is meant by 'alternativism'. The term implies a coherent, uniform, oppositional response to the mainstream, but it covers different approaches, attitudes and precepts that are sometimes defined in terms of modern versus traditional, progressive versus conservative, or even revolutionary versus reactionary. The so-called 'alternative' press that sprang up in the late 60s (magazines such as *Oz* and *International Times*) published material sympathetic to the drug culture of the time. In music industry parlance, 'alternative' music – for which 'indie' (short for independent) is a common synonym – is music neither aimed at mainstream audiences nor mainstream in attitude, though this does not stop some music being marketed as 'alternative' in order to stress its credibility.

RADIO AND OPPOSITION

Daniel Cohn-Bendit, one of the key protagonists in the mass student protests of the late 1960s, once commented that the reason those protests failed to translate into open revolution was because the students failed to capture the radio stations. At times of acute political tension, radio can be a means of instant access to a mass audience, of spreading disinformation or disaffection, a rallying point, and at time of war it may well be the only source of news.

The story of alternativism on radio is essentially one of how opposition to authority is organized, expressed and disseminated. This can take, and often has taken, an overt political form, particularly when that authority is embodied by government, its agencies or the services sanctioned by them. Indeed, clandestine radio has played a key part in the internal political struggles and civil wars of many countries over the years, especially as transmitting equipment is relatively cheap to obtain and easy to move. One example is Algeria, whose national station Radio Alger was, prior to the late 1940s, listened to almost wholly by French settlers and took values, emphasis and programming from the French National Broadcasting System. In effect, it was an instrument of colonial power. When the campaign for independence from France began in the 1950s, attempts were made to 'Algerianize' its output, but most Algerians turned to the Cairo station, the Voice of the Arabs, for a less slanted presentation of events as they were unfolding. As Julian Hale relates, the establishment in late 1956 of the Voice of Free Algeria as the voice of the Front National de Libération was 'the signal not just for a rush to buy any and every radio set, but also for a new unity between the leaders of the revolution and the ordinary people in whose name they were fighting the French colonists . . . the more the French tried to stop people listening, and hunted down the fugitive transmitters, the more credible became the persistent, elusive and sometimes less than audible Voice . . . [radio] created a new national speech and a new national consciousness' (Hale, p. 117).

Hale cites some other examples of clandestine radio at work. Radio Biafra was established in 1967 as an information and propaganda weapon in the fight for the region's independence from Nigeria and benefited from the input of novelist Frederick Forsyth, who acted as adviser, and the advertising and public relations company, Markpress, which ensured that charges of Nigerian genocide were circulated internationally. There were numerous examples during the 1970s of pirate stations springing up in Northern Ireland as mouthpieces for the IRA (Radio Free Derry), the Ulster Defence Association (Radio Free Nick) and the Ulster Vanguard Movement (Voice of Ulster), though their impact was minimal.

During the Bosnian war of 1991–95, scores of Serbian, Croat and Muslim stations came and went in a confused and confusing battle for military and psychological supremacy. When the US-brokered Dayton Accord brought an end to military action, the potential of such stations – which increased at one point to around 200 – to sow dissension and even reignite conflict was not fully appreciated. 'Frequencies for independents were obtained by backhanding the right politicians and kept by the same method, allegedly ... content was unregulated and certainly uncontrolled by any authority', John Ross-Barnard reported in *The Radio Magazine*. 'Wild stories about how the "other side" was out to get them were not only read out but embroidered into the lyrics of so-called folk songs to confuse the temporary international government called the Office of the High Authority.' To counter this, a re-education strategy was enacted by the OHA – including the setting up of a BBC journalism school in Sarajevo with funding from the Soros Foundation – and a Swiss-funded radio network, FERN (Free Election Radio Network), was established employing staff and journalists from the three communities. By 1998, an Independent Media Commission was in place to regulate all broadcasting and press activity throughout Bosnia.

The Bosnian experience is virtually unique, paralleled only by the internationally enacted reconstruction of German and Japanese broadcasting after World War Two. The intention in Bosnia, as it was 50 years ago, has been to recreate a hegemony of consensus that limits opportunity for further conflict.

COMMUNITY RADIO MODELS

Politicized radio, in war or peace, gives voice to the forces of opposition. By definition, it polarizes as much as it galvanizes. Events concerning oppositional radio in France and Italy during the 1970s, however, had a long-term effect not only on the particular broadcasting systems of those countries but on their domestic politics too, and also, albeit via a circuitous route, on the eventual shape that radio took in Britain and elsewhere. Out of the oppositional politics and alternative culture of the time came a new concept in community-based radio whose development was paralleled in Canada and Australia and, to a limited extent, in the US.

In *The Invisible Medium*, Lewis and Booth trace these developments in some detail. In Italy in 1974, a campaign for reform of the country's archaic broadcasting system (dominated by the right-wing Christian Democrat party through the state-owned broadcasting corporation, RAI) snowballed after the appearance of an illegal station broadcasting from the heartland of communist Italy, Bologna. When hundreds of other illegal stations came on air in a direct challenge to the authorities, Italy's Constitutional Court declared the RAI's monopoly of local stations invalid. The new stations were a mixture of ambitious commercial operators, cooperative ventures and anarchist stations, and taken together they drained the RAI of much of its listenership. In France at roughly the same time, '*radios libres*' (free radio stations) 'came to symbolise opposition to the centralised tradition of French broadcasting and the cultural and linguistic domination of Paris' (Lewis and Booth, p. 148). A collective of would-be operators, the Association pour la Libération des Ondes, published its own plans for legal local radio based on avoiding the relative anarchy of free radio in Italy and prompted the formation of a splinter group, the

Fédération Nationale des Radios Libres Non-Commerciales, with the philosophy that radio 'should be the means of expression of a particular group which already has its own identity. If the group disappears, so does the radio' (Lewis and Booth, p. 149). Together with trade union stations, these made an eclectic mix, and the new socialist government of 1981 created a Consultative Committee and High Authority to oversee the award of frequencies to non-commercial private local stations (RLPs); but with scores of groups applying for a limited supply of frequencies, there were inevitable casualties. In 1984, more radical changes were introduced to allow the licensing of 1,600 RLPs funded by advertising. With the election of the Chirac government in 1986, political control of radio licences was reintroduced and many openly left-wing stations lost their franchises.

Ultimately, as Lewis and Booth point out, what started out as alternative radio in France became institutionalized. What began as a disparate movement essentially radical and oppositional in nature – and favoured by the availability and relative cheapness of the technology – paved the way for change which in turn opened up unprecedented opportunities for commercial operators. It is a familiar pattern in the commercial development of radio, but it cannot necessarily be applied to the relationship between established radio and alternative radio in all territories. In some countries, for example, the pressure for change and expansion has come directly from the commercial sector: Britain had virtually no organized campaign for community-based radio until the 1970s, but the campaign for commercial radio had pre-war roots and predated that for commercial television. 'Alternativism' in British radio in the 1960s (and also in Holland, which enjoyed a similar boom) meant unlicensed offshore stations funded by US money that took advertising and played pop music on the American Top 40 pattern. The challenge was to the status quo. The big expansion in radio that followed the 1990 Broadcasting Act was the consequence of lobbying from two very different, opposing sectors.

At this point, it is useful to define what is meant by 'community radio' and the sources of its philosophies and principles. The Italian and French experiences give some clues, but the examples of Australia, Canada and the US are equally as instructive. The World Association of Community Radio Broadcasters defines community radio in terms of ownership, objectives and message, all of which are interlinked. Size of stations or coverage areas (which could be anything from a village location to many square miles of remote territory) are less relevant than ownership structures that embrace co-operative financing, administration and policy-making; funding may come in the form of subscriptions, listener donations, or even national or international agencies. Community radio does not eschew advertising, but the principle is to use advertising revenue to directly fund programming or running costs, not as a source of profit. The idealism behind this is best summed up by a community radio broadcaster from Ecuador, Jose Ignacio Lopez Vigil:

Do we work primarily for our own gain, or to help improve the social conditions and the cultural quality of life of the people in our communities?

> Community radio stations are not looking for profit but to provide a service to civil society. Naturally, this is a service that attempts to influence public opinion, create consensus, strengthen democracy and above all create community.
>
> AMARC web site

An Australian community radio historian defines the difference between commercial and community radio succinctly:

> . . . commercial radio broadcasts in order to make money. Community radio seeks to make money in order to broadcast . . . the primary reason for the existence of community radio is to provide entry to the public sphere for those who may normally be excluded.
>
> Hope-Hume, Broadcasting and the Public in Australia

The American experience helped establish the defining principles of community radio – a radio form which, in Lewis and Booth's words, 'reinstated the listener as subject-participant in a sharing of artistic and political power' (Lewis and Booth, p. 115). The pioneer station was KPFA in the university town of Berkeley, California, launched by the Pacifica Foundation in 1949 following an FCC decision to reserve 20 per cent of available FM frequencies for non-commercial operators. KPFA was non-profit making; financed by voluntary subscriptions; structured on a departmental basis (creating news, public affairs, music, drama, literature, third world and women's programming); and run by an elected board with a small paid staff and a team of volunteers, all of whom had union recognition. In time, the Foundation extended its operation to five stations across the US.

The Foundation's objectives were to provide the kind of serious discrete programming that was obsolete in most mainstream US radio from the 1940s onwards. It survived the anti-communist witch-hunts of the early 1950s and openly supported liberal political issues such as civil rights during the 60s. A former KPFA employee, Lorenzo Milam, took an even more radical approach from 1962 with a string of FM stations that were more experimental than Pacifica's. 'A radio station should not be just a hole in the universe for making money or feeding an ego, or running the world,' Milam wrote. 'A radio station should be a live place for live people to sing and dance and talk; to talk their talk and walk their walk and know that they, and the rest of us, are not financially and irrevocably dead.'

The year 1967 was crucial for 'alternative' broadcasting, following the FCC's instruction to AM stations to use their FM frequencies to offer different programming. The impact that this had on the American radio market as a whole – an object lesson in the commodification of alternativism – is the subject of the case study at the end of this chapter. In the same year, the US government set up a Corporation for Public Broadcasting to encourage 'high quality, diversity, creativity, excellence and innovation', through funding of National Public Radio. Under the funding formula, financial support was given to non-profit stations according to transmission power and hours of programming, though this tended to exclude low-power college stations. Though the idea was to encourage a publicly approved alternative to mainstream commercial radio, one of the effects of NPR was to prompt the formation of stations that were alternative to it. The creation of the National Federation of Community Broadcasters (NFCB) in 1975 re-emphasized a commitment to local community control, access and policy-making among the low-power stations affiliated to it. The deregulatory atmosphere of the 1980s and the trimming back of public funds for broadcasting encouraged greater concentration on programming to specific audiences and cost-efficiency, but the concept of community radio came through largely intact.

MICRORADIO

By the late 1990s, when the NFCB had a membership of 160 stations in the US, the advantages of ever-cheaper equipment and the exploitation of uncertainty within the FCC were combining to fuel a new surge in radio piracy and activism. This continues to centre around what is commonly called 'microwatt radio', 'micropower radio' or 'microradio' – stations operating at power levels of up to 100 watts. In 1978, the FCC stopped licensing stations of less than 100 watts, effectively forcing them underground. (Alaska was the only territory exempted by the ruling.) By 1998, a would-be operator could purchase a transmitter, 12-amp power supply, filter, limiter, antenna, cable, power meter and standard DJ mixer, from sources such as Free Radio Berkeley, for around $700.

Microradio campaigners have tended to fall into distinct groups. Its pioneers were civil rights activists who saw microradio as a vehicle for community radio in the fully local, grass-roots sense. Yet microradio also has 'a strong group of would-be broadcast entrepreneurs who see this service as a lower tier of the commercial industry. They want the FCC to authorise commercial, advertising-based low-power stations, and to auction the spectrum space to the highest bidders' (Peter Franck, Microradio Empowerment Coalition web site at www.nlgcdc.org). It was seemingly with one eye on the latter group that, after years of active opposition to authorizing microradio, the FCC indicated a willingness to explore its possibilities in January 1999, when it issued a 'Notice of Proposed Rulemaking' to legalize low-power broadcasting on FM. Politically, it seemed to be an attempt to mitigate the effects of the 1996 Telecommunications Act, which had caused a wave of 'merger mania' between radio groups in the US and a consolidation of ownership into just a handful of companies (see page 64). Here was an enabling measure that would simultaneously open up radio to new users (including community groups, ethnic minorities, high schools and church organizations) and make greater use of available spectrum, yet leave the economic base of the existing stations unchallenged. It was introduced at a time of intense and aggressive FCC action against unlicensed operators throughout the US.

The FCC proposals include the establishment of a two-tier system of community radio, through licensing FM stations of 100 to 1,000 watts (8.8-mile radius) and 10 to 100 watts (3.5-mile radius), with the possibility of a third tier (on which it invited comments) of stations of one to 10 watts covering a radius of up to two miles. Several of the campaign groups complained that this distinction would undermine the lower tier's status, particularly if a top-tier or full-power station in the same locality boosted its power; also criticized was the proposal to allow a single organization ownership of up to five low-power stations, which raised the prospect of small-scale broadcasting empires, and the lack of any requirement on licence holders to originate local programming.

Mainstream broadcasters, meanwhile – as represented by organizations like the National Association of Broadcasters – saw the proposals as unleashing new, disruptive voices on the airwaves and breaking with the American radio tradition of allowing market forces to dictate what (and who) survives on air. The unspoken fear was of competition – not so much from the radical, activist sector as from an impatient independent sector seeking to exploit gaps in the market. NAB president Edward Fritts commented that the proposals threatened 'the transition to IBOC [In Band On Channel] digital radio, will likely cause devastating interference to existing broadcasters, and will challenge the FCC as guardian of the spectrum . . . in its quest for "more diversity" we fervently hope that the FCC does not damage today's free, locally based system of radio that is the envy of the world' (quoted in *The Radio Magazine*).

AUSTRALIA AND BRITAIN

The Australian experience of community radio has some parallels with that in the US. In Australia, where a two-tier broadcasting system comprising the national public service broadcaster ABC and a commercial sector had been in place in 1936, pressure for a third tier linked to neither came from a powerful arts lobby, the universities (wishing to establish educational stations on the US model), the ethnic communities and radical students. Under Gough Whitlam's Labor government – elected on a platform of establishing a new national, and less Eurocentric, identity – a third tier of 'fine music' (classical), educational and ethnic stations was introduced between 1972 and 1975 on the FM band. Under the deregulatory Broadcasting Services Act of 1992, the three tiers were joined by a further three – subscription broadcasting and subscription narrowcasting (i.e. encrypted paid-for services) and open narrowcasting (freely available) – in which stations were made available to the highest bidders. Narrowcasting signified specialist stations offering services such as tourist information and sport. One of the effects of this, according to Jeff Langdon, was 'the blurring of the difference between some types of community licence and open narrowcasting. Already a number of open narrowcast licences have been issued to groups which would otherwise have sought community licences. Already the Australian Broadcasting Authority is finding it hard going to define what differentiates a narrowcaster from a broadcaster' (Jeff Langdon, 'The social and political forces that led to the development of Public Radio in the 1960s', www.adelaide.edu.au/5UV, 1995).

Britain's experience of community radio mirrors this problem of definition. Britain was a latecomer to the whole idea of local radio, commercial radio and community radio, and such pressure as there was for expansion was for commercial radio alone – heightened by the 1960s success of illegal commercial radio, broadcasting from offshore. The main thrust in expansion until the mid 80s came in developing local radio – a task handed to the BBC – and subsequently in creating a commercial alternative to it. The political appetite for deregulation in the 80s – coupled with pressure from within commercial radio for expansion, the boom in radio piracy and the crystallization of a vocal new lobby for community radio – led directly to the growth of radio at local, regional and national level. Community radio therefore became embraced and embroiled within the existing duopoly of commercial and public service broadcasting. In the legislation that enabled the new wave of stations to become a reality, there was no official distinction between kinds of station, merely an insistence on economic viability.

The post-1990 stations were all born in a spirit of alternativism of one kind or another, but they provided an object lesson in the difficulty of defining exactly what the terms 'alternative' and 'community' mean. Community radio on the French, Italian and American models was the inspiration behind the establishment of an umbrella group of academics and activists, the Community Communications Group (COMCOM) in 1977, which proposed to that year's Annan Committee on broadcasting the creation of a Local Broadcasting Authority to nurture locally accountable radio. Although this was rejected, the concept of local, non-BBC affiliated radio with greater accountability was responded to sympathetically by the Committee, and the IBA itself proposed to the Select Committee on Nationalised Industries that 'a new sector of autonomous, non-profit, community-based local radio, one that is not dependent on advertising' be set up. While this was not followed through, the lobby was sufficiently encouraged to campaign further, and the Greater London Council funded a number of active community radio workshops that were pivotal in providing training and meeting points for those interested. At the same time, both BBC radio and the IBA encouraged stations to become more involved in working directly with their communities.

Paralleling this – and likewise encouraged by the decreasing cost of transmitters and broadcasting equipment – came a new proliferation of unlicensed pirate stations in metropolitan areas. The new pirate radio echoed the old offshore variety, in that the outlawing of the latter in 1967 had led to the formation of groups (notably the Free Radio Association) dedicated to 'freeing' the airwaves for anyone with the money and enthusiasm to set up their own transmitter and play music. These groups in turn spawned a trade in information regarding transmitter technology. Meanwhile, the surge in listening to pirate radio – notably Radio Invicta, London Weekend Radio, JFM and Horizon in London – was in part a consequence of the stations' black music output, which had traditionally been relegated to specialist programming streams on legal stations. As action by the Radio Interference Department (later the Radio Investigation Service) became noticeably selective and the financial risks involved in unlicensed broadcasting diminished (because confiscated equipment could be easily replaced), so the stations began to operate quite openly.

A 1979 article in *Time Out* succinctly defined the new pirates as belonging to any one of five different categories – disc jockeys for whom 'pirating on the airwaves can be the ultimate in liking the sound of your own voice'; 'techfreaks' whose love of the technology tends to outweigh interest in programme content; 'music missionaries' intent on bringing their own tastes in the obscure to a wider public; and believers in 'community access', who argue that radio technology can put members of a locality in touch with each other and have a transforming effect on the political process; and those with undisguised political interests. If there was more than an element of hyperbole about the whole pirate boom, it was clear that they had the largest following in parts of London, Manchester and Birmingham, while ethnic stations like London Greek Radio and its offshoot The Voice of the Immigrant could fairly claim that they were reaching audiences – Greek and Greek Cypriot, with a high proportion of non-English-speaking elderly people – who but for their existence would not listen to radio at all.

An aborted 'community radio' experiment in 1985 led to 245 groups coming forward with applications, 64 of them in London alone. The sheer weight of numbers and diversity of applications underlined the potential but also prompted its postponement until the difficult process of selection and monitoring of the applications could be worked out. The 1990 Broadcasting Act subsequently created a Radio Authority that would supervise frequency allocation; however, in setting out the criteria for selection it acknowledged the need for new programming but not any structural or philosophical difference between different approaches to broadcasting. Any station would in theory be permissible so long as it kept within the bounds of decency and good taste, could demonstrate that the service it provided did not directly duplicate any existing service within the locality, and paid its way. This dovetailed with what the majority of the pirates had campaigned for – to programme as they like, legally, and with no interference – but only partly with the concept of non-paternalistic, non-commercial, democratically controlled and locally owned access radio developed since the 1970s by the various community radio pressure groups. The implicit assumption in the new legislation was that both perceptions of radio were tenable and could live together.

But a degree of antagonism was already apparent: some members of the pirate lobby had, as early as 1986, split from the Community Radio Association to join the Association of Small Independent Radio Stations. The common view within established commercial radio was that pirate stations were primarily interested in introducing unrestrained, low-cost commercial radio by the back door. And although the commercial stations, through their trade association the Association of Independent Radio Contractors (AIRC), campaigned hard for action against the pirates, the irony was that the pirates' success in broadcasting without fetters or regulation demonstrated the AIRC's own case for removing those regulations and creating a level playing field.

Numerous pirates grabbed the opportunity to 'go legitimate' after 1990, and there were some spectacular success stories including Kiss FM, which was eventually bought up by the EMAP media group. For the original community radio activists, however, it was a mixed story. The changing ecology of radio in the 90s – particularly the expansion of the larger ILRs into wider catchment areas, and the parallel broadening of BBC local radio stations into county or even three-county stations – suggested that highly localized services might flourish, but by the end of 1998 only 19 stations with permanent licences were operating under the code of practice of the Community Media Association (see Figure 4.1). Much more successful were the 'incremental' or Restricted Service

Community broadcasting services:

1. Serve geographically recognisable communities or communities of interest.

2. Enable the development, well-being and enjoyment of their listeners through meeting their information, communication or cultural needs; encourage their participation in these processes through providing them with access to training, production and transmission facilities; stimulate innovation in programming and technology; and seek out and involve those sections of the community under-represented in existing broadcast services.

3. Take positive action to ensure that management, programming and employment practices encourage non-sexist, non-racial attitudes and representation; for example by including such pledges in their constitutions or secondary rules and by instituting relevant training and awareness programmes.

4. Reflect the plurality and diversity of their listening community and provide a right of reply to any person or organisation subject to serious misrepresentation.

5. Draw their programming from mostly regional/local sources rather than national sources.

6. Have their general management and programming policy made by a broadly based Council of Management including the producers.

7. Are legally constituted as non-profit-making trusts, co-operatives or non-profit-maximising limited companies.

8. Are financed from more than one source, such as public and private loans, shares, advertising, listener subscriptions and public grants.

9. Have ownership solely representative of their locality or community of interest.

10. Recognise the right of paid workers to be unionised and encourage the use of volunteers.

Source: The Community Media Association

Fig. 4.1 Community Media Association Code of Practice

Licences – short-term (28-day) licences issued mainly to groups running specific events. Figures for 1997 showed that 34 RSLs had been allocated to London stations, 27 to West Yorkshire, 21 to Greater Manchester, 18 to the West Midlands and 14 to Glasgow. RSLs were particularly important for spreading broadcasting skills among largely volunteer teams and raising awareness of issues and causes, this at a time when BBC and commercial stations have been cutting back training schemes. A station in Sheffield, Forge FM, has at the time of writing broadcast under an RSL for a tenth time. Its community links include the involvement of the city's Northern Media School, which provides finance, training and daily news support, and joint broadcasts with the city's hospital radio services.

For many, gaining an RSL and proving their viability (financial and in terms of audiences reached) is a crucial step in applying for a full-time licence. This happened in the salutary case of Xfm (see pages 215–217), which then encountered severe problems trying to stay within its original 'alternative music' remit and attract the necessary advertising. A more familiar pattern is that former RSL stations become a smaller, much more localized version of ILR, drawing on backing from local newspaper groups and relying on a core of local advertisers. One example is Quay West in Somerset, which came on air in August 1998 and attracted national attention as the smallest station in England. Quay West is the epitome of small-scale radio, with a full-time on-air staff of two, a catchment area of just 32,000 people, investors including the West Somerset Free Press, and travel news provided by a local taxi firm and weather from the harbour master.

Quay West's 'alternativism' rests on providing a service that's far more localized than anything that the ILR operators could provide, except by means of opt-out stations. (Opt-out stations are local broadcasting centres offering a couple of hours of localized programming, literally 'opting out' of networked programmes for the duration.) The same applies to CTFM in Canterbury, which came on air in September 1997 with backing from the Kent Messenger newspaper group. As John Ryan, the station's managing director, put it a few months into CTFM's life:

> You do public service by stealth ... public service doesn't negate entertainment, and packaging things better doesn't negate its value as public service. It's an outdated term – if you said public service radio for Canterbury, nobody would listen. It's like the muesli that's got raisins in it, it's good for you but who wants to eat oats all the time ... community spirit is a fairly dead notion – you could live anywhere in the country and not know your neighbours. There are some very unusual circumstances in which it will work, for example – usually racial communities, if you're doing a black music station for Lewisham, the Asian radio station in Leicester gets close, but not if it was all about 'Whitstable community umbrella is getting together today and they want to take direct action for people with disabilities in the town'. A station can't just be there to be a community outlet, because that's not why people use the radio. People use the radio for all sorts of things, for entertainment, company, their use of radio is too sophisticated

just to run a community radio station. Even if you had a cheque coming every week from some benefactor, nobody would listen to it.

Interview with the author, 5 May 1998

A further issue is the increasing involvement of the major radio groups in RSLs, either in actively competing with community groups for the licences or in buying into them once the licence holders have proved themselves. Sometimes the involvement begins earlier, through the provision of support, facilities and financial help. For example, one of the smaller radio groups, UKRD, took 68.9 per cent of share capital in First Love Radio, which won the licence for Lewisham in late 1997.

CASE STUDY: FREEFORM RADIO IN THE US

The development of FM radio in the US during the 1960s and beyond provides a good illustration of how new technology can offer new outlets for new kinds of programming. It also demonstrates how, due to commercial and regulatory pressures, 'alternative' approaches can themselves become quickly absorbed into the broadcasting mainstream. For much of the 50s, FM was used primarily for foreign-language programming to specific ethnic groups, or (if AM and FM franchises were co-owned) for simultaneous broadcasting of an AM station's programmes. In 1966, however, the Federal Communications Commission introduced a new requirement that stations must from then on simulcast no more than 50 per cent of their programming. This put an immediate obligation on station owners to provide distinctive programming on FM.

In San Francisco, a traditional centre of American bohemianism and in the mid 1960s the home of a burgeoning 'drop-out' community, station KMPX-FM quickly evolved from a foreign-language station into one catering specifically for the city's underground culture. Disc jockey Tom Donahue moved from a daytime job on an AM station, KYA, to take charge of these changes: he reshaped the programming with an eclectic mix of blues, jazz, and classical music, as well as some of the more left-field rock music being released on albums which had hitherto had no natural home on radio. When local bands began recording, he was an early champion. In 1968 he moved across to KSAN and perfected what was, in effect, a blueprint of 'progressive' music radio identified with a cool, informed style of presentation. He derided Top 40 radio in print, describing it in *Rolling Stone* as 'a retarded child . . . aimed directly at the lowest common denominator. The disc jockeys have become robots performing their inanities at the direction of programmers who have succeeded in totally squeezing the human element out of their sound . . . Top 40 radio as we know it today is dead and its rotting corpse is stinking up the airways.' What Donahue developed was not wholly new, and it was paralleled in other American cities, notably by WABX in Detroit and WBCN in Boston. At KYA itself, Russ 'The Moose' Syracuse had experimented with free-form, play-anything music radio in the relative safety of night-time broadcasting (where DJs could work relatively free from advertising strictures).

FM radio was therefore very much a crusade against traditional chart-based radio formats. Donahue and his supporters favoured individual presenters' choices over playlists and rotation, were suspicious of advertising, and preferred to champion alternative music over mainstream commercial records. At KMPX, the new approach proved an instant success, with advertising revenues increased from $3,000 a month to around $25,000. A newly launched sister station, KPPC, produced even better results. However, here as elsewhere, there were tensions from the start, particularly between management and the presenting and engineering teams. A strike at KMPX led to sackings and policy changes, with some of the key staff (including Donahue) decamping to KSAN, one of the first FM rock stations to be owned by a major media corporation, Metromedia. Attacks by US Vice President Spiro Agnew on the supposed left-wing bias of the media brought a greater tendency on the part of station owners to steer clear of controversy and, in some cases, to actively censor or ban certain records.

By 1970, the neutralizing effect of all this was such that a writer in *Rolling Stone* could describe underground radio as 'just another spinoff of commercial, format radio' – the cosmetics of Donahue's original blueprint retained but the soul of the concept, the sense of experimentation and challenge, largely dissipated:

> The typical station comes on with waves of good vibes, builds an audience of loyal listeners by playing album cuts unheard on AM, by talking with instead of to listeners, and by opening up the station to the community. As the audience builds, however, the ratings climb and station owners suddenly have a marketable commodity. Suddenly the air is filled with increasingly uptight advertisers, national corporations and agency spots replacing local commercials; administration takes over, and everything is sterilised. Suddenly there are playlists; certain records have to be banned. No more interviews – can't stop the flow of music. No politicising – remember the Fairness Doctrine [of the regulatory body, the FCC] . . . in the end, FM rock stands naked. It is, after all, just another commercial radio station.

The FM rock format – for that is what it became – proved lucrative, because it captured a young, growing student market with money to spend. If the late-60s generation of record buyers was not as outwardly materialistic or aspirational as their parents or elder siblings, they were still in the market for leisure products (stereo albums, radio programming, fashion) that reflected their values and interests. It was through astute promotional use of FM radio that the major American record labels – Columbia (CBS), Atlantic, and Warner Brothers in particular – were able to achieve a breathtaking domination of the post-1967 record market. Meanwhile, FM rock radio metamorphosed into a plethora of new formats such as the 'Love' format launched by the ABC network. ABC subsequently pioneered the album-oriented rock (AOR) format, developing the primacy that FM radio gave to album tracks and the generally mellow presentation ambience but adding the disciplines of playlisting and re-establishing the power of the programme director. By the mid-70s, AOR was the prime format on American radio, consistently beating even the established

Top 40 stations. AM stations picked up elements of the format, depending on the particular demographics they wished to attract. KGB-AM in San Diego, for example, mixed album tracks and singles sequentially and broke with the tradition of basing airplay on what was in the chart. This style of programming was labelled 'Progressive AM'. By the end of the decade, AOR and Top 40 stations alike had switched their services from AM to the aurally superior FM waveband, and a wave of new formats followed that fine-tuned still further the more ratings-sensitive aspects of the programming.

The 1978 film *FM* helped legitimize FM radio's absorption into mainstream American culture by playing on the myth of small-time independence at loggerheads with centralized corporatism: it depicted a station's staff rebelling against a takeover by playing all the music that the new executives wanted to ban and gathering listener support by doing so. The irony was that much of the music featured on the soundtrack as being somehow radical or left-field was very mainstream indeed. Only the cynical title song by Steely Dan hinted at the passivity of listeners and the unquestioned acceptance of technical excellence for its own sake – as the lyric put it, 'no static at all'.

What happened to underground radio in the US mirrored the fate of the 'alternative' culture as a whole. What began as a genuinely radical departure from established norms became absorbed into the mainstream, owing to a mixture of political and commercial pressures. What remained – as in the worlds of music and fashion – was a veneer of radicalism exemplified by the cool tone, sober style and self-consciously hip language of the presentation, a winning out of cosmetics over substance.

Further reading

Denisoff, R. Serge (1975): *Solid Gold: The Popular Record Industry*. Transaction.
Eberly, Philip K. (1982): *Music in the Air: America's Changing Tastes in Popular Music*. Hastings House.
Fong-Torres, Ben (1974): *The Rolling Stone Reader*. Bantam.
Girard, Bruce (ed.) (1992): *A Passion for Radio*. Black Rose.
Hale, Julian (1972): *Radio Power: Propaganda and International Broadcasting*. Paul Elek.
Hope-Hume, Bob (1996): 'Broadcasting and the Public in Australia' in *Communication and Culture, Identity, Plurality, Equality*. Korean Broadcasting Academic Society.
Jankowski, N., Prehn, O. and Stappers, J. (1992): *The People's Voice*. John Libbey.
Keith, Michael C. (1997): *Voices in the Purple Haze: Underground Radio and the Sixties*. Praeger.
Ladd, Jim (1991): *Radio Waves: Life and Revolution on the FM Dial*. St Martin's Press.
Lewis, Peter M. (1978): *Whose Media? The Annan Report and After*. Consumers' Association.
Lewis, Peter M., and Booth, Jerry (1989): *The Invisible Medium: Public, Commercial and Community Radio*. Macmillan.
Partridge, Simon (1982): *Not the BBC/IBA: The Case for Community Radio*. Comedia.
Partridge, Simon (1990): *Radio for Ethnic and Linguistic Minorities*. Commission for Racial Equality.
Sakolsky, Ron, and Dunifer, Stephen (eds) (1998*): Seizing the Airwaves: A Free Radio Handbook*. AK Press.

Activity 4.1

Investigate the provision of radio in your locality and assess how well the existing services reflect and serve its demographic and ethnic make-up. Are there gaps in radio service that a more community-based station of the kind described in this chapter could fill? Outline what the gaps are and map out the main areas of programming that such a service could offer.

Activity 4.2

Contact a community radio station or association – preferably one you are familiar with. Prepare a two-sheet analysis of its ownership and management structure, its sources of funding and its main programming objectives. Compare its organization and day-to-day output and operation with that of a publicly funded local station (e.g. the BBC) or a commercial station.

Activity 4.3

Summarize the regulations and programming obligations under which small-scale stations operate in Britain. Taking the station you chose in Activity 4.2 as an example, and interviewing station personnel where possible, investigate how the station would cover – or has covered in the past – a community issue such as the proposed closure of a hospital or the construction of a bypass or a new private development. Point up any particular dilemmas that might arise out of the coverage and how the station might seek to resolve them.

Activity 4.4

Refer back to Activity 4.1 and list all the stations available to you in your locality. Delineate which are legal broadcasting operations and which broadcast illegally. How different are these 'pirate' stations in terms of style, attitude and programming to the legal stations? Who are they aimed at, and is there any on-air evidence (listeners' letters or e-mails, phone-ins, etc.) that the stations have an existing audience of any size?

Activity 4.5

Drawing on the Community Media Association Code of Practice (Figure 4.1) and your own research, identify the main factors that make 'community radio' different in practice and principle from established local radio. Investigate the history of any community radio station near to your home town or place of study and compare its ownership and funding structures with those of a commercial local radio station in the same neighbourhood. List the main ways in which the two stations interact with their audiences and, on the basis of listening to both stations over one week, assess the differences and similarities in their programme output. What are the strengths and weaknesses of each?

Activity 4.6

Consider the ethnic make-up of your village, town or city of residence and research the provision of programmes for these audiences by your local radio stations. How much broadcasting time is given to particular communities, and at what times of day?

Part Two

Audiences

Denis McQuail has described audiences as 'both a product of social context (which leads to shared cultural interests, understandings, and information needs) and a response to a particular pattern of media provision' (McQuail, p. 2). Though Paddy Scannell's *Radio, Television and Modern Life* is a pioneering text – an attempt to consider listening as an experience and how it affects the individual – radio audiences and their motivation (why people listen, in what circumstances, for how long, and why) remains a surprisingly underdeveloped area in academic studies. There does exist a mountain of commercially sponsored research, upon which many of the general assumptions about radio listening – and the consequent decisions on programming content and style – are based. This is valuable material, but it should not be viewed uncritically: apart from questions of methodology and research objectives, market research is primarily a marketing tool geared to the requirements of specific commercial interests within a competitive environment.

Market research also demands that we consider the audience as a mass, or as a series of communities of taste or interest, rather than a collection of disparate individuals with their own priorities and concerns. The concern in Part Two is to relocate the question of how radio is used around the *individual* listener – for no other broadcast medium speaks to the individual with the same level of intimacy – and to question what 'community' means in a radio context. To what degree is the sense of community on which radio stations draw not only an artificial construction, but one built from the findings of market research itself?

5

Listening – Measurement and Meaning

In marketing its stations to both its listeners and advertisers, GWR leads the commercial radio industry in its detailed knowledge of audience tastes and needs. This information is based on extensive telephone research, carried out for local stations by the Group at its base in Bristol, and for Classic FM in-house at Camden, North London. The research operation makes more than 30,000 random telephone calls each year, quizzing respondents about their listening habits, tastes in music and preferences for news. GWR Group audience research runs alongside the industry-wide RAJAR research which issues figures every six months.

The most important benefit of the GWR system is the frequency of the results which allow programmers to see the effect of changes they have made and of changes made by competitors [. . .] Says Group Programme Director Steve Orchard: 'the facility to test audience reaction to particular prices of music is a unique ability, allowing GWR stations to plan their music on the basis of real listener tastes, not the teenage fad-driven pop sales charts, the hype-driven pop music industry of publicity-influenced classical music CD sales'.

Listeners' response, telephone lines, listener panels and local partnership groups all help to ensure the stations accurately reflect the communities they serve.

GWR Group plc press release, web site

The centrality of the audience to broadcasters and broadcasting content is a given: without an audience of some kind, the broadcasting of any message by any means is meaningless. A radio station may exist primarily as a profit source for its owners or as a means of serving a public, but in each instance the audience is pivotal: the 'quality' of the audience that the station may deliver to potential advertisers may mean the difference between profit and loss, while an ostensibly 'public service' station such as a BBC local radio station might see high numbers of listeners as confirmation of its right to exist and to command a proportion of the licence fee.

In Britain alone, commercial operators and the BBC spend huge amounts annually on monitoring radio audiences both quantitatively (the gathering of numerical data related to radio usage) and qualitatively (research into attitudes, tastes and preferences, usually undertaken by means of interviews with listeners). Possibly the most over-used word in radio circles is 'demographics' – meaning the analysis of audiences according to age, gender, environment and social class. The Radio Authority will grant broadcasting franchises only to those would-be operators able to demonstrate detailed research into the potential appeal of their proposed services within the prescribed locality.

Superficially, then, radio *is* an audience-led medium: one might assume that the intensity, scale and diligence of research into listening patterns and listener expectations and preferences reflects positively on the responsiveness of the radio industry to those who bankroll it. Certainly radio is a medium in which changes to content and style of presentation can be effected quickly – far more quickly than in television, where programmes tend to be individually produced items conceived and executed over a period of time. It is not unknown for stations in the US, faced with sudden downturns in performance (i.e. the station's achievement in targeting particular audiences within the locality), to be 'repositioned' overnight and reappear with an almost completely different staff and programme line-up.

Research that the stations undertake not only illuminates but often *defines* the programming decisions that they make. It can confirm or identify the existence of 'communities' of listeners (consumer communities by another name) that match the particular marketing aspirations of station and advertiser. Radio programming cannot be understood without reference to the research undertaken into its effectiveness in delivering listeners, and particularly as a vehicle for linking advertiser and listener. If the research seems, at close sight, limited and limiting, and if the 'communities' that research appears to identify appear artificial and even incoherent, this at least gives clues to the limited and limiting nature of the programming material that results.

MARKET RESEARCH AND RADIO HISTORY

Market research's defining role in radio broadcasting is a matter of history. In the US, many of the most popular networked programmes were, by the early 1930s, developed, written and produced for advertising agencies on behalf of their clients, who chose presenters, artists, music and format according to up-to-the-minute research findings:

> audience measurement made commercial control over broadcasting all the more stringent. No longer did a sponsor have to rely upon mail solicitation

campaigns to know the extent to which his commercials were being heard. This meant, of course, that if a show did not produce favourable listener statistics, it probably would be dropped by the advertiser and therefore the network.

J. Fred MacDonald, Don't Touch That Dial! p. 35

The prime sources of audience measurement were: the Crossley ratings, produced by the Co-Operative Analysis of Broadcasting and based on telephone polls of random listeners in 30 cities; the 'Hooperatings', developed by C.E. Hooper Inc., based on telephone polls of listeners while the programme itself was being broadcast; and the A.C. Nielsen Company's ground-breaking system of monitoring listening (including changes of station) by means of an electronic audimeter in radio sets.

At the BBC, the concept of audience research arrived late, in 1936, and only after sustained pressure from programme producers whose only feedback regarding the quality and content of their programmes came from the unreliable source of listeners' letters. Reith had held out against it for many years, but competition from Radios Luxembourg and Normandie and the need to counter their claims with hard data made audience analysis imperative. (Figures from the Advertising Institute suggested that Luxembourg was attracting 45.7 per cent of listeners on Sundays, when the BBC broadcast no entertainment.) The head of the BBC's listener research, Robert Silvey, was recruited from the advertising agency the London Press Exchange; he introduced a random sample system of questionnaires to a few thousand listeners on the basis that 'conclusions about large populations can be inferred from data about a limited number of them' (Silvey, p. 44). In 1938, for example, the BBC discovered through this research that 85 per cent of listeners listened regularly to the news, and mid-morning listening was twice as prevalent in rural areas as in urban centres. The BBC also undertook exhaustive qualitative research by means of listener panels. The first head of the Light Programme, Maurice Gorham, later characterized Silvey's approach as a twin-track one, a 'daily barometer . . . which showed how many people listened to each item, and the weekly thermometer, which gave an indication of what they thought of it' (Gorham, p. 165). The biggest effect was on programme planning and particularly scheduling: 'The notion of sequencing programmes through the day began to be worked on in a rational way, in an effort at matching different kinds of programmes with different kinds of listener at different times of day, according to their availability. This study of listening habits was a key factor in the normalization of the schedules' (Scannell, p. 10). 'To study these figures, as we did, day by day seven days a week, gave you a feeling of being in touch with your audience,' Gorham confirmed in his autobiography. 'They confirmed many things that I had thought but not known, such as that the audience starts shrinking fast before 10pm, and after 11pm it is smaller than the early morning audience; that there are comparative peaks during the early afternoon; that a popular programme will usually increase the numbers listening to the items before it and after it; and so on' (Gorham, p. 166).

THE PURSUIT OF RATINGS

In contemporary radio, quantitative research is undertaken on a quarterly basis by RAJAR (Radio Joint Audience Research), funded jointly by the BBC and the Commercial Radio Companies Association since 1992. RAJAR results are an industry yardstick, an independent and 'neutral' reflection of rises and falls in audience between stations over the given period. For national networks and local stations alike, RAJAR offers proof of the impact that a change of identity or ownership, a particular repositioning, the introduction of a new presenter at peak listening time, or a change in music policy has had. Because of its cross-industry backing, broadcasters and advertisers accept its status as objective. See Figure 5.1 for notes on the process of data gathering and measurement.

RAJAR ratings – which allow the stations to be ranked alongside national and local competitors – are not just market indicators but marketing tools for station owners and programme controllers. They show recurrent weaknesses and strengths in the daily and weekly programming sequences, enabling fine-tuning or wholesale changes, but they do not index audience appreciation, neither do they indicate the depth of attention listeners give a programme. As Andrew Crisell suggests, the very term 'listener' is problematic because the radio audience will listen or hear with different degrees of concentration that may reflect on the programme content, on the proclivities of different types of listener, or on the particular circumstances in which a programme is heard.

Market research is usually undertaken by agencies working to objectives set out by the commissioning companies, and any other value is incidental. As Denis McQuail writes, it focuses on media *consumption* rather than pure reception: 'the view of the audience as market is inevitably the view *from the*

Much of the RAJAR-collected data on audiences and reception included in this book derives from a measurement system based on a pre-printed diary that participants in the research complete, with an ever-lengthening list of stations printed across the top of each diary page. This system was modified at a cost of over £500,000 in early 1999 with the introduction of a new personalized diary customized to include only those stations that the individual uses. Under the new system, only one adult per household is interviewed, instead of everyone in a household, and data for each service is measured over a period of three to 12 months, to build a fuller picture of how a station is performing. The chief flaw in this method of collecting data – that its reliability depends on participants' recall of what they have listened to – is being addressed in the long term by the development of electronic 'radio meters' which measure the time that participants spend tuned in to particular stations. Testing of Arbitron's 'Personal People Meter', which is the size and weight of a pager and records what it hears and for how long, is underway at the time of writing. Other equipment under development includes a radio wristwatch with built-in logging technology.

Fig. 5.1 A note on audience measurement

media (especially of their owners and managers) and *within the terms* of the media industries' discourse' (McQuail, p. 9, emphasis added). It focuses on communities of consumers, actual or prospective, which may be defined according to social group, age or gender and the particular tastes and preferences of those predisposed to the product or service.

For commercial radio stations, the value of market research goes beyond gauging consumer reaction to the station. It analyses the audience in terms of its propensity to purchase particular products or types of products – information which the station's media sales department will then use in selling the station itself to advertisers, as a vehicle appropriate for their advertisements. It is not a neutral process, nor is the station a disinterested party in the research. The audience is in fact *itself* a 'product' which advertisers buy; it has a literal value in the form of advertising rates that are variable according to the time of day and who is listening. Ultimately, then, the volume and/or 'quality' of audiences – mediated through market research and interpretation of that research by media sales departments – determines advertising rates and sets price differentials.

Market research may also be used as a tool for *exclusion* as well as inclusion, for finding niches – of high-income earners, possibly, or young people with high disposable incomes – within the collective market. Interpretation, or rather a creative reading of the data, is all. Follow-up research may then be commissioned to test out consumer reaction within the identified 'community'. (See Figure 5.2 for a definition of socio-economic groups.)

A TYPOLOGY OF LISTENERS

The major argument against reliance on audience research is that it encourages the broadcast media and programme-makers in particular to create

Social grade	Social status	Occupation of main income earner
A	Upper-middle class	Higher managerial/administrative/professional
B	Middle class	Intermediate managerial/administrative/professional
C1	Lower-middle class	Supervisory/clerical/junior managerial/administrative/professional
C2	Skilled working class	Skilled manual workers
D	Working class	Semi and unskilled workers
E	Subsistence level	State pensioner/casual workers

Source: Market Research Society

Fig. 5.2 Definition of socio-economic groups

		1977 Q2	1988 Q2	1994 Q4	1995 Q1	1996 Q1	1997 Q4	1998 Q2	1998 Q3	1998 Q4
All radio	Reach	92	86	86	86	86	85	85	84	85
	Hours	22.9	21.4	20.8	21	21.6	20.6	20.7	21	20.5
Radio 1	Reach	48	37	23	22	24	20	20	20	20
	Hours	11.2	11.9	8.7	8.7	9.9	8.7	8.4	9.1	9
	Share	25.9	23.9	11.3	10.8	12.7	9.9	9.5	10.5	10.6
Radio 2	Reach	41	28	19	19	18	19	18	19	19
	Hours	10.2	11.7	12.2	13.1	12.7	12.2	12	13	12.2
	Share	19.8	17.8	12.8	13.4	12.2	13	12.6	13.6	13.1
Radio 3	Reach	10	8	5	5	5	5	5	5	5
	Hours	4.2	4.7	3.4	3.2	3.5	4.5	4	4.5	4.3
	Share	1.9	2.1	1	0.9	0.9	1.4	1.2	1.3	1.3
Radio 4	Reach	30	21	18	18	18	17	17	16	17
	Hours	10.5	11.9	10.6	10.1	10.6	10.7	10.4	10.1	11
	Share	14.7	13.3	10.6	9.8	10.5	10.4	10.3	9.2	10.5
Radio 5	Reach			10	11	11	11	11	10	11
	Hours			4.7	5	5.3	5.9	5.9	6.2	5.9
	Share			2.7	3.1	3.1	3.6	3.7	3.6	3.6
BBC local radio	Reach	19	19	21	21	20	18	18	17	18
	Hours	7.2	8	8.9	9.3	10	9.2	9.3	10	9.3
	Share	6.5	8.2	10.2	10.7	10.9	9.6	9.6	9.6	9.3
ILR	Reach	49	42	49	49	49	49	50	49	50
	Hours	12.4	13.5	14	14.3	14	13.9	14.3	14.8	13.9
	Share	28.3	30.8	38	38.5	36.7	39.5	40.8	40.5	40
Classic FM	Reach			10	10	10	10	11	10	11
	Hours			5.7	5.8	5.8	5.8	6.1	6.1	6
	Share			3.2	3.1	3.3	3.4	3.7	3.4	3.7
Virgin	Reach			9	8	7	7	7	7	6
	Hours			8.3	7.9	8.2	6.6	7.4	7.3	7.1
	Share			3.9	3.5	3.1	2.6	3	2.7	2.6
Talk Radio*	Reach				3	4	5	5	5	5
	Hours				5.1	6.6	6.7	6	6	5.7
	Share				0.9	1.6	1.9	1.8	1.7	1.6
Atlantic 252	Reach			10	9	8	7	6	5	5
	Hours			7.2	6.4	6.6	5.1	4.9	5	4.3
	Share			3.9	3.3	2.9	2.1	1.7	1.5	1.4
Luxembourg**	Reach	7	2							
	Hours	3.2	2.8							
	Share	1.1	0.3							
Others	Reach	NR	10	7	8	6	6	6	6	6
	Hours	NR	7	6.5	6.3	6.4	7.3	6.7	7.2	6.7
	Share	3.2	4	2.4	2.9	2	2.6	2.1	2.3	2.2

Notes:
1. Q = calendar quarter.
2. Figures are weekly averages. Data are for listeners above the age of 15.
3. Reach = % of national adult population who listen to station for at least five minutes in average week.
4. Share = % of total listening time accounted for a station in the UK or its designated area.
5. NR = not reported.
6. * First survey shown was for less than full fieldwork period.
7. ** Luxembourg closed down in 1991.

Source: JICRAR (1977–92); RAJAR/RSL

Fig. 5.3 Audience ratings by station or network

		1997 Q4	1998 Q2	1998 Q3	1998 Q4
All BBC	Reach	56	56	56	56
	Hours	15	14.7	15.2	15
	Share	48.5	46.8	47.8	48.5
All commercial	Reach	60	60	59	60
	Hours	14.4	14.9	15.1	14.4
	Share	49.3	51.1	49.9	49.3

Source: JICRAR

Fig. 5.4 Audience: BBC radio and commercial radio compared, 1997–98

programming geared to majority tastes, and that it encourages an over-familiarity and over-formatting of output. Against this, broadcasters on all sides of the spectrum – echoing Maurice Gorham's comments – have argued that research enables radio stations to be more responsive not just to the tastes and expectations of listeners but to their *uses* of radio. These are problematic issues because radio's 'responsiveness' to audiences is a selective one, the 'audience' being primarily determined according to pre-set and widely diverging criteria: a national audience of people aged 25–55 in the case of BBC Radio 2, for example, or an audience of country music fans in the London area in the case of Country 1035. Within both commercial radio and the BBC there has been a marked lack of interest in what in advertising parlance is called the 'grey' market – the over 60s, though the buying power of the latter audience segment in particular is strong and growing as the population ages. There is always a danger of disenfranchising sections of the audience when fashioning programming to particular age or social groups.

The other issue is one of defining the audience. When 'narrowcasting' – the industry term for niche programming aimed at minority audiences – became a part of the radio scene in Britain in the 1980s, it was praised in the trade press as another example of responsiveness to the demands of listeners for whom '*broad*casting' (in its literal sense) did not fully cater. But how far was the listening 'community', in Radio 2 as much as Country 1035, a contrived one, constructed for marketing convenience? What determines a station's performance among that community?

Part of the answer lies in the typology of listeners that radio stations use as an aid to market research and, ultimately, as a justification for the content and style of their programming. Typology involves compartmentalizing listeners according to particular criteria – social class and/or income bracket, means or manner of listening (domestic, in-car, at work), engaged or non-engaged (passive) listening, tastes in music, ethnic background, preference for news or speech and so on. Typologies are problematic because they are basically

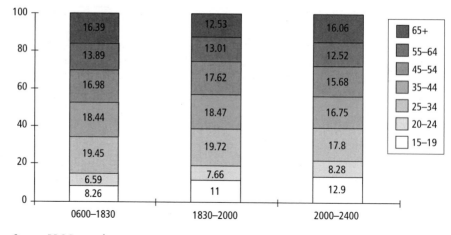

Source: BBC Research

Fig. 5.5 Radio audience by age group (weekdays)

simplifications of convenience, because the 'types' they identify tend to be unrealistically exclusive, and because of the baggage of stereotyping that they bring with them – that is, assumptions of common behaviours on the basis of one characteristic. But, again, they illuminate the thinking behind the programming – or, more specifically, the assumptions made by the broadcaster regarding the audience's level of receptivity and comprehension.

In the very early years of the BBC, the perception of the audience was as a unified mass, broadly united in terms of educational background, social class and artistic appreciation; by wartime, thanks partly to listener research but also to the influx into the BBC of personnel trained in advertising and publicity, the perception had changed to one of a mass audience united in purpose and in nationhood but made up of different publics with different uses of radio. The Forces Programme was the product of painstaking study of the listening needs of the British Army in France, who were found to favour news, entertainment, music and diversion. This typology informed much of the broadcast output on BBC radio during the war, and subsequently it was preserved and expanded in the form of a tripartite division in services – Light Programme, Home Service and Third Programme – effected according to what Jean Seaton has called 'a new psychology of the listener' (Seaton, p. 188). According to the BBC's post-war Director-General, William Haley, the idea rested 'on the conception of the community as a broadly based cultural pyramid, slowly aspiring upwards' (quoted in Barnard, p. 24): the Light as a populist network, aimed at a broad span of mass taste, leaning heavily towards variety and popular music; the Home as a middlebrow network of talk, news, drama and a mixture of musics; the Third Programme as a highbrow network specializing in serious music, new drama and the arts in general. In reality, the concept of listeners 'aspiring' to better things as they made their way through the networks was a non-starter: though there was a great deal of cross-listening between the Light and the Home, listeners tended to stick with what they knew and liked.

When the networks were replaced by Radios 2, 4 and 3 respectively in 1967, the balance of listening was broadly retained. The audience was still a range of publics defined by culture, class and their use of radio, but now with the added factor of taste and age: Radio 1 (not immediately, but over a period of years) took over and expanded upon the youth- and pop-oriented element of programming previously found in relatively small measure on the Light Programme, though precisely who Radio 1's programmes were aimed at was at first a source of contradiction and confusion. Even as late as 1986, the then Controller, Johnny Beerling, could claim that the main aim of daytime Radio 1 was to target 'people listening in their own houses – that has to be generically housewives' (quoted in Barnard, p. 145), while the main focus in the evening was the student audience, with an interest in the music as music rather than as a passively received background sound. Because they identified Radio 1 and Radio 2 as their main sources of competition, the new commercial stations that opened from 1973 onwards adopted a similar typology, despite the IBA's own findings that, during the peak morning hours of 9am to 12.30am, the ratio of women to men listening to ILR was only 6:4. More pernicious than the simple attempt to translate a female bias in listening into 'female programming' was the tendency to stereotype that listenership as housewives alone – and worse, the tendency to stereotype housewives as passive home-makers with limited imaginations. (For further development of the theme of female stereotyping by radio, see pages 226 to 229.)

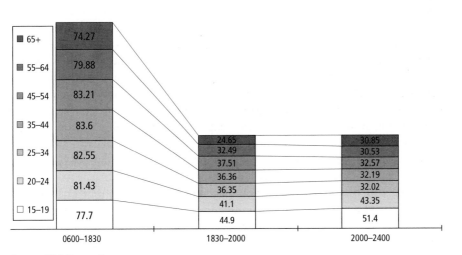

Source: BBC Research

Fig. 5.6 Percentage of age groups listening to radio (weekday evenings)

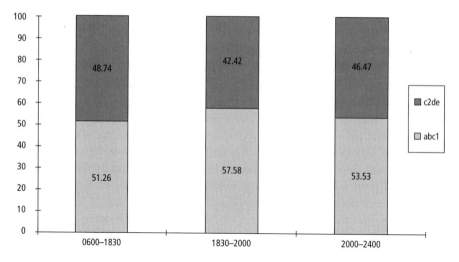

Source: BBC Research

Fig. 5.7 Radio audience by social group (weekdays)

CONSTRUCTING COMMUNITIES

Traditionally, radio stations maintain fixed and limited perceptions of the audience as a matter of deliberate policy. Stations *choose* their audiences on the basis of available data, targeting those sections of the audience of most interest to advertisers – and often reassessing that targeting if the programming fails to deliver. This was so even during the days of pre-deregulated ILR, when the remit of stations was to provide a broad range of entertainment, news and information to a broad range of audiences: stations found they could circumvent this by focusing on different audiences at different times of day and shifting a large part of their 'public service' output (programmes for minority audiences) to the evening. To adopt a music policy calculated with particular audiences in mind – 'housewife'-appeal music was, in this definition, heavily dominated by ballad singers and 'the gentler end of the Top 40' – enabled a kind of surreptitious targeting, effectively discouraging the older or younger sections of the audience from staying with the station. The straightforward concept of treating the local radio audience as a geographically defined homogenous community was therefore distorted in practice.

On the other hand, ILR station management frequently complained that to treat the local audience as a mass audience in miniature – in effect, to try to please all the people all the time – was unrealistic, and that audiences with 'minority' tastes or interests were well catered for during off-peak evening and weekend programming. Here again, however, this policy had its problematic aspects: how were such minorities defined, and why were particular tastes in music prioritized over others? Why are certain 'specialist' music programmes run on a shoestring budget – sometimes on the understanding that they do not eat into the station's allocation of needle-time – while others make healthy use of specially recorded sessions or out-of-studio recordings (local classical concerts, for example)? Even 'geographical' communities are not really as straightforward to define as they might first appear: one of the consequences of cost-cutting in BBC local radio in the late 1980s was the merger of a number of locally bordering stations and an expansion of coverage to areas on the fringe of existing stations. So Radio Sussex and Radio Surrey became BBC Southern Counties, and BBC Radio Bedfordshire became Three Counties Radio, covering not only Bedfordshire but Hertfordshire and Buckinghamshire as well.

One of the main benefits of deregulation in the 1980s for existing ILR stations was the chance to shift away from the public service concept of serving a mass (albeit local) audience to more market-led specialisms. These tended to be based on extensions of traditional typologies – particularly a homing in on tighter age groups – but some stations also took advantage of the opportunity to split their AM and FM services to appeal to consumer communities supposedly differentiated by lifestyle. Lifestyle research has roots in pioneering studies of social and psychological types such as Maslow's theory of basic needs and the categorization of people as 'belongers', 'emulators', 'achievers' and so on. Traditionally, such research has been of particular benefit to marketers as it identifies not just tastes or interests but proclivities, attitudes and values. This kind of attitudinal typology enables advertisers to target their message more skilfully by adopting language and tone of voice appropriate to the potential consumer.

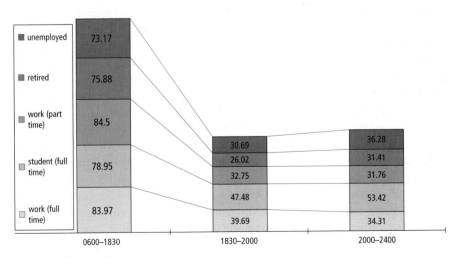

Source: BBC Research

Fig. 5.8 Percentage of occupational status groups listening to radio (weekdays)

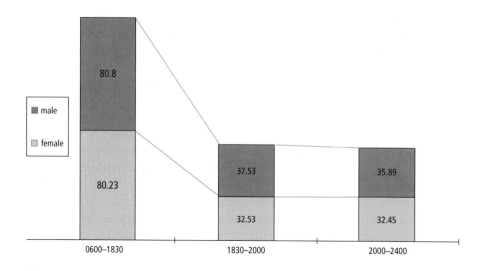

Source: BBC Research

Fig. 5.9 Percentage of gender groups listening to radio (weekdays)

The problem with applying these kind of considerations to radio lay in the basic self-consciousness of the lifestyles they wished to attract and implicitly celebrate. While it made marketing sense to aim a service at the potentially lucrative group of young, middle-class, upwardly mobile listeners (what one trade magazine called 'Sunday supplement radio', drawing an analogy with readership of up-market Sunday newspapers), the reality was programming which tended to confirm the worst prejudices against 'yuppies'. McQuail suggests that 'a lifestyle is in the end no more than a construct of theory or research that posits, or claims to discover, connections among several out of a vast array of potentially relevant variables' (McQuail, p. 94); as such, lifestyle considerations may have a marketing value, but they depend on consumers themselves making the connections and being sympathetic to them, and – in radio or television – on the skill of broadcasters in interpreting the data in a way that makes attractive programming. The creative challenge here is immense.

In the 1980s, 'yuppies' formed a basically artificial, self-conscious community, but the general concept of differentiating markets for streamed radio services has since been institutionalized by the Radio Authority, which, while it does not predetermine the content of prospective services when advertising licences, invites applications on the basis of their distinction from existing services. The range of applications which the RA has received in its decade of existence represents a wealth of interpretations of listener communities, some focusing on generic strands (talk, music), some focusing on shared concerns (religion, ethnic backgrounds), some on age and even gender.

London's current mix of RA-licensed stations shows, on paper at least, a wide variety of definitions of such communities. It contains a mix of stations aimed at geographical communities (e.g. Choice FM in Brixton, Millennium Radio in Thamesmead), taste communities (Country FM, Jazz FM), ethnic communities (Sunrise Radio for listeners of Asian or Anglo-Asian background), communities of interest (Premier Radio, a Christian music station) and even one (Liberty) which started life as a women's station. But many communities are not catered for at all, suggesting a degree of prioritization between communities on the RA's part, based on pragmatism: stations came on air because of the dovetailing nature of their projected programming in relation to London's established radio services – Capital FM and Capital Gold, LBC and News Direct.

Traditionally, creating a separate stream of minority programming enables mass-market stations to remove from mainstream programming anything that might question the majority consensus, while at the same time conferring a limited legitimacy on the minorities concerned. It is as if the minorities are expected to trade their right to be heard for the knowledge that few outside these minorities are likely to hear them anyway. On local radio stations, such programmes are sometimes little more than 'conscience slots', designed with the specific purpose of enhancing a station's public service profile. The prevalent assumption is that there is a distinct qualitative difference in radio *use* between daytime and (much smaller) evening audiences – in effect, that the night-time audience comprises active and attentive listeners rather than the passive, inattentive consumers of daytime.

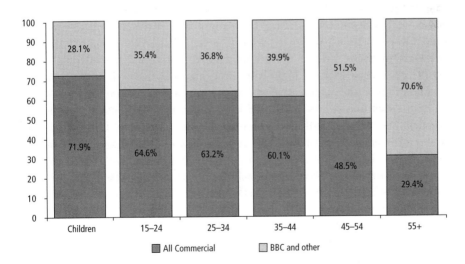

Source: RAJAR, January 1999

Fig. 5.10 Commercial radio share of audience, by age group

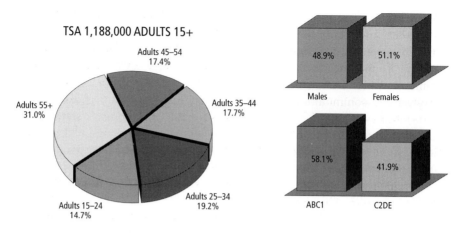

TSA 1,188,000 ADULTS 15+

Source: Essex Radio Group

Fig. 5.11 Population profile of the TSA (total survey area) covered by Essex FM

Radio 1's evening and weekend shows have traditionally been repositories for alternative or indie rock music, aimed primarily at students and sixth-formers and reflecting what Simon Frith has suggested is a fundamentally middle-class interpretation of pop music, i.e. not simply as an accompaniment to leisure but as a focus of it. It is also an example of the BBC's Light Programme inheritance in its marginalization of (and simultaneous reverence towards) musics of a supposedly more intellectually appealing character. Just as jazz had always figured on the periphery of Light Programme schedules, kept separate from the mainstream as an act of deliberate intellectual apartheid, so 'progressive rock' and its descendant student-appeal styles were so treated after Radio 1's launch in 1967. Followers of these styles often complained of discrimination against them, but the very separation of night-time programming (and for some years the broadcasting of the progressive shows in full stereo on an FM frequency, unlike the daytime shows) indicated a distinct split between the serious and the trivial, the intellectually valid and the inconsequential and disposable, the elitist and mass-appeal, the difficult and the easy – and cultural validation of *some* aspects of the musical margins. Frith and others have argued that, in the case of the BBC, this kind of validation of certain supposedly 'fringe' tastes over others has a class base, reflecting middle-class values of education, achievement and progression.

RECEPTION AND LISTENING

However defined and however perceived, the radio audience is a collection of individuals, and radio's impact is felt individually in a whole range of different ways. It is fundamentally a personal medium, favoured for its companionability and implicit intimacy, and in this respect it is simultaneously much more accessible than television or print media – it can be taken anywhere and does not demand visual attention – yet is also more disposable. Yet one of the great paradoxes of radio is, according to Andrew Crisell, that 'consumption is apparently vast but its impact minor' (Crisell, p. 191). What sense does the individual listener make not just of the aural material aimed at him or her, but of its sequencing and predictability? What kind of impact and influence does radio programming actually have on our lives?

Historically, much of the focus in communications studies has been on the effect of media messages on society in general and on the individual listener or viewer. Individual television programmes may be criticized for portraying excessive or gratuitous violence; whole strands of TV programming may be analysed for giving stereotypical and detrimental portrayals of ethnic minorities or age groups; during the 1990s, the rapid growth of satellite and cable TV was blamed for encouraging Britain's terrestrial TV operators to 'dumb down' their output in a bid to retain viewers. The cause for concern in each case – not just among academics but in political and cultural circles and sometimes within the media itself – may include encouragement of antisocial behaviour or a risk to standards of literacy among the young.

In radio, these kind of debates have been less prevalent, though in recent years there has been ongoing controversy over the broadcasting of rap records containing 'bad' language. The earliest academic studies of radio nevertheless assumed a direct correlation between mass-media messages and effects, drawing heavily on the lesson of print media and specifically the use of anti-

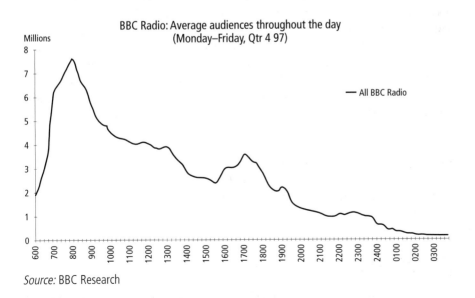

Source: BBC Research

Fig. 5.12 BBC Radio: Audience patterns of listening (weekdays)

German propaganda during the First World War. Cultural commentators like Walter Benjamin and Theodor Adorno wrote at length on radio's potential to corrupt and demean by playing to the gallery, while the tight state control of radio operated by the Nazis during the 1930s in Germany – where propaganda messages were relayed into the streets – offered a powerful example of how media could be used to manipulate a whole nation.

That radio could mislead to the point of causing mass panic was demonstrated by the reaction to Orson Welles' dramatization of H.G. Wells' *The War of the Worlds*, syndicated across the US by CBS in 1938. So realistic was the adaptation – which made skilful use of mock news bulletins and eye-witness reports – that thousands left their homes in fear of a Martian invasion. But the incident was important mainly as an example of what happens when the boundaries between fantasy and reality (in this case between drama and news) are blurred and the trust between audience and broadcaster is (albeit unwittingly) broken. Only occasionally in today's media world are the codes of radio confused or subverted to the point that this trust is questioned: minor examples in the 1990s included comedian Steve Coogan's portrayal of the blundering radio talk-show host Alan Partridge (which later moved to television and upset even more people before the joke was understood) and Chris Morris' late-night shows for Radio 1, on which he subverted such radio conventions as the abrasive phone-in show host and reports into the paranormal.

But concentration on the 'effects' of particular programmes rather misses the point: radio's impact is of a much more pervasive, more general and perhaps ideological kind and consequently much less easy to measure. Taking John Downing's point that it is 'the daily operation of media which is at the heart of their role', what one finds in radio is a communications media of low-key but singularly insidious impact, its messages and conventions repeated relentlessly, round the clock, day in and day out, year after year, by station after station. And while effects research in the academic field has been to a great extent overtaken by work related to other theoretical interpretations of audience receptivity, radio's strength as an advertising medium – and as a promotion medium for pop music – suggests that *repetition* of messages is indeed the source of its impact.

SOME THEORETICAL APPROACHES

Much tends to be made, in both academic and commercial studies of radio, of how the medium is used by the listener as background entertainment, as a source of information, as a 'portable pal'. One of the classic contemporary media theories is the 'uses and gratifications' model proposed by Blumler and Katz and later developed further by Graham Murdock, Richard Dyer and others. According to this, audiences use the media to gratify certain personal needs, namely for diversion (escape from everyday routine); integration with others (companionship, relationships); self-identity (comparing one's own life with those of others, including fictional personalities); and surveillance (information about the world beyond the front door). But are these 'needs' genuine and universal or created by the medium itself? Radio existed for decades without any apparent 'need' for regular time-checks or traffic reports; even the 'need' for local information via the radio is, in Britain, a comparatively recent development. The difference is perhaps that, in radio, fulfilment of such needs is *accepted* by the listener rather than actively *pursued*; news summaries and air-quality bulletins are part of the everyday fabric of the day, welcome if not especially necessary. There are degrees to this: the level of commitment and loyalty to a station varies from listener to listener, and a listener may find some needs met by one station (say, an analysis of that day's stock market trading) and others met more thoroughly by another. But the evidence in Britain is that listeners are not particularly promiscuous in their listening habits, and that around 40 per cent of listeners to any one station are likely to tune to that station exclusively (source: the advertising industry magazine *Admap*, November 1994).

Richard Dyer describes the mechanisms by which the media temporarily fulfil these needs as obliteration, contrast and incorporation. In radio's case, we can see the *obliteration* of the discomfiting by exclusion of the discordant record or complex news story (news summaries on the hour often exclude international stories altogether) and the weight given to programming that celebrates fantasy and romance; Dorothy Hobson, in a 1970s study of a group of female listeners to Radio 1's Tony Blackburn show, suggested that daytime radio could be seen 'as providing women with a musical reminder of their leisure activities before they were married' (Hobson, p. 109). This assumes a passivity, even a helplessness, which is perhaps questionable, but fantasy and memory are potent qualities that underlie much of the appeal of music radio in particular.

Developing Dyer's analysis, where radio programming does acknowledge the real world, it *contrasts* that reality against 'the warmth of the immediate moment' provided by good-time camaraderie and reinforced by the paraphernalia of listener response. Finally, radio puts forward an alternative, positive world-view by selective *incorporation* of 'elements of the real world' into its programming. It 'tries to deny that the world is, after all, so bad' by emphasizing the comic side of life and feeding off other media (television, newspapers, cinema) for confirmation of the alternative scenario it favours. The emphasis on the tendency of the media user to seek confirmation of one's beliefs, attitudes, fears and tastes through the media, forms the basis of *reinforcement* theory developed by Lazarsfeld and Merton in the 1940s, one of their starting points being a study of media influence on voting outcomes.

Although the uses and gratifications theory focuses the listener as a user and interpreter and not as a passive, easily manipulated consumer, it stops short at considering the circumstances in which the messages are received and the listener's own understanding of the codes and language at work in the framing of the message itself. It does not answer the classic Marxist argument that the media has a preset agenda defined by those who own, control and supervise it, nor does it give much account of what listeners bring to their experience of the media they use – their levels of cultural competence, the knowledge and experience that inform their tastes, opinions and tolerance or otherwise of different forms of media content. The perception of different *levels* of cultural competence has informed the development of BBC radio since its inception. The theory as developed by Katz, Gurevitch and Haas underlines a predilection for audiences to use certain media for certain uses or gratifications at certain times of day, and shows that listeners, viewers and newspaper readers are never mutually exclusive.

Katz, Gurevitch and Haas found that, of all the principal media, radio was not a prime source of gratification for any of the needs for diversion, information and social integration. This is not as curious a finding as it might seem, for radio's strength since the 1950s has been to give the listener immediate, if casually received, access to information and entertainment. In other words, its effectiveness and appeal lie in its functionality and particularly its apparent disposability and the *instant* gratification it can offer. A seminal academic study in this respect was Mendelsohn's 'Listening to Radio' in 1964, which pointed to how listeners use radio programming to structure their day, almost regardless of the content offered.

Contemporary radio, essentially a vehicle for programming rather than programmes, operates on the principle of a continuity of items – records, interviews, news items – held together by a presenter and punctuated by familiar time-points such as traffic reports, weather forecasts or stock market bulletins. Stripped programming represents an organization of time on the listener's behalf, which he or she will adapt to his or her own routine. Its alliance with daily routine enables radio to ingratiate itself into listeners' lives by making itself simultaneously indispensable yet unimposing. Paddy Scannell puts this more positively, in *Radio, Television and Modern Life*, by explaining radio's appeal, function and relevance in terms of its 'dailiness', its integration with the dynamics and rhythms of daily life. In other words, radio (and television) may well be disposable, transient, of-the-moment, but they *matter* and make sense of the world: he describes broadcasting as 'the taken-for-granted, meaningful background that constitutes the horizon of all possibilities for all actual foregrounded social relationships and practices. In modern societies radio and television are part of both the background and foreground of our everyday dealings with each other in a common world' (Scannell, p. 5). He links this to what he calls the *temporality* of broadcasting: 'the effect of the temporal arrangements of radio and television is such as to pick out each day as this day, this day in particular, this day as its *own* day, caught up in its own immediacy, with its own involvements and concerns' (Scannell, p. 149). In other words, every day in broadcasting is familiar yet new, a continuation of yesterday and a link with tomorrow, mirroring human life in its continuity and daily regeneration.

Scannell's study, which draws on the writings of philosopher Martin Heidegger, represents a brave and rare attempt to look beyond traditional media studies concerns – production, consumption, decoding of message – in its consideration of broadcasting. It attempts to define the appeal and *meaning* of the listening experience as, primarily, a link to and with the world. We can continue this line of thought by asking what differentiates radio listening from any other aural experience we could otherwise choose: why tune in to a radio programme rather than play a CD or cassette? Why let someone we have never met choose music to play when the facility to choose is at one's fingertips? Why choose music or a football commentary in which one might have no particular interest over silence?

The answer is that the listener chooses to make a connection with the outside world at that moment, not out of any particular desire to be part of a shared experience or a community of anything, but out of a simple, human desire to be 'in touch'. Radio lets the world in, but on the listener's own terms; it enables the listener to becomes as close or as distant as he or she prefers. Through radio, a listener can connect without engagement or commitment.

Further reading

Baehr, Helen, and Ryan, Michele (1984): *Shut Up and Listen! Women and Local Radio.* Comedia.

Barnard, Stephen (1989): *On the Radio: Music Radio in Britain.* Open University Press.

Crisell, Andrew (1986): *Understanding Radio.* Methuen.

Downing, John (1980): *The Media Machine.* Pluto Press.

Dyer, Richard (1973): *Light Entertainment.* British Film Institute.

Frith, Simon (1977): *The Sociology of Rock.* Constable.

Gorham, Maurice (1948): *Sound and Fury: 21 Years in the BBC.* Percival Marshall.

Hobson, Dorothy (1980): 'Housewives and the Mass Media' in Stuart Hall et al. (eds), *Culture, Media, Language.* Hutchinson.

Katz, E., Blumler, J.G. and Gurevitch, M. (1974): 'Utilisation of mass communication by the individual' in Blumler and Katz (eds), *The Uses of Mass Communication.* Sage.

MacDonald, J. Fred (1979): *Don't Touch That Dial! Radio Programming in American Life from 1920 to 1960.* Nelson-Hall.

McQuail, Denis (1997): *Audience Analysis.* Sage.

Mendelsohn, H. (1964): 'Listening to Radio' in L.A. Dexter and D.M. White (eds) *People, Society and Mass Communication.* Free Press.

Scannell, Paddy (1996): *Radio, Television and Modern Life.* Blackwell.

Seaton, Jean (1985): 'Broadcasting History' in James Curran and Jean Seaton, *Power Without Responsibility: The Press and Broadcasting in Britain.* Methuen.

Silvey, R. J. (1974): *Who's Listening? The Story of BBC Audience Research.* Allen & Unwin.

Activity 5.1

A station in your locality wishes to research the impact that its programmes have within the student community. List the main areas that the research might focus on – tastes in music, listening habits, whether passive or concentrated listening, and so on – and assess the kind of methodology that could be used. How might the station apply the results of the research?

Activity 5.2

Figures 5.5 to 5.12 are examples of the kind of research undertaken by BBC radio and the commercial radio industry into the demographic make-up of the audience and listening patterns in general. How might such information be used by programmers to help shape programme content, and by the sales departments of commercial radio stations to encourage advertisers to buy advertising space?

Activity 5.3

How far do the general patterns of listening depicted in Figures 5.5 and 5.12 reflect your own use of radio? Identify the points in the day where your listening habits differ from those of the majority, and assess the factors in your lifestyle (and particularly your working and leisure patterns) that determine the differences.

Activity 5.4

How complete is the BBC research analysis in Figure 5.8 in terms of the occupational status categories it depicts? Suggest some reasons why the full-time parental care of young children is not identified in the research as having 'occupational status', and the implications that this apparent omission might have for programming.

Activity 5.5

Figure 5.9, which depicts the make-up of the radio audience by gender group according to times of day, suggests some variance in radio listening between men and women. Suggest reasons why men constitute the majority of listeners during weekday evenings. Drawing on your own listening experience, assess how far evening broadcasting reflects this apparent male bias.

Part Three

Forms

'Genre' is a term commonly used in a publishing, film or television context, to denote distinctions in content or style between types of novels, films or programmes – mysteries, romances, thrillers, musicals, soap operas, docu-soaps and so on. Each carries its own 'repertoire of elements', as Gill Branston describes them – a set of conventions which the author or producer manipulates to produce a text that is new yet fulfils the reader or viewer's expectations of the genre. Genre has a particular application to media texts or products with distinct narrative structures, and so has some validity in a radio context, as a means of differentiating between programming strands (music, news, talk, sport, comedy, drama and so on) or between broadcasting styles or content within those strands.

In television and particularly in BBC radio, generic distinctions not only shape different approaches to production but locate them in an institutional sense, as different centres of production – separate departments for news and current affairs, for example, or for drama and entertainment. The drive towards merger and takeover in contemporary radio has led radio groups to set up separate, centralized production centres with particular programme-making or commissioning responsibilities.

If only as a kind of industry shorthand, genres clarify the process of commissioning, publishing and producing. They give media 'gatekeepers' a set of conventions, rules and professional standards by which to select and present content. They can also act as a validation of *other* media – in the case of music radio, providing a vehicle for the publicizing of music industry products. Genre is also a limiting concept, in that a concentration on established genres discourages development beyond fairly fixed boundaries. The next four chapters examine radio's principal generic streams, their characteristics and dynamics.

6

Fictive Forms

Contemporary radio is so dominated by music and speech formats that traditionally fictive (i.e. non-factual) programme forms – the situation comedy, the variety show, the made-for-radio play, the daily serial, the panel game – can seem antiquated and irrelevant. In Britain, on daytime commercial radio and Radio 1, they hardly exist at all; on Radio 2, they appear tucked away on the periphery of the schedules, during the evening and at weekends. The BBC's attempt to create a network built around this kind of discrete programming, the original Radio 5, had an image from the start as a cost-heavy repository for programmes which did not fit comfortably anywhere else on the networks, and it was relaunched within two years as a rolling news station.

It would be easy to see radio soap operas or variety showcases as leftovers from an earlier era of radio's primacy as a source of home entertainment, or as throwbacks that owe their continuing existence on Radio 4 to the legendary loyalty (and age profile) of the network's listeners. But this is simplistic. Historically, such programme forms were not only products of their time but were the means (especially in the case of radio drama) by which the BBC built its reputation and its power as a cultural producer. In the very different broadcasting environment of the US, these same programme forms became the vehicle by which manufacturers and advertising agencies achieved a massive ascendancy within American commercial life and a proactive role within broadcasting itself. The genres that were developed by radio producers also formed the bedrock of television programming in its early days and to a large extent continue to do so – indeed, it was television that all but killed US radio's generic programming in the 1950s by robbing radio of many of the programmes that had been its lifeblood for years – soap operas like *The Goldbergs*, variety show vehicles for entertainers such as Jack Benny and Bob Hope, adventure serials like *The Lone Ranger* and *Dick Tracy*, quiz shows like *You Bet Your Life*.

CULTURAL RING-FENCING

From the 1950s onwards, the genres on which radio was built fell victim as much to the cost of production, loss of a funding base and the breakdown of network syndication as changing audience tastes or habits. Records, news and phone-in chat proved an infinitely cheaper and more cost-effective source of programming. Today, the faith-keepers of discrete programming remain organizations like National Public Radio in the US and the BBC in Britain: Radio 4 is not that greatly different in character, structure, daily schedule or audience profile from its 1945-created predecessor, the Home Service. It is therefore possible to view the continuation of drama, comedy, panel games and documentary on Radio 4 as a kind of ring-fencing, effected to keep faith with the old public service values and traditions of the BBC. The rationale is that these kind of programmes are precisely what a publicly funded, culture-moulding body such as the BBC should be making, regardless (up to a point) of cost and size of audience. This is a familiar argument, which is also used to justify the funding of classical music performances on Radio 3 and the 'specialist' music shows of Radios 1 and 2.

There is a certain irony in the way the BBC now puts its comedy and entertainment output on a pedestal, in that the very place of entertainment on the schedules, its value and what exactly should constitute it were issues of often furious internal debate during the first two decades of the Corporation's existence. What we know now as 'classic BBC comedy', for example (and what its catalogues of commercial spoken-word cassettes tell us *is* classic comedy), such as *Band Wagon, The Goon Show* and *Hancock's Half Hour*, were in their day subject to regular negotiation between performers, writers, producers and network heads as to what was permissible in terms of content and language. Situation comedy in particular did not arrive at the BBC as a fully developed form but rather evolved over a period of time in the light of ongoing cultural tensions, especially regarding working-class accents, music hall ribaldry and the mocking of authority.

RADIO COMEDY AND VARIETY

The initial thrust in radio, wherever services were established, was to reproduce established features of culture and entertainment – the stage play, the concert, the variety turn, the public lecture. This could be complicated by constraining factors such as the refusal of powerful interests in the theatre, variety and press industries to co-operate with a directly competitive medium. The BBC's entrance into variety production (the Revue and Vaudeville Section was set up in 1930) disrupted the economy of the entertainment industry, creating new demands on performers for material – a whole year's music hall material could be used up in one radio appearance – and turning some acts into overnight national stars. The character of variety underwent a change as radio embraced it: some of the most popular dance bands, for example, found new demand for appearances on the music hall as well as ballroom circuits, playing a made-for-radio music that was more a sweetened hybrid of dance music and light music – domesticated, frothy, easy to listen to – than the strictly made-for-dancing music they played in the dance halls. This was emblematic of a process of domestication – taking entertainment out of its original social context and rendering it suitable for the domestic environment – which the BBC institutionalized through its move into the production as well as dissemination of variety (notably the creation of its own dance orchestras) and the exercise of strict control over the output of bands and performers selected for broadcasting. As Simon Frith puts it, 'the BBC's "non-commercial" principles of entertainment now determined what commercial entertainment itself sounded like' (Frith, p. 40).

There were parallels in the US where the major programme providers, the advertising agencies, and their sponsors wielded similar power. If their perspective was less one of cultural well-being than maximization of audiences, the programming they created was rife with dilemmas that were even more intense, such as how to portray America's melting pot of racial and regional division in a way that acknowledged difference yet also projected a basically Anglo-Saxon, English language-speaking ideology. As Michele Hilmes shows in *Radio Voices*, programmes like *The Goldbergs* (concerning a Jewish family in New York) and *Amos'n'Andy* (in which two white actors played two lovable but stereotypically dim-witted blacks coping with life in Chicago) were powerful indexes of both assimilation and place-putting – representing multi-ethnic America to itself and its newcomers as comic and colourful but knowing its place in a predestined hierarchy of races. Hilmes contrasts the huge amount of broadcasting time devoted to entertainments derived from 19th-century blackface forms like minstrelsy with the almost total exclusion of blacks from employment in American radio, even as members of dance bands.

In Britain, variety was virtually the only context in which regional voices were heard on national radio prior to World War Two. Northern comedians like George Formby and Gracie Fields – also stars of music hall and cinema – became what Richard Middleton has called 'licensed eccentrics . . . [who] could be mostly contained by the stereotypes of class humour, fatalism and exotic folk custom' (Middleton, p. 39). The BBC approach to entertainment was to refashion it as something tasteful and decorous enough to be allowed into people's homes:

> Working-class entertainment was collective, disorderly, immediate – 'vulgar' by definition. Middle-class entertainment was orderly, regulated and calm, and it was this aesthetic that informed the BBC's understanding of listeners' leisure needs . . . the problem was to fit entertainment as occasion into an intimate routine, to take pleasures that were essentially live (with the elements of risk and uncertainty) and script them so that nothing untoward happened.
>
> Frith, *Music for Pleasure*, pp. 32 and 36

The very term 'light entertainment', which for decades became the accepted BBC synonym for variety, suggested a particular perception of what entertainment constituted and what it was for. The programmes that resulted were routinized productions created around the disciplines of a programme order and script and placed within the schedules in palatable half-hour or 15-minute chunks. They also benefited from the injection of pace and novelty that was characteristic of the programmes made by London advertising agencies for broadcast on Radio Luxembourg, many of whose writers and producers entered the BBC at the start of World War Two.

The massive expansion in BBC light entertainment during the war reflected the need to keep morale high and the nation diverted, while programming as a whole took on a new inclusiveness in terms of tone, manner and accent. New influences infiltrated programme production, especially with the creation of an Allied Expeditionary Forces Service in 1944, incorporating American and Canadian shows, and with the establishment of the Light Programme in 1945. The impact of the war on subsequent entertainment broadcasting was huge, in that it cemented the appeal of particular types of variety programmes – star showcases like *Sincerely Yours* with Vera Lynn, which linked servicemen overseas with their families, panel shows like *The Brains Trust*, and particularly situation-based comedy shows with a fixed cast, like *Band Wagon* and *ITMA*. For the first time, it brought a vein of participatory broadcasting to the BBC and allowed 'representative' ordinary voices to be heard – albeit in scripted form. This included meet-the-people shows that played up working-class camaraderie, like *Harry Hopeful* (which had started in Manchester in 1935), *Billy Welcome* and *Have A Go*, all with bluff but genial northerner Wilfred Pickles in a mediating role. The same spirit of discovery – finding in life 'out there' a mixture of the eccentric, the exotic, the funny and the reassuring – lay behind the post-war *Down Your Way* and even Radio 1's *Savile's Travels* in the 1970s.

The war also brought to the BBC a strand of service humour that was to permeate radio comedy for decades. This came through in variety programmes made for specific branches of the services (*Ack-Ack-Beer-Beer* for the anti-aircraft units, *Shipmates Ashore* for the Navy, *Mediterranean Merry-Go-Round* for the RAF, and so on), some of which continued under a new name after the war. (*Mediterranean Merry-Go-Round*, for example, was the precursor of *Much Binding in the Marsh*.) Many of these programmes had an undercurrent of nose-poking at authority as represented by the upper ranks and the BBC itself. *Band Wagon* had the archetypal cheeky northerner Arthur Askey and the snooty Richard Murdoch living in a flat at the top of Broadcasting House, while *ITMA*'s repertory of daft characters included a civil servant called Fusspot, a drunken military type called Colonel Chinstrap, and straight man Tommy Handley as (among other roles) the Minister of Aggravation.

Band Wagon and *ITMA* were particularly influential because they built the comic action around a repertory of characters and a single situation – a departure from the usual mix of sketches and a musical turn or two. Significant, too, was the creation of a Script Section under Michael Standing and the recruitment to it of new writers mostly fresh from the services – Eric Sykes, Bob Monkhouse, Denis Norden, Frank Muir, Ray Galton and Alan Simpson among them. *Take It From Here*, centred on the everlasting engagement between the clueless Ron Glum and his ever-optimistic fiancée Eth, began as a parody of a BBC radio soap opera, *Mrs Dale's Diary*, while *The Goon Show* echoed *ITMA* in stretching radio's ability to work on the imagination, notably via bizarre voices, sound effects, endless comic references to the war and service life (and ferocious caricatures of Army types in particular), and a parodying of radio conventions like the mock-sincerity of announcers and *Dick Barton*-like incidental music. As one of its producers, Peter Eton, put it, *The Goon Show* 'was less a criticism of any social system than a bold and melodramatic rearrangement of all life. It was obliged to create a nightmare landscape of its own and to people it with men, beasts and machines terribly at variance with the observable universe' (quoted in Foster and Furst, p. 164).

Although it enjoyed a long run, from 1952 to 1959, *The Goon Show* was not a typical example of BBC radio comedy. Much more characteristic were character-driven shows like *Hancock's Half Hour* or standard situation-based comedies that had a lampooning element *(The Navy Lark, The Men from the Ministry)* but followed a by now well-trodden formula. That situation comedy was a flagging form on radio was clear by the early 1960s, when *Hancock's Half Hour* was transferred to television and much of the effort in comedy production went on re-recording television hits for radio, *Steptoe and Son* and *Dad's Army* included.

The flowering of new comedy shows that occurred in the 1980s *(The Mary Whitehouse Experience, Naked Radio, After Henry)* was partly a result of the opening up of programme provision to independent production companies and the development of a youth-oriented comedy stream (since largely abandoned) on evening Radio 1. As if to underline radio's status as a recruiting and training ground for television, most of the writers and performers moved quickly into the latter, while *The Mary Whitehouse Experience, Today's the Day* and *After Henry* were all transferred successfully to television – the latter to ITV.

RADIO DRAMA

On both sides of the Atlantic, radio's institutions initially embraced drama as a demonstration of cultural commitment. The US networks could point to their investment in series of one-off, discrete dramas to counteract criticism of the space given to daily serials and the heavy involvement of advertising agencies in their production: CBS's *Mercury Theater of the Air*, for example, was a direct response to the Roosevelt administration's hardening attitude to monopolies in commercial radio. Drawing on the skills of New York's Mercury Theater repertory team, led by Orson Welles, the series included innovative radio adaptations of prestigious novels, including *A Tale of Two Cities, The Count of Monte Cristo, The 39 Steps, Treasure Island* and – in a broadcast that created panic throughout the US and gave Welles his entry into Hollywood – *The War of the Worlds*. The Mercury productions were almost unique in US radio in that they attempted to break the mould of dramatic production by playing with listener expectations and narrative codes. More typical of the general dramatic output was *The Lux Radio Theater*, which was produced in Hollywood by the J. Walter Thompson advertising agency and was framed by the mediating presence of film magnate Cecil B. De Mille, who introduced each production as if coming live from a real theatre and (despite virtually no involvement in the productions themselves) imbued each with a characteristic blend of showmanship and a Hollywood version of culture.

The BBC's involvement in drama production was guided until the 1950s by Val Gielgud, who identified two distinct periods of development – an experimental period when 'the machinery was tested; its components were largely fixed; and interest, both professional and listening, was almost entirely confined to the means, with deplorably little regard for the end'; and the war years, when 'the broadcast play ceased to be a producer's toy, a highbrow's hobby' (Gielgud, *Radio Theatre*, pp. vii–viii). The change came with improved facilities and technology – not least the ability to record plays, which not only enabled mistakes to be corrected but also made programmes repeatable – and with a new conception of the audience as requiring drama of a more accessible and relevant kind. Gielgud developed his own rules for presenting drama on radio, such as an insistence that writers should 'write for the microphone' and develop the art of interior monologue (a more intimate equivalent of a stage soliloquy) and use music and sound effects sparingly to establish scene changes or to delineate character. Like Orson Welles, he sought to exploit the unique qualities of radio to dramatic effect – what Paul Donovan describes as 'its dependence on one sense only, its ability to reach inside the imagination with silences, pauses and the tiniest linguistic subtleties' (Donovan, p. 85).

Gielgud's openness to experimentation with dramatic forms like the verse play created the climate for landmark productions like Dylan Thomas' 'play for voices', *Under Milk Wood*, which in both form and theme was an exercise in memory and imagination and the tricks they play. This was not a Drama Department production but the responsibility of its offshoot, the Features Department, which specialized in a peculiarly BBC form of drama-documentary ranging from mixtures of music, archive material and dramatic reconstructions to *Radio Ballads*, which blended folk songs, interviews and actuality evoking different aspects of working-class life. Produced in Manchester by Charles Parker, the latter used a core of talent who later became associated with the political theatre of Joan Littlewood and the Theatre Royal, Stratford East.

BBC radio drama was a production house with, from the late 1930s onwards, its own repertory theatre of actors, fixed budgets and a commitment to fulfil certain slots in the schedules. Though it never paid well enough to attract the best West End writers – Gielgud himself and other BBC insiders like Variety Head Eric Maschwitz contributed many plays of their own, without fee – it did provide a platform from which dramatists such as Robert Bolt, Harold Pinter, Giles Cooper and James Hanley could launch their careers. Its relatively low public profile rises occasionally with productions like *The*

Hitchhiker's Guide to the Galaxy (1980) and *Spoonface Steinberg* (1997), both of which were recreated for television. Annually, drama as a whole still accounts for 1,174 of BBC radio hours (just under three per cent of total output, according to 1997–98 figures) and the Drama Department itself remains the largest commissioner of new plays (around 300 a year) in Britain; its productions are still calculated to reach more people than the total number attending professional theatre productions in Britain each year.

SERIALIZED DRAMA

One-off productions represent only one aspect of programme-making in drama on radio. Although radio serials are now almost non-existent on American radio, and limited on BBC radio to the six-nightly *The Archers*, the form was for a long time one of the most prevalent and popular of all genres of speech programming. It was the one form of radio that offered listeners a parallel, ongoing reality: 'a fictional world that exists in parallel with the actual world . . . is the basis of the cumulative pleasures it offers to its listeners and viewers' (Scannell, p. 155).

The radio serial was important to broadcasting history on several levels. In the US, it was the means by which sponsors and advertising agencies achieved a huge degree of influence on programming and scheduling decisions. It helped routinize the schedules: it gave listeners points at which to tune in, and so helped integrate radio with the working day. Its development of narrative codes and conventions such as the cliffhanger gave sponsors and networks a regular, returning, captive audience. It established the main sub-genres, narrative codes and conventions, and production routines that came to underpin television series production (many early TV shows were simply adaptations of radio favourites); its economics were particularly attractive, in that most serials were produced in assembly-line fashion, by teams of writers and actors working to an intensive weekly routine. The serial also represented – especially in commercial radio, but also in BBC daytime serials like *The Dales* – the most explicit example of radio's preoccupation with 'the woman listener'. Daytime radio became 'the staging ground for more continuous dramatic narratives directed specifically toward women that any other medium has offered before or since' (Hilmes, p. 150).

By the mid 1930s, over half of the US networks' daytime shows were made not by the networks themselves but by advertising agencies producing programme packages on behalf of clients. These were largely scripted and supervised by women, working in teams in a nine-to-five assembly-line fashion, and were aimed at women at home. The argument for this female bias was that women constituted almost all the daytime listenership, and that they were the family's main purchaser of the domestic goods that manufacturers sought to promote. The conceding of daytime ground to the agencies by the networks – a reversal of evening programming, for which NBC in particular initiated most of its own shows – also allowed them to distance themselves

Meet 'The Archers'

A serial play of country life, 'The Archers,' begins in the Light Programme today. GODFREY BASELEY explains here how the programme originated

IT all began a long time ago—over two years ago, in fact, when the BBC in the Midlands called a conference of farmers to discuss programmes that were being done for their special benefit. After a long discussion, one farmer got up and said —' What we really want is a farming *Dick Barton!* ' Everybody laughed. But somehow or other the idea kept cropping up in my mind, and after a while I began to realise that there was a good deal of truth in this appeal. Slowly but surely, a number of characters that could be called symbolic of the farming community took shape in my mind.

Part of the job of the Agricultural Producers of the BBC is to meet people who get their living from the land, and as time went on it became

more and more evident that there was a fascinating story—not only for the farming community, but for listeners generally—in the latest scientific developments and the use practical farmers are making of them. On my visits to the countryside I soon appreciated that if a farmer wanted a day out, he had a walk round someone else's farm, talking shop. Everything that happened in the countryside was of interest to everyone else—and I include the townsman, because every year the number of people who spend their spare time in the country grows. The BBC has of course produced many programmes about the countryside, but as far as my memory serves there has never been a daily serial based on everyday happenings.

We started with farming folk: *Mr. and Mrs. Archer* farming a hundred-acre farm; their eldest son *Jack*, married to a town girl, working on a smallholding of four-and-a-half acres; their second boy, *Philip*, educated at a farm institute; their daughter, *Christine*, a bright girl at school, making the most of every opportunity to further her education and interest in rural affairs. But we couldn't stop there; the squire and his wife forced their way into the programme as the leaders of village society; the district nurse; the policeman; the doctor; the publican, and the parson were all linked to this real centre of country activity—the farm; and before we knew where we were, we were dealing with the everyday affairs of the whole rural community.

This picture of the countryside must be accurate, and to make sure that every detail of the programme shall be as acceptable to the countryman as it is entertaining to the townsman we are keeping records of the daily happenings on an actual farm. Behind us a team of experts will be always ready to keep us up to date with the latest developments.

Last, but perhaps strangest of all, Edward J. Mason and Geoffrey Webb, who write *Dick Barton*, will be responsible for the script.

Source: Radio Times

Fig. 6.1 An article in *Radio Times* introduces listeners to the BBC's new radio serial, *The Archers*, January 1951.

from the serials when questions of 'quality' arose. The disparagement of serials as 'women's shows' reflected the then-common equation of female appeal with low culture. Some examples of the most popular daytime serials of the 30s are listed in Figure 6.2.

The ideological genesis of the serials was traditional women's magazine fiction, both of the sensationalist 'true confessions' kind and dramatizations of dilemmas arising from infidelity, life choices (most commonly, marriage or career), impending motherhood, estrangement and divorce. Serialization meant open-ended narratives, which allowed themes and characters to be developed or dropped as audience research dictated; it also meant that the convention of resolving plots according to moral scruples (compulsory in Hollywood film) was not always followed, creating an ambiguity of message that added to the serials' 'vulgar' image but also gave them a more realistic dimension. Though some have argued that the hidden agenda of daytime soap opera was and remains (through its TV reincarnation) one of reinforcing the dominant ideology of female subservience, there was in 1930s US radio a high degree of ambivalence in the serials' presentation of a woman's lot and a sense of the soap opera being jealously guarded by its listeners as women's territory. Qualitative audience research, for example, consistently noted the serials' position as a talking point, a meeting ground, in everyday conversation. In contrast to the vacuous female characters in the more male-oriented action series broadcast at night-time, soap heroines were often strong-willed and articulate: if they did put marriage before a career, the decision was theirs.

US-style serial drama eventually reached Britain in the 1940s via a circuitous route, in the form of *The Robinson Family* on the BBC's North

Serial	Sponsor
Against the Storm	Procter and Gamble
Amanda of Honeymoon Hill	Phillips
Beyond These Valleys	General Mills
Hilltop House	Colgate
Houseboat Hannah	Procter and Gamble
Life Can Be Beautiful	Procter and Gamble
Mary Noble, Backstage Wife	Lyons Products
Our Gal Sunday	American Home Products
Second Husband	Lyons
Stella Dallas	Phillips
The Right to Happiness	Procter and Gamble

Fig. 6.2 Examples of daytime serials and sponsors in 1930s US radio

American Service – created for an American audience to depict an ordinary British middle-class family coping with the war. It transferred to the Light Programme but was soon eclipsed by *Mrs Dale's Diary* (subsequently retitled *The Dales*) which began in 1948; this was a continuing tale of a doctor and his practice, as seen through his wife's eyes. Scheduled specifically as a daytime serial for women at home, it was overwhelmingly middle-class in tone: Peter Black recalls that 'the lower orders were brought in exactly as Shakespeare had brought them in, as comedy relief in the characters of servants, charwomen, gardeners etc.' (Black, p. 175). The programme rarely touched the serious emotional issues that were always at the heart of American serials, however sentimentally they were treated.

After *The Dales* closed with the doctor's retirement in 1969, there were various attempts to replicate its success with more 'topical' fare – notably *Waggoner's Walk* and *Citizens* – but these were generally in the context of Radio 2 and sat uneasily in sequences of music-dominated programming. In 1998, Radio 3 experimented with a daily serial, *Quartet*, about a group of four young musicians, which was scheduled at the strategically important time of 4.45pm, to attract listeners to the station's drive-time period. It exemplified many of the problems in starting a new serial from scratch: that a serial needs possibly a year to bed in, which cost may prohibit; that characters take time to establish themselves with listeners; that content and characters must be finely matched to the desired audience; that the programme has to be effectively launched and promoted.

Mrs Dale's Diary apart, the BBC's one major success in this field has been *The Archers*, which began in 1951 as a vehicle for keeping farmers informed of developments in agriculture. Its broader popularity prompted its move from mornings to a 6.45pm slot, the timing of which marked it as a weapon in BBC radio's battle against evening television; on the night that ITV opened in 1955, the programme stole the headlines by killing off a lead character, Grace Archer, in a barn fire. As late as 1998, changes to its scheduling were a key part of the strategy to revitalize Radio 4. From the start, *The Archers* had a core appeal to folk memory in its idealized rural English setting in which all classes knew their place, yet was always tempered by a streak of realism on farming matters; it gently stressed family values while exploring conflicts between the old and new ways in the relationship between patriarchial Dan Archer and his go-ahead son Phil; and its supporting characters included a few rural stereotypes straight out of the popular fiction of H.E. Bates or Stella Gibbons – warring families of yokels, a village eccentric, wayward daughters, gamekeepers and poachers, all seen from the perspective of a tight-knit, sensible and supportive middle-class family. *The Archers'* continuing remit to the farming community (it still has an agricultural story editor) ensured that the serial did keep pace with genuine change within agriculture and to the social fabric of village life – well-to-do newcomers settled in houses that the tenant workers couldn't afford, landowners sold fields for housing, teenage vandals sprayed graffiti over the pub walls, and old-timers grumbled about a female vicar in the parish. In 1999, the programme tackled the issue of genetically modified crops by involving one of its young characters, Tommy Archer, in criminal action against an experimental crop being grown by his uncle, landowner Brian Aldridge.

ACTION DRAMAS

The other main sub-genre of radio drama, though even less prevalent today than the daily serial, is the action adventure series. In the US, the origin of a show such as *Gangbusters* clearly lay in crime fiction magazines like *True Detective*, while *Superman* was a straight radio adaptation of an already established comic-book series; but of equal impact on the form, tone and especially subject matter of the serials was Hollywood, where many of the shows were produced by advertising agencies using locally based scriptwriters and small-time film actors and where production was routinized on the conveyor-belt model of cinema serials.

Narratives rarely deflected from the classic 'hero versus villain' scenario of the western movie (itself an infant genre in the late 1920s) or the emphasis on action and pace over character development. The programmes were targeted mainly at men (hence their early-evening siting in the schedules) and especially juvenile males: the radio western was initially almost wholly child-oriented, its recurrent themes characterized by J. Fred Macdonald as championing the oppressed or weak (often lone female ranchers or cowmen fallen on hard times) and establishing a civilized code in the midst of anarchy. The character of *The Lone Ranger* embodied this idealization of the American male, while one of radio's numerous singing cowboys, Gene Autry, even published a Cowboy Code (reproduced in Figure 6.3). Much of this ideological perspective was carried over into radio detective fiction: 'Whether or not a program openly declared that "crime does not pay", this was the message expounded in all broadcasts. In a civilisation established upon the principle of private ownership of property – be it land, coin or life – such a proclamation is

> 1. A cowboy never takes unfair advantage, even of an enemy.
> 2. A cowboy never betrays a trust.
> 3. A cowboy always tells the truth.
> 4. A cowboy is kind to small children, to old folks, and to animals.
> 5. A cowboy is free from racial and religious prejudice.
> 6. A cowboy is always helpful, and when anyone's in trouble, he lends a hand.
> 7. A cowboy is a good worker.
> 8. A cowboy is clean about his person, and in thought, word and deed.
> 9. A cowboy respects womanhood, his parents and the laws of his country.
> 10. A cowboy is a patriot.

Source: J. Fred MacDonald, *Don't Touch That Dial!*

Fig. 6.3 Gene Autry's Cowboy Code (published 1951)

functional necessity' (Macdonald, p. 158). Yet there were variations within the detective genre, from the cerebral *Sherlock Holmes* to the detective-as-loner depiction of *The Adventures of Sam Spade* (where his status as *private* detective emphasized his separateness) to the more stylized *Dragnet* of the 1950s. As Hollywood crime films became darker and more ambivalent in the 1940s – the era of *film noir* – radio production teams pushed the genre as far as sponsors and networks would allow into what Macdonald calls 'neo-realistic programming', though there was a double-edged aspect to this. On the one hand, this was no more than radio attempting to keep up with film and upstart television in maintaining popular attention; on the other, the emergence of a new kind of solitary, almost existentialist hero in America's prime time chimed in with growing paranoia about the world outside (manifested in the who-can-you-trust scenario of the anti-communist witch-hunts) and with the rise of adolescent-oriented culture, with iconic figures like James Dean and Marlon Brando personifying a dangerous sense of alienation.

BBC radio's action dramas had some parallels, especially in the upright but strong male heroes of *Dick Barton, Secret Agent* and *Journey into Space*. The BBC's first real venture of this kind in 1943 was *Appointment with Fear*, a series of late-night horror stories, whose narrator 'The Man in Black' (the actor Valentine Dyall) inspired a later series of the same name. *Dick Barton* started in 1946 and signalled a new move into serialized populist drama, whether in the form of serials or series with self-contained weekly episodes such as *Paul Temple* and *PC49*. This came about partly because of the deliberately populist flavour of the Light Programme – aiming to achieve, in its first year, an internally set target of 60 per cent of the listening audience – and partly because of the shift to tight daily scheduling and recorded rather than live programming that wartime broadcasting had necessitated.

Again, the genre's antecedents were in popular fiction: *Dick Barton* was an escapist mix of thrills and fun inspired by the Bulldog Drummond stories, with a fight against foreign subversion – a legacy of the war years but now reinterpreted for a new Cold War era – its explicit theme. Yet it was a sign of the times that *Dick Barton* changed in response to Listener Research's discovery that its main audience were schoolboys. The tone changed, Dick's girlfriend was abandoned, a Gene Autry-like code of conduct was introduced to ensure that Dick always represented fair play, and the all-action drama from then on became a mainly child-oriented genre that all but died with the end of children's programming in 1964.

Some of the dilemmas of drama on contemporary radio are well illustrated by the fate of *Dr Who* on radio. *Dr Who* started as a children's TV serial in 1963 with clear roots in BBC radio's science fiction adventure series of the 50s like *Journey into Space* and *Quatermass*. It lasted for over 20 years through several changes of actors. Some years after being controversially dropped from BBC TV, the series was revived on radio by a team led by established *Dr Who* writer-producer Barry Letts with Jon Pertwee (the third Dr Who) in the lead role. It had a clear pedigree and faithfully adhered to the mythology of the TV series, but it faced two related dilemmas. One, who was it for – children, BBC radio's committed drama followers, existing *Dr Who* fans, science buffs with a sense of fun? Reflecting the uncertainty, the series was shunted from Radio 4 to Radio 2 and eventually appeared on Radio 5. Two, without an obvious constituency – long-time *Dr Who* fans apart – the series had no real strategic role in building a network audience. The eventual abandonment of the radio *Dr Who* seemed like an ominous paradigm of BBC radio drama as a whole – cost-rich, overshadowed by its television counterpart, universally seen as worthwhile and carrying much goodwill, yet also ill-fitting and out of place. Ironically, however, the radio *Dr Who* did find a certain niche within the new, commercially-minded BBC of the 1990s: *Dr Who: The Paradise of Death* found a place in the BBC's cassette catalogue as a part of BBC heritage, and on release it became the first spoken-word cassette ever to sell well enough to reach the album chart. It did have an audience after all.

Further reading

Black, Peter (1972): *The Biggest Aspidistra in the World.* BBC.
Branston, Gill (1995): *The Media Student's Book.* Routledge.
Colin, Sid (1977): *And the Bands Played On.* Elm Tree.
Crisell, Andrew (1986): *Understanding Radio.* Methuen.
Donovan, Paul (1992): *The Radio Companion.* Grafton.
Foster, Andy, and Furst, Steve (1996): *Radio Comedy 1938–1968.* Virgin.
Frith, Simon (1988): *Music for Pleasure.* Polity Press.
Gielgud, Val (1946): *Radio Theatre.* Macdonald.
Gielgud, Val (1949): *The Right Way to Radio Playwriting.* Right Way.
Gielgud, Val (1965): *Years in a Mirror.* Bodley Head.
Hilmes, Michele (1997): *Radio Voices: American Broadcasting 1922–1952.* University of Minnesota Press.
Horstmann, Rosemary (1988): *Writing for Radio.* A & C Black.
Macdonald, J. Fred (1979): *Don't Touch That Dial! Radio Programming in American Life from 1920 to 1960.* Nelson-Hall.
Middleton, Richard (1985): 'Popular music, class conflict and the music-historical field; in David Horn (ed.), *Popular Music Perspectives 2.* IASPM.
Nichols, Richard (1983): *Radio Luxembourg: Station of the Stars.* Comet.
Nobbs, George (1972): *The Wireless Stars.* Wensum.
Parker, Derek (1977): *Radio: The Great Years.* David & Charles.
Pickles, Wilfred (1949): *Between You and Me.* Werner Laurie.
Scannell, Paddy (1996): *Radio, Television and Modern Life.* Blackwell.
Snagge, John, and Barsley, Michael (1972): *Those Vintage Years of Radio.* Pitman.

Activity 6.1

Using sources such as pre-recorded cassettes of radio programmes available from public libraries, compare a current radio comedy show with a comedy programme from an earlier period. Assess the degree to which each is a product of its time. And what lines of continuity (narrative structure, conventions, archetypal characters, etc.) can be traced between them? Which is funnier – and why?

Activity 6.2

Evaluate the strengths and weaknesses of radio as a medium for drama, from a production perspective and as a listening experience. What would be the particular problems in presenting a Shakespeare history such as *Henry V*, a Molière farce or a stage musical such as *The Sound of Music* on radio?

Activity 6.3

Why should comedy and drama on radio continue to be ring-fenced in terms of the budgets they receive? Make a case for and against the continuance of this special treatment.

Activity 6.4

ANNOUNCER: The English Channel 1941. Across the silent strip of green-grey water – in England – coastal towns were deserted, except for people. Despite the threat of invasion and the stringent blackout rules, elderly gentlefolk of Bexhill-on-Sea still took their evening constitutions.

SOUND FX: (Ebb tide on a gravel beach)

CRUN: Ooh – it's quite windy on these cliffs.

MINNIE: What a nice summer evening – typical English.

CRUN: Mnk yes – the rain's lovely and warm – I think I'll take one of my sou'westers off – here, hold my elephant gun.

> From 'The Dreaded Batter Pudding Hurler of Bexhill-on-Sea'
> by Spike Milligan (1954) published in
> *The Goon Show Scripts* (Sphere).

What radio conventions are being parodied in this extract? What image of the BBC does it portray, and how does it express the social and cultural milieu of the period? Evaluate whether such dialogue would work as effectively in a television or film context.

Activity 6.5

Consider the examples of daytime serials listed in Figure 6.2 on page 117. Based on your understanding of soap opera texts as described in this chapter and/or your researches on the Internet, what kind of content and what type of target audience do their titles suggest?

Choose any one title and, with a potential sponsor in mind, sketch out a plot summary for a pilot episode (around 200 words) aimed at a 1930s audience. Assess how different your plot and characters would be if you were writing for a daytime radio audience today.

7

Music Radio

Music has formed the core of radio programming almost since the medium's inception, largely for reasons of tradition and cost. In contemporary radio, music enables the medium's utilitarian aspects to function smoothly and effectively – framing the talk and information content, setting a mood conducive to continued listening, providing an environment in which advertisements can be heard to most positive effect, matching the very pace of domestic life and the working day itself. Even on stations which have no musical content – BBC Radio 5 Live, for example – theme tunes and stations identifiers convey and establish a sense of drama or urgency. Correctly chosen, music can be a covert means of targeting particular socio-economic audiences and excluding others. Music selection, from the general (which musical style, which age group to target) to the specific (which artists to play, which records to feature and in what kind of sequence and rotation), helps determine the tone, image and personality of a station – a crucial factor in a competitive and saturated market.

Traditionally, music has been used by radio stations as an aid to relaxation (for example, the 15- and 30-minute interludes of live dance band music – 'tea dance' music – heard on BBC radio in the 1930s), as a means of establishing a link with the audience (record request shows), and to provide a background to working activities. The latter function was particularly widespread in the US in the 1930s, when factories relayed music from both radio stations and organizations like the Muzak Corporation as a means of keeping workers alert and attuned to their work. The wartime BBC programme *Music While You Work* – aimed at munitions factories and featuring continuous dance band medleys of even-tempoed tunes – was based on the same principles and endured on the Light Programme until 1967.

TOP 40 RADIO

The concept of a station or network devoted entirely to music of whatever kind emerged in the US during the early 1950s, in response to the loss of audiences and advertisers to television. Underpinning it was the basic economic fact that programming built around commercially available records was cheap, requiring none of the level of investment in variety programmes, drama or news. One of the most influential developments was the emergence of Top 40 radio in 1949, by stations affiliated to the Mid-Continent Broadcasting Company, owned by Todd Storz which broke with the familiar pattern (known as the 'bandstand' concept) of playing 15-minute segments of records by a single artist or dance band. Storz had noticed that jukebox users, in choosing what records to hear from a list of up to a hundred discs changed weekly, tended to select the same discs again and again. Applying this to radio, he developed the principle that the most popular current records (i.e. those in the Top 40 chart) should be given the most plays, and often. Supposing that more listeners would tune in if they could be sure of hearing their favourite records, a rotation system was introduced to ensure that the biggest current sellers were played at set intervals. Top 40 radio predated rock'n'roll – music of primary appeal to teenagers, stylistically linked to black rhythm and blues and white country music – but came into its own once the economic power of teenagers was fully appreciated. Top 40 radio could deliver a ready market for commodities such as hair grease, skin cleanser, sportswear, jeans, chewing gum, make-up and fan magazines, while the electronics industry saw sales of transistor radios soar past the two million mark between January 1956 and July 1957, the period spanning Elvis Presley's breakthrough.

The spread of Top 40 radio in the US aided the record industry's own exploitation of the teenage market, with companies concentrating their promotional efforts on getting their new releases on to the playlists of the highest-rated stations. For a time, 'payola' (payment for airplay) was rife, with the smaller labels fighting for their share of a congested market by trading cash and gifts for radio play from the most powerful disc jockeys. A congressional inquiry led to the outlawing of such practices and the end of several influential radio careers, but it left Top 40 radio strengthened as a genre: station managers now assumed responsibility for selecting the playlists, and the format became refined to prevent abuses, to the extent that disc jockeys became almost anonymous figures, 'making the disc jockey a mechanical figure, an automaton from which all humanness was drained' (Eberly, p. 201). This trend reached its nadir in 1965, when radio consultant Bill Drake introduced a new version of the Top 40 format in the form of 'Boss Radio' (derived from the Beatles' frequent use of the word), which featured a much-reduced playlist (the top 30 only) and a 20-second limit on talk between discs.

Top 40 radio established characteristics of pop radio which are still applicable today: an emphasis on topicality via the latest hits and fastest risers; and on pace and excitement, engendered by the breathless patter of disc jockeys, jingles, trailers, and technical developments like reverberation units to create a 'big' sound. For many years, British radio had nothing comparable: the BBC continued to treat its Light Programme audience as a broad church, with individually produced programmes to suit different musical tastes or interests, albeit selected and prioritized in curious ways. Jazz followers, for example, had programmes on both the Light and the Third Programme. It is not true to say, as some histories of pop radio have it, that there was little or no coverage of pop music on BBC radio between the mid 1950s and the mid 1960s: there were pockets of individual programmes, some featuring records exclusively (because they were produced for the network by the Gramophone Department) and some featuring BBC-hired bands and singers recreating the hits of the day (these produced by the Popular Music Department).

Beyond the BBC, the main outlet for pop music on record was Radio Luxembourg. From its relaunch after the war right through to the mid-1950s, Luxembourg remained a family-oriented variety station offering panel games, request shows and artist showcase programmes. It then fought the loss of audiences and advertisers to television (and Independent Television in particular) by following the American pattern of switching to a format centred almost exclusively on commercially made recordings, aimed primarily at teenagers. But Luxembourg neither produced nor commissioned programmes: instead it sold airtime to Britain's record companies in 15- or 30-minute sections, enabling them to promote what records they chose without having to negotiate around 'gatekeepers' of radio such as programme producers, network controllers, station owners and disc jockeys. For listeners, Luxembourg's version of music radio could be frustrating as such shows were subject to the practice of 'top-and-tailing' the records – missing out the introduction and the ending, leaving only about a minute of music, to leave listeners wanting more.

In Britain, the style and sound of Top 40 radio was in time recreated in often ramshackle circumstances by a handful of pirate radio stations, most set up with American financial backing, broadcasting from ships and forts just outside British territorial waters. Although the stations had relatively limited coverage – most were based on the east coast, meaning that huge swathes of the population never heard them at all – the pirates had a major impact on the course of British radio by giving the BBC a model for a new service, Radio 1, which came on air six weeks after the pirates were outlawed, in September 1967, with many ex-pirate presenters aboard. What the pirates offered was wholly record-based and mostly pop music-based (Radio 390 was the major exception, choosing to fashion itself as a 'sweet music' station aimed explicitly at housewives) but the BBC could only emulate its format and style up to a point. The pirate stations not only pirated wavelengths, they pirated the music: whereas BBC radio had to adhere to agreements made back in the 1920s and 30s regarding payments to record companies for records broadcast on air and to composers and music publishers for all songs broadcast, the pirates had no such obligations. What was cheap radio for the pirates turned out to be very expensive for the BBC – with the added complication that the BBC was obliged, through long-standing agreement with Phonographic Performance Limited (PPL) and the Musicians Union, to limit the use of records on the air (needle-time) to just eight hours a day.

Radio 1's identity as a pop station was therefore undermined from the outset by its inability to devote the core of its programming to the one element at the core of American pop radio – the commercial record. This was quite apart from the prevailing tendency of those Light Programme traditionalists within the two production centres – the Popular Music Department and the Gramophone Department – to see the station's daytime core listeners as housewives uninterested in teenage pop. The coming of legal commercial radio encouraged the BBC to review Radio 1's remit and particularly its music policy. Organizational changes led to the disbanding of the two production departments; needle-time agreements were renegotiated to ensure the BBC and the commercial stations had parity of operation; there was more investment in the specialist fringes of Radio 1's activity, and its commitment to the 'progressive' end of pop music became a key policy, justifying the network as more than just a purveyor of lightweight pop and giving it cultural weight.

The new commercial radio stations, meanwhile, found themselves too handicapped by the programming requirements set down in their franchise agreements to develop as true all-music stations, though they all (with the exception of LBC, whose terms of operations were as a news station) retained a music format of some kind. The most important development was the IBA instruction to stations to provide different services on their FM and AM frequencies. This led to some experimentation with music services differentiated on age lines, with Capital's split into Capital FM (Top 40, young profile) and Capital Gold ('oldies', targeted at 35s and over) providing a much-copied template.

FRAGMENTATION AND FORMATS

The Radio Authority-fostered expansion of radio created new opportunities for music radio, especially in metropolitan areas. By 1998, London had 22 commercial stations, all but four music-based and each of these ostensibly specializing in a specific genre. In 1992 Britain's first national commercial station, Classic FM, came on air; Virgin Radio (already established in London on an AM frequency) was awarded the second national franchise in 1993. In format, the new stations competed directly with neither existing commercial services nor established BBC services; the rock album-based menu of Virgin, for example, was aimed at the older end of Radio 1's audience and eschewed both the Top 40 bias of Capital FM and the oldies orientation of the gold stations.

The problem for genre-based stations (and especially those outside London) is in establishing and maintaining an audience base strong enough to support advertising. Classic FM could survive on a comparatively low base because its music policy gave advertisers (especially in the lucrative financial sector) access to a stable market of over-50s with high disposable income. Kiss FM, a former pirate, quickly established itself because it identified with, and gave exposure to, the burgeoning dance culture that daytime Radio 1 ignored. Jazz FM's many programming swings were symptomatic of the most basic problem of all – how to define what *kind* of music the station was meant to represent in the face of falling profits and patchy audiences. Jazz FM began with high hopes of pleasing both traditionalist and modern jazz followers but switched to a much higher content of jazz-*influenced* sounds (jazz-funk, acid-jazz, R&B) designed to attract a broader listenership.

Britain's patchwork of generic music stations follows loosely the American pattern of commercial radio, which since the heyday of Top 40 radio and its various offshoots has evolved into a fluid, ever-changing (but increasingly centrally owned) mix of stations covering distinct musical avenues (see Figure 7.1). American radio broadcasting is defined less by musical differences *per se* than by demographics: stations tailor their programming to match what market research defines as the tastes and preferences of particular age groups, social groups or communities of interest. What may seem like a plethora of musical niches is in fact more reflective of subtle differences in presentation and musical nuance, calculated by constant monitoring of the audience and marketed via skilful promotion. Established formats like Top 40 have been constantly refined not only in reaction to changing public taste but as part of a constant pursuit of a distinctive selling point – some emphasis in delivery or repertoire that makes a station *sound* different from its many competitors and register a few extra points in the weekly ratings.

Often supposedly new formats are in fact experiments in crossover between existing formats. So Top 40 radio evolved into CHR (contemporary hit radio), while AOR (album-oriented rock) radio grew out of the album-based freeform FM base of the late 1960s and paralleled the rise of AC (adult contemporary) radio, aimed at the maturing 'baby boomer' generation. AC in turn fragmented into formats centred on oldies, easy-listening (anything from orchestral mood

1.	Country	2,667	14.	Jazz	392
2.	Adult contemporary	1,892	15.	Christian	390
3.	News/talk	1,008	16.	Diversified	317
4.	Oldies	999	17.	Urban contemporary	314
5.	Religious	925	18.	Progressive	251
6.	Rock/AOR	548/136	19.	Alternative	246
7.	CHR	546	20.	Educational	243
8.	Classical	458	21.	Big band	172
9.	Sports	456	22.	Ethnic	166
10.	Spanish	453	23.	Beautiful music	137
11.	Gospel	445	24.	Nostalgia	120
12.	Classic rock	423	25.	Agriculture and farming	94
13.	MOR	393			

Note: This lists only the top 25 genres. The same source lists 40 other genres with fewer than 90 stations each.

Source: *Broadcasting and Cable Yearbook,* 1997 (R. R. Bosken)

Fig. 7.1 Number of US radio stations by genre

music to the Carpenters or Barry Manilow), new age music and 'quiet storm' (the mellow end of urban black soul music). Club-based music styles such as disco, with a strong crossover appeal between black and white audiences, were incorporated into the 'urban contemporary' format. Much more problematic – and indicative of American radio's relative inability to handle disruptive styles originating outside the professional music mainstream – was the rise of hip-hop, house and garage. KDAY in Los Angeles was the first rap-only station in the US, but the street language and references to gang violence and sexual prowess in some rap lyrics made rap a particular focus for new political demands for curbs on content, with the FCC urged to withdraw licences from stations that transgressed. Leading rap band NWA (Niggas With Attitude) sold three million copies of their 1989 album *Straight Outta Compton* with virtually no airplay.

■ GATEKEEPING IN MUSIC RADIO

The 'gatekeepers' of music radio are the programme controllers and producers who oversee not only what is played on the radio but the environment in which it is heard, the frequency of its playing and its positioning within programmes. They, far more than presenters, are the source of power in music radio; they both represent and control the twin ideologies of consensus and consumer sovereignty, and they keep the airwaves free of tension, conflict and disruption. Like gatekeepers in other media (newspaper editors, for example), they put their own tastes and preferences to one side in favour of a professional assessment of which music will most fit the editorial profile of their station. The main concern of radio gatekeepers is to serve the *particular* publics that the station's managers or owners have delineated.

Chart-based radio, by definition, is overwhelmingly concerned with topicality: it draws on those records which are currently selling well or which are likely to sell in large numbers in the near future. From the 50s through to the 70s, the Top 40 sales chart was the major frame of reference in choosing records for airplay because the record-buying audience and music radio listeners were interchangeable – that is, mainly teenage. When radio stations began targeting more lucrative older markets, it made sense to either ignore the Top 40 altogether or draw selectively from it. Britain's first legal commercial music station, Capital, began in 1973 with a distinctly middle-of-the-road (MOR) edge, mixing in album tracks with the latest single hits by artists with appeal to the station's target audience of over 25s (with a bias towards women). As the programme controller of Nottingham's Radio Trent put it in 1976, 'record purchasers are only a small proportion of the public and it would be foolish to base a station's programming intended for all the public on the demands of a minority . . . the last way to promote a record here is to tell me it's going to sell a million copies. I don't care. I want to know whether it'll sound good on the radio' (quoted in Barnard, p. 132).

Only at Radio 1 did an overwhelming allegiance to the sales chart remain in place, only to be seriously abandoned as part of the station's 'repositioning' in the early 1990s. The logic here was to view the chart as an expression of consumer sovereignty – a reflection of what people are buying, therefore of what is most currently popular. This ignored the fact that, such was Radio 1's predominance in music radio throughout the 70s and 80s, a record was only likely to reach the sales chart after being heard on Radio 1: frequently, the station only played those records that its own producers had *preselected* as potential chart hits. Although scrupulous in its insistence that the chart should be seen to be accurate and fair – which is why the BBC co-funded the Gallup chart in the 1980s with the British Phonographic Industry (BPI) and the industry's newspaper, *Music Week* – Radio 1's use of its information was and continues to be selective: records were not given an equal number of plays, chart positions did not automatically merit a certain ratio of airplay, and Top 40 records deemed to be salacious or politically unacceptable were occasionally banned altogether.

At almost every music-oriented station, a weekly playlist – usually compiled by the station's Programme Controller or a committee of producers, and often divided into A, B and C lists – dictates what will be played and its frequency. This is gatekeeping in its purest form: a selection of items chosen to match a professional judgement of what the listener will prefer to hear at a particular point in time, informed by a variety of factors including a record's appropriateness for the station's target market, whether it matches the brand image of the station and its generic base, and perhaps only incidentally its sales performance as reflected in the chart. Still echoing Todd Storz's jukebox principle, stations tend to draw on a narrow field of records to make their choices: those commercially available and currently selling in quantity; new releases earmarked as *potentially* matching the listener profile, because the artists concerned are established or because the record in question is already known through outlets such as clubs; records that are no longer selling well but which continually appear as preferred listener choices in the spot research that stations undertake; and records of still older vintage that fit with the audience profile – for example, records from the post-1990 period (matching what the 15–25-year-old age group is likely to be familiar with) in the case of Radio 1.

Another criterion for selection in a competitive market is what other stations are playing, as measured by the airplay rankings (compiled by Music Control UK) featured in *Music Week*. The airplay chart may verify the playlist compilers' choice or point him/her/them towards records that their peers are prioritizing – either way, the effect is self-fulfilling and reinforces the sense of narrowness, familiarity and repetition in what finally reaches the listener. That the Pepsi-sponsored Top 40 chart, widely used by commercial stations in preference to the BBC-BPI chart, incorporates an airplay factor into its rankings makes those stations' music choices yet more self-fulfilling. Even at stations which are not primarily Top 40-oriented, where the demand for topicality is not so rigid, the concentration on the *already popular* is marked: 'gold' stations, targeted at a 35-plus listenership, base their selections on records that their target group would have bought in numbers during the 60s,

Position	Last week's position	Weeks on chart	Position on sales chart	Title	Artist	Record company	Total Plays	Total audience (m)
1	1	8	10	Beautiful Stranger	Madonna	Maverick/ Warner Brothers	2462	79.56
2	3	13	45	Canned Heat	Jamiroquai	Sony S2	2056	62.69
3	6	5	7	If You Had My Love	Jennifer Lopez	Work/Columbia	1818	62.55
4	12	6	1	Livin' La Vida Loca	Ricky Martin	Columbia	1539	62.42
5	5	8	4	My Love Is Your Love	Whitney Houston	Arista	1932	62.00
6	4	8	3	Wild Wild West	Will Smith	Columbia	1791	56.87
7	7	6	2	9PM (Till I Come)	ATB	Sound of Ministry	1331	54.46
8	8	12	9	That Don't Impress Me Much	Shania Twain	Mercury	2184	53.71
9	2	13	28	Kiss Me	Sixpence None The Richer	Elektra	1844	53.37
10	9	7	8	Sometimes	Britney Spears	Jive	1968	45.42
11	26	3	0	When You Say Nothing At All	Ronan Keating	Polydor	1139	39.34
12	13	5	13	Secret Smile	Semisonic	MCA	1024	36.67
13	11	15	56	Every Morning	Sugar Ray	Lava/Atlantic	1206	35.92
14	16	4	18	Coffee + TV	Blur	Food/Parlophone	602	34.69
15	22	2	0	Lovestruck	Madness	Virgin	582	33.47
16	15	7	24	Everything is Everything	Lauryn Hill	Columbia	610	32.46
17	17	5	11	Tsunami	Manic Street Preachers	Epic	563	32.35
18	18	19	37	No Scrubs	TLC	LaFace/Arista	842	29.04
19	10	6	38	She's in Fashion	Suede	Nude	860	26.94
20	23	4	23	The Animal Song	Savage Garden	Columbia	1184	25.61

Source: Data reproduced by kind permission of Music Control UK. Music Control UK monitors the following stations 24 hours a day, seven days a week: 2 Ten FM, 2CR FM, Aire FM, Alpha 103.2FM, Atlantic 252, B97FM, BBC Radio 1, BBC Radio 2, BBC Radio 3, BBC Radio Scotland, BBC Three Counties, BBC Radio Ulster, BBC Radio Wales, Beacon, BRMB FM, Broadland FM, Capital FM, Century FM, Century 105FM, Chiltern, Choice FM, City Beat, City FM, Classic FM, Clyde One FM, Cool FM, Crash FM, Downtown FM, Dream 100FM, Essex FM, Forth FM, Fox FM, Galaxy 101FM, Galaxy 102FM, Galaxy 102.2, Galaxy 105FM, GLR, GWR FM, Hallam FM, Heart FM, Heart London, Heartbeat 1521, Horizon, Invicta FM, Isle of Wight FM, K1y 103, Kiss FM, Leicester Sound, Lincs FM, Magic 1170, Manx FM, Mercia, Metro FM, MFM 1034/971, Minster FM, Mix 96, Northants Radio, Ocean, Orchard FM, Power FM, Q103, QFM, Quay West Radio, Ram, Red Dragon, Rock FM, Scot FM, SGR Ipswich, Signal One, Signal Cheshire, Southern FM, Spire FM, Stray FM, TFM, The Pulse, The Vibe, Viking FM, Virgin 1215, 96.4FM The Wave, Wave 105 FM, Xfm.

Fig. 7.2 Airplay chart data, 17 July 1999

70s and 80s while, at the other end of the spectrum, Classic FM has been criticized for failing to move beyond a carefully researched core of pieces by a handful of well-known composers. In every case, the fear is that sudden confrontation with the unfamiliar, unexpected or difficult will disrupt the easy flow of daytime radio and cause listeners to reach for the dial or off-switch.

As stations are bought and sold and the primacy of the format (which is often spread across all the stations owned by a national group) becomes established, so programmers in music radio have come to rely more and more on computerization as a means of facilitating and controlling the selection process. The use of computers in music programming dates from the early 1980s; then as now, the field leader was the US-originated Selector software system, which selects from a pre-entered base of records (a playlist), divides them by artist, title, tempo, mood, chart position or (with 'gold' or oldies stations in mind) the age of the record, and provides running orders that take into account such variables as the required frequency of play across a day and 'timbre sequencing' (flowing together tracks of similar pace), 'conditional dayparting' (selecting tracks for particular times of day) and 'audience appeal requirements'.

The advantage of such a system is that it keeps the station 'sound' (its aural branding) consistent, as well as reducing the time and money spent on music programming itself and on filling out logging sheets and copyright returns. The wholesale switch to in-studio computerization during the 1990s brought the Sony CD jukebox into common use and the storing of all tracks on hard disk, both of which allowed instant access to the required music. A further development was the DAMS system, which added advertisements, promos and trailers to the mix, to be similarly accessed at the touch of a screen or keypad.

The development of automation systems took the principle of computerized output still further. Enco Dad is one of around 20 such systems which enable the complete station output of music, identification jingles and advertisements to be recorded and stored on the hard disk of a computer and then run automatically. The advantage to the stations is that it saves on time, labour and employment costs, while imposing a uniformity of style and output on a station's programming. That it may also lead to a loss of a sense of 'liveness' is a heated source of debate in radio circles. Nevertheless, automation is now commonplace in music radio, especially at relatively low listening periods such as overnight. A significant part of the daytime programming on London's Magic FM station (previously Melody FM) is automated, with verbal content limited to links after every three or four items of music, and then mainly to identify the station.

Computerization is a tool, not a substitute for human thought or ingenuity: programmers constantly point out that the running orders or sequencing that a computer system produces can only be as effective as the information with which it is supplied, or the instructions it is given, enable it to be. But the fact that many competing music stations use similar systems and software and work from the same selection basis contributes to a uniformity of output that undermines the very distinctiveness they profess to seek.

RADIO AND THE MUSIC INDUSTRY

Radio's emergence as a mass medium in the 1920s profoundly altered the very *sound* of popular music. This was most dramatically seen in the US with the sweetening of syncopated music into a form of light dance music similar to that heard as a background to dining in society hotels; the exposure of rural communities in the US to urban popular music, resulting in hybrid musical forms like the country music/big band crossover known as 'western swing'; and, most dramatically, the relabelling and reshaping of rhythm and blues music, an urban black music form, as a music (rock'n'roll) heard by, promoted to and subsequently recreated by white teenagers.

Radio's presence also changed the dynamics of commercial music-making, as stations suddenly became a major source of income for musicians and as America's music publishers – through the protectionist American Society of Composers and Publishers – enforced licensing and revenue agreements. ASCAP's growing revenue demands to America's radio networks in the 1940s led to the latter setting up its own licensing body, Broadcast Music Incorporated, and giving exposure to forms of regional music (country, Latin American, rhythm and blues, calypso) which had previously not had a national platform. This in turn brought new opportunities to regionally based record labels to market their products nationally. One of the consequences, music historians have argued, was a major reshaping of popular taste in music (and record-buying patterns) from the mid 1950s onwards. Changes within radio can also impact directly on record company strategies. In 1967, for example, the emergence of an 'alternative' stream of rock music on urban FM stations (see page 79) gave some of the nascent players in the US record industry – particularly Warner Brothers, Elektra and Atlantic – not only a source of new signings but a new medium through which to reach the lucrative album-buying student market.

Radio's demand for and use of music has a profound effect on the repertoire and promotional strategies of record companies: prior exposure on radio can influence a company to sign an artist; and how a songwriter, record producer or band approaches the process of creating a single or album may be influenced not only by what is currently selling but what is likely to be chosen for airplay.

If a record is not heard on radio, its chances of selling are limited. Compared to television and video, radio is cheap in terms of promotional resources and has a sustaining quality that the visual medium cannot match: while the impact of a television spot dissipates over a period of days, radio maintains the impact by regular repetition. But radio's main promotional value is that it reaches an audience comprised at least in part of the target group of potential record buyers – those listeners who use the medium not just as a source of entertainment or companionship but as a consumer's guide. Radio play is in this sense a form of free advertising for record companies, though the process of encouraging the gatekeepers to choose a record for airplay – 'plugging' – incurs a range of costs including the running of in-house promotional teams and the hiring of expert teams of independent pluggers.

The aim of promotion is not to maximize sales, but rather to create a climate in which sales will happen. So the promotion effort is centred on getting a record included in a station's playlist, usually six weeks ahead of the record's official release: once this is achieved, the record will get heard on a regular basis and build up a momentum for sales. (The number of plays will then be reflected in the *Music Week* airplay chart, which may in turn influence other stations to pick up on the record.) Once released, the record should then sell in sufficient quantities to guarantee a high chart entry. Responsibility for the playlisting push lies with a team of pluggers, often working independently of one another, whose mode of working can include delivering records personally to the station and sending duplicate records by mail to producers and disc jockeys. Working in tandem with a co-ordinated publicity campaign (press advertising, news stories fed through to gossip columns, flyposting, the release of a promotional video to TV shows and music channels MTV and VH1), the plugger capitalizes on the 'buzz' around a new release: if interest has been sparked before a plugger comes to call, half his job has already been done. Mostly, a plugger lives on his or her wits, cultivating contacts and relationships, his/her chief skill lying in persuading the broadcaster not of the quality of the record or even its capacity for sales but its suitability for the audience that the broadcaster is required to serve. Independent pluggers act on behalf of either the record labels or (more commonly) the artist's own management. Their growth period was the 1970s, the new demand for their services paralleling that for other independently functioning professionals (arrangers, producers, sleeve designers, management consultants) in the shift away from the centralized, imposed decision-making that characterized the recording and marketing processes of major record companies in the 60s.

Pressure for results leads to abuses, including the practice of 'hyping'. Hyping is based on the paradoxical notion that sales of a record will only begin to pick up once it has shown itself in the sales chart: if a record enters the lower reaches of the chart, it will automatically come into consideration for airplay. The aim of hyping is therefore to buy sufficient quantities of the single in question from those shops designated as chart return shops and thereby achieve a chart position.

MINORITIES AND SPECIALISMS

Frances Line, while head of BBC Radio 2 during the 1980s, referred to her station's main objective as 'ratings by day, reputation by night'. This is a familiar dichotomy in British radio, and a convenient one: Radio 2, like Radio 1 and the ILR stations of the 70s and 80s, caters for a mass audience during prime-time hours of listening but fulfils its image-enhancing 'public service' obligations to so-called minority audiences outside these hours. Radio 2, for example, broadcasts regular evening programmes of country music, folk music, brass bands, organ music, rhythm and blues, show music and jazz; at weekends, the emphasis shifts to specialist shows of vintage music, religious music, light classics and operetta. The effect of this is to sweep these non-mainstream musical tastes to the margins, and it implies a process of cultural prioritization and categorization that requires close study.

Underlining the dichotomy are a number of assumptions: that daytime listeners use radio in a secondary way, as background, while evening listeners make a deliberate choice to *listen*; that minority musical tastes do not fit comfortably with the mainstream; that minority tastes are more valid cultural forms than mainstream forms. Such assumptions have informed BBC music programming since the 1920s, when policy debates raged about how jazz should be treated on air. Jazz was an improvisational music with a following among the country's intelligentsia that could be classed as neither pure entertainment (such as dance music) nor classical music, though it shared common roots with the former. BBC policy was to accept the existence of internal distinctions within the dance music mode yet confer intellectual validity only on those styles or approaches favoured by an expert elite. While sequences of live dance music were scattered through the radio day to provide decoration and relaxation, jazz sessions were framed as recitals and often prefaced by distancing explanatory remarks – prime examples of how, as Paddy Scannell writes, 'a non-cultural category (dance music) is transformed and renominated as a cultural category for the connoisseur' (Scannell, p. 251).

The same tendencies were evident in the early days of Radio 1, when the station's programming was clearly divided between the Top 40-dominated daytime shows (which were granted the lion's share of needle-time) and what was loosely called 'progressive rock' – music with an experimental bent and bohemian appeal, mainly album-based and with a supposedly 'alternative' thrust. The latter's popularity with a young, educated, streetwise elite, together with its existence on the fringes of commercial pop music, gave it an oppositional edge. Instead of seeking to incorporate it into the daytime schedules, Radio 1 emphasized its distinction from Top 40 pop by giving in airtime at weekends, in the early evening and (from 1970 onwards) late at night. Progressive rock fans complained of discrimination against them, but the very separation of their programmes from the conventional disc shows (and their transmission on Radio 2's FM frequency) suggested compliance with the notion of a distinct split between the serious and the trivial, the valid and the disposable, the elitist and mass-appeal. The late-night shows in particular had a premise of featuring 'adventurous contemporary sounds' within what appeared to be a fairly free format and a style of low-key, almost conspiratorial presentation modelled on American FM radio. In reality, however, the musical policy of these shows was narrow and unquestioning, presenting the latest industry product wrapped in the trappings of exclusive interviews, pre-release scoops and affirmative critical comment that were so criticized as elements in Top 40 radio.

This programming dichotomy was briefly undermined by the emergence of punk rock in the late 1970s, which gave John Peel the opportunity to make a break with his progressive rock past and attempt to redefine the notion of 'alternative' music as something that was oppositional to the point of being disruptive. Peel and his producer John Walters continued their policy of hiring unsigned bands for Radio 1 recording sessions, with the result that almost all the punk bands exposed for the first time on the station won contracts with record companies. Although Peel's programmes were viewed very ambivalently at the time, it was on their success in effectively setting the agenda for late 70s and 80s rock music that Radio 1 built a new myth for itself – that of a network not only interested in entertaining the largest number, but one with a role to play in the life of the country's culture. But when (in the mid 1990s) Radio 1 management attempted to put these principles into practice across daytime as well as evening programming, the result was a disastrous slide in audience.

NEEDLE-TIME AND PERFORMANCE FEES

Radio stations cannot help but become embroiled in the marketing strategies of the companies originating the music. But they pay another price, quite literally, for their dependence on commercially recorded music, in that they are obliged to pay the music industry, through its collection agencies Phonographic Performance Limited (in Britain) and the International Federation of Phonogram and Video Industries (IFPI), for the privilege of broadcasting such material. This is in addition to fees paid to the Performing Right Society (PRS), and its equivalent societies in other countries, for distribution to songwriters whose work is featured on air.

The British music industry takes a collective view, through organizations like PPL and the BPI, that excessive airplay harms sales and that, as one ex-BPI chairman has put it, 'a record played on the radio is a record sale lost'. This does not stop companies within the BPI investing in promotion teams whose sole responsibility is securing airtime for their products. In fact, the industry is simply exploiting a revenue entitlement that is enshrined in law and which, particularly in times of economic downturn, represents a significant (and recession-proof) source of income. PPL has argued that radio stations *choose* to use music as their main source of programming, and that while airplay may promote sales of particular recordings for the benefit of individual companies, it does not expand and may well substantially limit the total market for records.

Under the terms of the 1956 Copyright Act (ratified internationally by the Rome Convention of 1961), public performance of a record company's products requires not only permission but also recompense, while at the same time safeguarding (at least in theory) the interests of the musicians who create the records. Well before the Act, the BBC had accepted the principle of payment for recorded music to copyright owners, while agreements on 'needle-time', restricting usage of records to a certain number of hours per week, were negotiated with the Musicians Union as a safeguard against records being used as a cheap substitute for live music. (Currently, the Musicians Union receives 20 per cent of PPL revenue for distribution to the credited artists and a further 12.5 per cent for distribution to the unnamed musicians who play on sessions and backing tracks.) Commercial radio stations, on air from 1973 onwards, inherited needle-time and performance fees negotiated by the IBA against BBC precedents. These became a running source of conflict between PPL and the stations (to which combined PPL and PRS fees could represent as much as 10 per cent of annual turnover) throughout the 1980s that eventually led to a High Court ruling in the former's favour.

All this is in contrast to the situation in the US, where a tradition of mutual investment between the radio and record industries stretches back to the 1920s and the Radio Corporation of America's creation of the record company RCA. There, their symbiotic relationship meant that radio was never perceived as a threat by the record manufacturers and that the issue of payment for the broadcasting of records, and of limiting radio's use of them, never seriously arose. The US was a significant absentee from the list of signatories to the Rome Convention.

Historically, the PPL/IFPI position reflects an industry-wide suspicion of technological developments that challenge the music industry's control of its products and its markets. Protectionist actions taken by the industry represent just one aspect of its attempts to adapt to fundamental changes in technology, in patterns of leisure, and in the domestic and world market for music. The pursuit of 'secondary' revenue such as performance payments ('primary' revenue being that generated by sales) is part of a switch from direct sales to the public to generating income through exploitation of ownership. As Simon Frith has suggested, 'for the music industry the age of manufacture is now over. Companies (and company profits) are no longer organized around making *things* but depend on the creation of *rights*' (Frith, p. 67).

Further reading

Barnard, Stephen (1989): *On the Radio: Music Radio in Britain*. Open University Press.

Chambers, Iain (1985): *Urban Rhythms: Pop Music and Popular Culture*. Macmillan.

Eberly, Philip K. (1982): *Music in the Air: America's Changing Tastes in Popular Music*. Hastings House.

Frith, Simon (1978): *The Sociology of Rock*. Constable.

Frith, Simon (1988): 'Copyright and the music business' in *Popular Music 7*. Cambridge University Press.

Garfield, Simon (1998): *The Nation's Favourite: The True Adventures of Radio 1*. Faber & Faber.

Gillett, Charlie (1971): *The Sound of the City*. Sphere.

Hardy, Phil (1985): *The British Record Industry*. IASPM.

Harris, Paul (1968): *When Pirates Ruled the Waves*. Impulse.

Hebdige, Dick (1979): *Subculture: The Meaning of Style*. Methuen.

Henry, Stuart, and Von Joel, Mike (1984): *Pirate Radio: Then and Now*. Blandford Press.

Hind, John, and Mosco, Stephen (1985): *Rebel Radio: The Full Story of British Pirate Radio*. Pluto Press.

Keith, Michael C. (1997): *Voices in the Purple Haze: Underground Radio and the Sixties*. Praeger.

McFarlane, Gavin (1980): *Copyright: The Development and Exercise of the Performing Right*. John Offord.

Nichols, Richard (1983): *Radio Luxembourg: Station of the Stars*. Comet.

Peacock, Alan (1975): *The Composer in the Market Place*. Faber Music.

Scannell, Paddy (1981): 'Music for the multitude' in Paddy Scannell et al. (eds), *Media, Culture and Society*. Sage.

Skues, Keith (1968): *Radio Onederland*. Landmark Press.

Activity 7.1

Choose any music station and listen in regularly for a period of at least a week. Define, in no more than 100 words, with examples, what its music policy is in terms of musical style and playlisting priorities.

What does its music policy tell you about the target market of the station, especially as regards age, gender and income level?

Discuss any differences between daytime and evening output.

Activity 7.2

Based on your own continued listening, and drawing on the national airplay charts in *Music Week* or any other music industry publication, assess the distinctiveness of the playlisting policy of the station you chose in Activity 7.1. To what degree do its music choices appear to concur with those of other stations? Account for any particular singles which figure strongly in the station's playlist but not in the airplay chart.

Activity 7.3

Choose any single in the Top 40 chart and trace the reasons for its sales success. Build as complete a picture as possible of the marketing strategy behind the single's release and promotion, with particular emphasis on how (and which) radio stations were targeted and promoted. Take into account such factors as the familiarity of the artist, the origin of the record (for example, as a club hit or featured on the soundtrack of a newly released film), the level of in-house and independent plugging, and the single's context in a wider cross-media campaign, e.g. a national tour or a forthcoming album release.

Activity 7.4

Prepare a running order of 10 records to be played during an hour of a breakfast-time show on (1) a station targeted at a 15–24-year-old audience, and (2) a station targeted at a 35-plus audience. Order the records in relation to points in the hourly sequence – news summaries, advertisements, weather and traffic reports, etc. – and note the reasons for your choices in each case. Drawing on the discussion in this chapter, evaluate the assumptions you may have made regarding the tastes of the particular age groups and the recency (or otherwise) of the music selected.

8

News Radio

> The very best any broadcaster can do is to give you a generalised
> approximation of what is going on in the world. The editorial process is a
> way of trying to impose some sort of order on chaos, and it is not for nothing
> that all items in news journalism are known as 'stories'.
>
> Patrick Hannan, former BBC Industrial Correspondent, in *The Welsh Illusion*
>
> News is not reality, but a supply of sources' portrayals of reality, mediated by
> news organisations.
>
> Leon V. Sigal, quoted in Manoff and Schudson, *Reading the News*

The importance of news to radio extends beyond bulletins or even regular updates: for talk stations, news is a constant source material for debate, controversy and expression of opinion. Even at stations that are not primarily speech-based, news can sometimes be the major source of programming expenditure, requiring the most staff and resources. Nowhere is the pressure for fresh content more keenly felt than by those involved in gathering, selecting, writing and presenting news.

Even if limited to just a minute or two at the top of each hour, news acts as a punctuation mark, a transitional mechanism between programmes or time periods. (The hourly news bulletins on weekday Radio 4 attract the highest level of listening – the dips between the bulletins are referred to within BBC radio as 'hammocks'.) The news is part of the very fabric of broadcasting, often a measure of a station's credibility and increasingly a major factor in the buying and selling of media on an international scale. All this inevitably impacts on the processes, mechanics and ideology of news broadcasting.

What constitutes 'the news'? Accurate, balanced and timely reportage on the events of the day, or a ragbag of disparate items ordered and prioritized according to an editor's sense of what will interest and engage his or her public? What makes a multiple pile-up on the M1 more of a 'story' than an earthquake in a remote part of China, and why should a forthcoming royal betrothal generate more coverage than a newly published set of divorce figures? These are age-old questions that apply across all news media and can be partly answered by exploring news sources, editorial values, issues of ownership, audience expectations, and the political and economic context in which the press and broadcast media operate. The primary point is that news never just 'happens': what appears in a bulletin or a newspaper is an attempt at a comprehensible interpretation of selected events, and as such is never wholly value-free.

NEWS INSTITUTIONS

A starting point in analysing the selection and prioritisation of news on radio is the internal structures, editorial philosophies and practices, and the place of the news division within the news institution. What defines the perspective of the 'gatekeeper' in news radio? How is a particular institution's news culture perpetuated? The policies and practices of the BBC's news division tend to dominate any history or analysis of news radio in general, primarily because it has been and remains so influential on a local and global scale, and because its output on a domestic level alone is massive – over 20 per cent of total broadcasting hours (see Figure 8.1 for a network-by-network breakdown). Although UK commercial radio draws on material provided by a handful of established news supply organizations, they were born and have matured in a BBC-dominant environment; the very legislation that brought the first of them (Independent Radio News) into being placed obligations and requirements on it that were modelled on BBC conventions.

BBC news matured in a political atmosphere in which the public service ethos went largely unchallenged. From the 1980s onwards, BBC management had to respond to a political sea-change that forced a fundamental economic review of its public funding and altered the landscape of the broadcasting industry by allowing the commercial exploitation of new technologies such as

Network	Total broadcasting hours	News hours	% total hours
Radio 1	8,760	389	4.4
Radio 2	8,760	506	5.8
Radio 3	8,760	23	0.3
Radio 4	7,697	2,281	29.6
Radio 5 Live	8,760	5,683	64.9
Total	42,737	8,882	20.9

Source: BBC Annual Report, 1997–98

Fig. 8.1 BBC network radio news: total broadcasting hours, 1997–98

satellite and cable TV alongside new terrestrial TV channels and a massive expansion in non-BBC radio. Out of these pressures came the splitting of BBC programming into five massive directorates as described in Chapter 2, including BBC News, an independent bi-media news division whose remit included the continuous news station, Radio 5 Live.

The merging of the BBC's radio and television news operations had logic. It refocused one of the BBC's key perceived strengths in preparation for the launch of the BBC's all-day satellite and cable news channel, News 24, which put the BBC in direct competition on a world stage with CNN and the News International-owned Sky News. It has economies of scale, in that it reduces or eliminates duplication of effort and resources allocation in news gathering and analysis – reporters and correspondents now prepare material across the board, for every level of the news operation (local radio, Ceefax, the five national radio networks, individual news and current affairs programmes across radio and TV, News 24, BBC Online). It restructured news gathering from the ground up, with the news teams at the local stations and regional news centres acting as news 'scouts' for the other services and feeding stories upwards; similarly, it restructured news provision on the reverse route, with the national news centre (based in new headquarters within BBC Television Centre) providing news material and commentary for bulletins and news programmes on local stations. BBC News became, as a result, the biggest single news gathering operation in the world, with a 2,000-strong staff of journalists including 250 correspondents in 50 countries.

These changes were made in a spirit of expansion, not contraction or concentration of resources for their own sake: the concept was the creation of a single news resource, including correspondents in any number of specialist fields, from which the different media could draw. News on BBC radio expanded massively in the 1990s with the launch of a rolling news station, Radio 5 Live, the idea for which had been piloted during the Gulf War of 1991 by a news service on Radio 4's FM frequency. Radio 5 Live's remit is to follow news as it breaks with on-the-spot reporting and expert analysis, interspersed with phone-in programmes and sports commentaries, but the flexibility of its format is such that in times of national or international crisis it can devote its attention to the one story alone. This is somewhat removed from the traditional BBC news approach of sharply concentrated and tightly edited coverage of current news stories on programmes like *Today*, *The World At One* and *The World Tonight*, but the BBC's argument is that of 'horses for courses' – different news services tailored to different audiences with differing expectations and requirements.

How has this impacted on journalistic standards? Some see a wide gulf between *Today*, which is often claimed to set the news agenda for the day through interviews with political figures, and news on a BBC local station, where the reporting team may be only three or four strong and local news is limited to road accidents, court cases and council meetings and – in a classic case of raiding other news sources – a noticeable flurry of fresh stories on the day that the local newspaper is published.

Extended research into the preferences of particular audiences for particular stations has, since the 1980s, brought a conscious departure from the traditional BBC model of news broadcasting. BBC news provision is more audience-led than ever before, which makes it a major focus in the debate over 'dumbing down' – the aiming of content at (and the styling of programming to meet) low attention spans and low levels of understanding.

NEWS VALUES

John Hartley, in *Understanding News*, suggests that the purpose of news is to *translate* what is happening in the world in terms that make it comprehendable – that is, understandable according to listener expectations and experience. This tends to encourage a dichotomizing of the news into familiar arenas of right and wrong, acceptable and unacceptable, sensible and bizarre, fair and unfair. The resulting news-discourse is 'hostile to ambiguities . . . [its] task is to prefer particular meanings for events over against other possible meanings' (Hartley, p. 24). He explores the everyday language of television and radio news and finds it rife with value-laden simplifications, classifications and 'preferred meanings' that are in part a consequence of pressures on the journalistic process, partly a matter of convention and precedent, and partly a reflection of the *institutional* concerns and practices of the news medium itself.

What lies behind news selection, and what characterizes the particular treatment that radio broadcasters give the news? Part of the answer is historical and lies in the institutionalisation of news and particularly the growth of an industry dedicated to the sourcing, gathering, publishing and broadcasting of news in all its many forms. From the spread of newspapers during the latter half of the 19th century through to the mass availability of information via the Internet, the production and dissemination of news has become ever more sophisticated while still adhering to many of the traditions and conventions established in the earliest days of professional journalism. Galtung and Ruge, in a famous exposition of cross-media news values based on close analysis of news bulletins, produced a list of criteria for news coverage that has since been quoted and added to many times, notably by John Hartley and Andrew Boyd, and it is worth summarizing here.

> **Frequency:** a concentration on events happening now and their immediate effects, rather than the undercurrents behind the news.
> **Threshold:** to be reported, a story must reach a certain threshold of importance.
> **Unambiguity:** stories tend to be reduced to simple levels, in pursuit of clarity.
> **Proximity** or **relevance** to the audience, whether geographical or cultural.
> **Predictability:** news stories related to known events such as anniversaries, launches, release of statistics, award presentations.

Unpredictability: conversely, an event's rarity or suddenness lends it dramatic value.

Continuity: the running story – for example, a disaster or death of a major political figure – whose impact lasts days or even weeks.

Composition: a story which in other circumstances may not have been considered important enough for coverage receives attention to balance an 'excess' of stories on other topics (for example, a balance of foreign versus local stories).

Personalization: a concentration on personalities (especially politicians) as the primary news drivers and as personifications of issues, political positions and social attitudes.

Negativity: a particular focus on crime, the judicial process and human drama in general (disasters, accidents, scandal).

To this one can add an overriding concern with topicality, immediacy and freshness – with capturing the story *as close to the moment of its happening* as is possible. (This is why newspaper headlines are invariably written in the present tense.) All these predilections have their roots in the competition for mass readership among national and (in the US in particular) regional and local newspapers, alongside which developed – in the interests of instant clarity – journalistic conventions of simplification, cliché and what Michael Schudson identifies as 'subjunctive' reporting, where single incidents are taken to illuminate larger meanings.

The now-classic argument against media news coverage is that it over-simplifies issues, is too preoccupied with the timeliness of an event to analyse its context or meaning in sufficient depth, that its vocabulary, language and style of presentation over-dramatizes, that it depicts people and events according to stereotypical, ever-ready, warmed-over assumptions about human behaviour and that its frame of reference is primarily one of conflict and consensus. Stuart Hall has summarized the picture of our immediate world – our national community – that emerges as *fragmented* into distinct spheres categorized by the internal bureaucracy of news production – the division of business, home affairs, foreign affairs, sport and so on; as *individualized*, events happening as a consequence of an individual's action; as *hierarchical* by nature, the political and celebrity elite having a kind of ingrained importance; and as *consensual*, built around an assumed consensus embodied by Parliament (democracy in action), the family (a 'natural' order of relationships) and structures such as the educational system and even the broadcasting institutions themselves (Hall, 1986, pp. 40–48). This inevitably means that those acting outside the consensus are marginalised as deviant, outcast or at best eccentric, while the news journalist is cast in the role of the voice of common sense, as a representative of the public.

Yet it is debatable how far the news media is the *inventor* of such ideological meanings:

> The mutual confirmation of ideological meanings between news and agencies like the family and the school . . . is the product of a complex historical process and is deeply embedded in the discourses through which

> we learn to interact with the world, and in which we make sense of it. This
> goes just as much for news-people as for anyone else. It suggests, further,
> that news is not a *producer* of ideological meanings in the sense that they are
> originated here and nowhere else. News reproduces dominant ideological
> discourses in its special areas of competence.
>
> Hartley, *Understanding News*, p. 62

The phrase '*the* news' suggests definitiveness, which is reinforced by the
apparent consensus between news media as to what makes up the main news
of the day. But news media are notoriously self-referential, simultaneously
looking to each other for corroboration and confirmation of a story's
importance while seeking out new angles or information to call their own and
claim a lead over competitors. So while every day has its core stories, what
varies is the particular spin that the news provider may put on them and the
prominence that they are given – in radio's case, the weighting of a story within
a bulletin according to the editorial team's perspective of its audience's
interests.

Figure 8.2 offers a case in point. It lists the news stories, in the order in
which they were heard, on the 7am news bulletins on Radio 4 and Radio 5
Live on 30 September 1998. News of a massacre in Kosovo was the lead item
on Radio 4 but the seventh item on Radio 5 Live, although both bulletins were
the responsibility of the same news organization and drew on the same basic
source material. In February 1999, a further massacre became the lead story on
Radio 4's *Today* while Radio 5 Live led with the first appearance of Prince
Charles and Camilla Parker-Bowles together in public. In both cases, the BBC
news division made clear and conscious editorial decisions based on the remit
of the respective stations: Stephen Mitchell, deputy head of BBC news, has
likened the difference between news on Radio 4 and Radio 5 to the difference
between the *Daily Telegraph* and the *Daily Mail* – the former a strongly
analytical, internationally minded newspaper, the latter a more populist-toned
tabloid newspaper noted for accessible journalism and a more domestic
orientation.

NEWS SOURCES

News is a construction made from a variety of sources. That 'core stories'
emerge in all news media is a reflection of similarly held news values, but it also
demonstrates how they draw on the same 'primary definers' – 'those sources of
information, usually official, that generate control and establish initial
definitions of particular events, situations and issues' (O'Sullivan et al., *Key
Concepts in Communication and Cultural Studies*, p. 242). The most important
of these in terms of everyday use are international news agencies such as APTN
and Reuters, which act on a subscription basis as suppliers of pre-sorted news
to major domestic news outlets across the world. The agencies have a
particularly influential role in setting the foreign news agenda, as the cost of

Fig. 8.2 Lead news items on BBC radio, 7am, 30 September 1998

Radio 4
Bulletin on *Today*
Newsreader: Peter Donaldson

Order of item	Subject	Material	Timing (seconds)
1	Serbian forces accused of fresh massacres in Kosovo, contradicting Yugoslav claims that the offensive against Albanian rebels is over.	Report from David Loyn	90
2	Deputy Prime Minister John Prescott announces tougher controls for privatized rail operators. Report from BBC Political Correspondent.	Report from John Piennar	60
3	Announcement of inquiry into number of National Health Service beds.		40
4	Secretary General of the Commonwealth urges G7 action to tackle economic crises around the world.	Report from Ed Crooks	60
5	Rover car company warns of job losses at Longbridge factory.		20
6	New German Chancellor, Gerhard Schröder, visits France.		20
7	EC working time directive, limiting working hours, comes into force from midnight.	Report from Stephen Evans	60
8	Tony Blair meets Northern Ireland political leaders to try to end dispute over decommissioning of arms.		30
9	Police say man wanted in connection with murder of Sussex schoolboy has been arrested in Holland.		25
10	Builders of Millennium stadium seek permission to work round the clock.	Report from BBC Welsh correspondent	65
11	The Navy's first amphibious helicopter carrier, HMS *Ocean*, to be commissioned in Plymouth.	Report from David Sillitoe	60

Fig. 8.2 *continued*

Radio 5 Live
Bulletin on *Five Live Breakfast*
Newsreader: Victoria Derbyshire

Order of item	Subject	Material	Timing (seconds)
1	Rover car company warns of job losses at Longbridge factory.	Report from Isobel Mathison	60
2	Tony Blair meets Northern Ireland political leaders to try to end dispute over decommissioning of arms.	Report from John Campfner	60
3	Labour Party conference at Blackpool: tougher controls on privatized rail companies, statement on NHS beds.		30
4	EC working time directive, limiting working hours, comes into force from midnight.	Report from Stephen Evans	50
5	New powers of curfew on disruptive children come into effect.		15
6	Family of murdered teenager Stephen Lawrence's family calls for Metropolitan Police Commissioner Paul Condon's resignation.		15
7	Serbian forces accused of fresh massacres in Kosovo, contradicting Yugoslav claims that the offensive against Albanian rebels is over.	Report from David Loyn	30
8	Germany's new Chancellor travels to France.		15
9	Arrests after football match between Millwall and Manchester City.		10

blanket foreign news coverage is frequently prohibitive. Individual news organizations may also draw on strategic alliances with foreign broadcasters to ensure coverage that has a head start over that of its competitors.

Peter Golding suggests that the world view that emerges from this centrality of sources is limiting and distorting. Broadcast news gives a picture of international relations that 'reflects the distribution of agency and organisation correspondents rather than world power structures. Roughly 60 per cent of these correspondents are in western Europe and North America. For many

European audiences, Latin America is virtually invisible, while Africa and Asia emerge as occasional locations of unrest, war, disaster, or as exotic locales for inspection by western leaders' (Golding, p. 255). Other primary definers of news include the police and emergency services, transcripts of court cases or the on- or off-the-record comments of media relations sections of government departments or political parties. In a profession based on a culture of newness and immediacy – where filling airtime and newspaper space is paramount – the simple availability of such news usually guarantees some level of coverage.

Of course, the sources themselves may well have their own agendas, and media awareness within all levels of government and business is usually sophisticated and acute: ministries, companies, pressure groups, political parties, religious organizations, all employ media spokespersons determined to put their own spin on a story that may directly impact on their reputation, profitability or goals. The resulting story, as it appears in the press or broadcast media, is therefore *doubly* mediated, drawing on a reporter's interpretation (sympathetic, hostile or neutral) of a selective and probably slanted account. (In fact, there is an interim stage of mediation, as well, in that the journalist's copy will need editorial approval – for accuracy, newsworthiness and style – before reaching page or microphone.)

News management can take particularly cynical forms. In December 1998, US and UK forces launched four days of air attacks on Iraq just as pressure was building on President Clinton to resign in the face of impeachment proceedings: if it was debatable whether they were deliberately launched to improve the President's image, the specific *timing* of the announcement that the raids had begun – by Clinton himself, on national television and radio, at 5pm on a weekday evening – seemed a classic case of news manipulation, with the media a willing participant. The timing ensured a whole evening of prime-time news coverage of the raids, thus deflecting attention from the domestic crisis at a crucial point.

Another source of news is other media. Radio news staffs constantly monitor news television in particular, for updates of ongoing news and the first inkling of a new story breaking. Dedicated Internet sites have become a major news source in recent years for specialist news sections like business or finance. Local newspapers provide radio news staff with ready-made stories to follow up – usually without acknowledgement. Radio's biggest dependence of all is on daily newspapers, which can set the news agenda by means of exclusive stories and special investigations and, on a more mundane level, provide breakfast programmes and phone-ins with a constant supply of talking points. This is especially true of tabloid newspapers like The Sun and The Mirror, whose own news values encompass television soap opera comings and goings, celebrity scandals, film premieres, and 'surveys' (often paraphrased from research reports) into sexual misbehaviour. The sources of these snippets of news are openly acknowledged, to reinforce their topicality. This is 'news' that's second hand, easily sourced, cheap to process, and free to use.

Some have argued that radio has nothing like the power of television or the press to set the news agenda, that it functions primarily as a summarizer or anticipator of events rather than a source of analysis. One of the biggest news stories of the last half of the 20th century – the death of Diana, Princess of Wales – was broken by radio but rapidly transformed into a week-long television event interpreted and manipulated by newspapers with circulations to maintain. For all the quality of a considered, analytical news programme like *From Our Own Correspondent* – with its long track record of identifying stories of international importance well before they reach 'front page' status – radio is such a stripped, formulaic and pre-packaged medium that its journalism rarely moves beyond a straightforward blending of reportage (what has happened and why, and what may happen as a consequence) with interviews that provide a platform for 'expert' discussion. The emphasis on the *now* – instant reaction, informed speculation – is radio's greatest strength, but all too often the analytical ground, the sense of context, is conceded to other media.

While news values in radio differ according to the geographical areas that stations serve, all news, national or local, focuses on the familiar categories of politics, crime, accidents, basic economics and entertainment, sport and celebrity matters – all mixed and put in order according to the criteria of timeliness (is it happening now or has it just happened?), relevance (will this impact on listeners' lives?), and proximity (is it relevant to the area served?) which Andrew Boyd identifies.

NEWS PRESENTATION

The listener hears nothing of the process by which news appears on the radio. It arrives apparently fully formed – pre-selected and sorted, ordered, condensed, written and timed – and seemingly mediated only by the voices of newsreader and reporter(s). News radio's unseen gatekeepers are the editors, sub-editors and writers who package the selected news not only according to qualitative considerations – what is important, what is interesting to the audience – but also according to practical considerations such as the availability of a journalist to file a live report on it.

News is packaged for radio in a number of standard forms – the news summary or bulletin, the news programme (amplifying and analysing the news), magazine or omnibus programmes (mixing music, news, interviews and lighter material: Radio 2's *Jimmy Young Show* is a classic example), and documentary. Rolling news has elements of all these formats and in any given hour will feature a standard progression of summary, amplifying news reports and live interviews, presided over by an anchor person or team.

A characteristic of news programming is that much of it is scripted, including the spoken links between items or introductions to news reports. In the case of bulletins or summaries, the news is announced as being, literally, a *reading,* and the effect is to place a deliberate sense of distance between the (relatively anonymous) newsreader and the text itself, thereby rendering the news text 'authorless . . . [the newsreader's] reading will maximise the symbolic function – the meaningfulness of the words – while minimising her voice's function as an index of her personality' (Andrew Crisell, *Understanding Radio*, p. 61). This adds to the weight or gravity of the news being imparted, and to the sense of neutralism which is a key part of the unspoken ideology of broadcast media, which we will return to later in this chapter.

Yet while the newsreader is usually announced by name ('this is the Radio 2 news read by Colin Berry'), those responsible for collating or writing the text are not. This curious convention maintains the illusion of authorlessness and ensures that the skill of writing news remains one of the least appreciated in the whole of broadcasting, despite the attention it receives as a key part of editorial training. Andrew Boyd points out that text that is written to be spoken has to take into account the limitations of reception – particularly how listeners will lose attention or patience if a sentence if convoluted, and how what has been heard cannot be instantly retrieved or re-read by the listener. Broadcast news text must be clear, declarative and use few clauses; points must be made succinctly, in an ordered fashion, using plain terms and simple syntax; delivery must be at a pace with which the listener can keep up, yet at the same time brisk and flowing.

News reports – short or long features using actuality recording, written and presented by reporter or correspondent – follow similar literary rules yet have a clear authorial voice. In a bulletin, such a report will add detail, set the event in context, and suggest possible ramifications. In the context of a news programme, a report may use the paradigmatic technique of focusing on how the event affects an individual or group (for example, how the closure of a factory impacts on a family) or may present reaction to a particular story by means of 'vox pops' (street interviews). Both kinds of reports are constructions, as tightly written as any newspaper piece and following similar conventions of openings, illustrations and closures.

The news interview, by contrast, can be planned but not scripted. Either they are spontaneous conversations between the anchor person and the reporter or correspondent on location or in the studio; or they comprise discussion between the anchor and a participant in, or witness to, the news story in question. The characteristic of each is that the questioning and answering is *contrived on the listeners' behalf*: the questioner acts as the listener's representative, drawing out information that either clarifies the how and why of the story or takes it forward (or both).

THE OBJECTIVITY OF NEWS

A radio news report represents journalistic objectivity in microcosm. Within its structure the listener hears a brief summary of the known facts; an articulation of different perspectives on the facts; and verification of the facts by reference to authoritative sources. The journalist sublimates any opinion he or she might have about the event. But total objectivity is not possible, however committed a journalist may be to the concept through training and instinct. The very act of summarizing or *re*-presenting involves a process of selection and prioritization – certain 'facts' have to be discarded in favour of others according to concepts of significance and importance; not every event or development will necessarily have two neatly opposing viewpoints to represent in the interests of balance; there may be a multiplicity of authorities to comment on a story, but constraints of time allow room for just one. What emerges is a selective re-presentation informed by the *intention* of objectivity – a report that is *not knowingly biased* towards one side or another.

If objectivity in news journalism is a problematic concept, it has been central to the notion of journalistic professionalism and integrity since the 19th century. In the US and UK, radio inherited it from newspaper journalism and institutionalized it by means of regulation, particularly with regard to political issues. Radio news had to reflect, yet be detached from, the political process in a democratic society. Intricate strategies of balance were developed in BBC news to ensure that the three parliamentary parties received coverage in proportion to the number of votes cast for them at the previous general election. The problem with this has been that political coverage tends to centre on the three parties alone and indeed on Parliament itself, at the expense of regional or local politics. In the US, the primacy of the First Amendment and the individual's right to free expression of opinion ensured a commitment, at least in theory, to putting a variety of opinions to the public – albeit mediated by an anchor person acting as umpire-cum-arbiter. The 'Fairness Doctrine', introduced by the FCC in 1949, formalized the duties of American broadcasters in this regard and introduced a long period of what has been criticized as 'stenographic' news reporting.

Complete objectivity is never possible, especially when reporting the effects of war, famine or disaster. Pressure of deadlines, constraints on time allotted to stories, difficulties over access to places and key people, all make giving a complete picture an unachievable ideal. Human emotion inevitably colours certain stories: former BBC war correspondent Martin Bell has written eloquently of the difficulties of maintaining even a semblance of an objective tone when reporting on ethnic cleansing in Bosnia, especially when also trying to convey the complexities of a civil war involving three belligerent parties and hatreds going back centuries (Bell, p. 151). What matters is the objective *stance* – the measured tone and the clarity and directness of the language as much as the stating of evidence and conflicting viewpoints. There are aspects of news reporting, too, where dogged pursuit of the middle ground would lead to an unrevealing blandness: the most impactive documentary reporting invariably has a didactic or campaigning edge. No documentary could be made from a completely neutral starting point: every investigation by a radio or TV news team begins with an assumption to be tested.

'Objectivity' in broadcast journalism can imply a mythical consensus, the adopting of a middle ground of common sense to which opposing sides refuse to commit: this was a common feature of much industrial relations reportage in Britain in the 1970s. Conversely, it can *overstate* conflict. Brian McNair describes liberal democratic societies such as the US and Britain as being concerned with 'conflict and negativity. The negative – crime, industrial dispute, disasters – is more newsworthy than the positive' (McNair, p. 30). What the news brings us is palpably *not* an objective reflection of the totality of a day's events, but a selective representation that elevates the *non*-common-place events over the unremarkable. The cumulative result may be a portrayal of life that is fundamentally false – that muggers lurk at every corner, that factory workers strike at the drop of a hat, that every train or bus journey may be an accident waiting to happen. Jock Young has centred on the portrayal of *deviance* in British media to show how particular groups such as young blacks receive a negative labelling by being persistently associated in the news with deviant activity such as street crime and rioting (*The Manufacture of News*).

Even the language used in bulletins and news reports can be loaded with associations and meanings that have the effect of sanitizing a subject – terms such as 'colateral damage', 'carpet bombing' – or are so assumptive that they give an erroneous impression. During the 1999 war between NATO and Yugoslavia, for example, the phrase 'the international community' – previously used in a United Nations context – was used as a synonym for the NATO countries. This ignored the opposition to the action within countries unaligned with NATO.

THE BUSINESS OF NEWS

News has always been an expensive element in broadcasting, requiring a high level of skills and resources on almost constant demand. Traditionally, news broadcasting has not been judged according to its cost-effectiveness – that is, its propensity to deliver either mass audiences in high volumes or niche audiences of interest to advertisers. However, the biggest change in news broadcasting over the last two decades of the 20th century has been its expansion as a commercial enterprise, fuelled by new technology such as satellite and cable television and by a global political climate generally favourable to its exploitation.

News always has been a means to profit, as the history of the newspaper industry shows. But the basis of press profitability and the nature of ownership changed from the 1970s onwards, away from competitive but family-owned mass readership newspapers serving particular communities towards corporate ownership of multiple titles targeted at particular segments of the audience. Major economic recessions in the 70s and again in the early 90s led to papers closing down, takeovers, wholesale staff cuts and greater orientation towards 'lifestyle' reporting. In the US, the television and radio industries underwent a similar transformation, the effects of which included a streamlining of news coverage and a concentration of resources on on-the-spot reporting rather than investigation and analysis. Relaxation of broadcasting regulations meant that radio and TV networks were no longer required to provide news services, while the key safeguard against media bias, the Fairness Doctrine, was repealed in 1987.

But if the profit potential of news within the domestic broadcasting media of the US and UK was limited, its global potential was tested by the 24-hour news channels CNN (owned by Time Warner) and Sky News (owned by Rupert Murdoch's News International). The success of these channels altered the ecology of broadcasting at several levels. In Britain, though its audience was and remains comparatively small in number, Sky News in particular impacted on established services such as BBC News and ITN by recruiting senior news staff from both organizations and prompting the wholesale reshaping of the BBC's networks in the manner described earlier. Sky News and CNN represented competition on a global scale, to which the BBC responded with the creation of World Service TV (as a counterpart of World Service radio) and, in 1998, the satellite and cable channel BBC News 24.

This was not the first time that BBC news coverage had been subject to competition. Most broadcasting historians agree that the introduction of competition in the form of ITN in the 1950s drastically improved the BBC's own pedestrian and colourless news coverage. In the 1970s, the setting up of Independent Radio News (IRN) to serve the new ILR stations and supply LBC Radio in London with constant news also had an impact, building experience in rolling news and the news phone-in format that BBC local radio and Radio 5 Live in particular were to draw from. But the framework under which both ITN and IRN were established and operated was public service-based and subject to Act of Parliament; the new news channels, because they were registered overseas, were not subject to comparable regulation.

The deregulatory climate of the 1980s onwards and the introduction of new technology such as electronic news gathering (ENG) affected the economics of news production across all media and brought costs down by loosening the power of media-based unions. Wholly in-house staffs gave way to a mix of staff journalists and freelancers; 'producer choice' at the BBC opened up current affairs programming to independent production; training, too, became increasingly part of the commercial arena as the BBC cut back on its budgets. In commercial radio, IRN lost its status as the medium's sole news supplier as new providers moved in, among them Reuters, Metro Networks and Sky News itself; ITN was itself a competitor for a while before buying up IRN. With the 1996 Broadcasting Act, the ending of checks on cross-media ownership enabled newspaper interests to invest heavily in television and radio services – Mirror Group Newspapers with the cable station Live TV, for example – and use them for cross-promotion.

Changing economics and particularly falling costs account in part for the expansion of news broadcasting services since the 1980s. Diversification within media as a whole has seen radio playing an increasing role in the cross-media strategies of multinationals and national players alike: concerns that are lean, profitable and have a high saliency or brand value in the marketplace can be bought and sold like any other commodities. The move to independent production in radio is just one aspect of a new commission-and-supply culture in broadcasting, with news agencies moving beyond simply providing news to offering a complete news package to stations. In television news, battle lines have been drawn over the ownership and exploitation of rights – especially the paying of fees for use of archive news material

Newly established news agencies have developed specialisms in particular types of news. Entertainment news is one growth area, as new stations have started with special requirements for a flow of news or gossip relating to fields such as film, television and pop music. The biggest growth of all has been in business news targeted at the financial sector but with a constituency, too, among share-owners and mortgage-holders. In Britain, this has its roots in the expansion of share-ownership and the privatization measures of the Thatcher government in the 1980s, while the explosion in business information ties in closely with the demand for constantly updated news (on share fluctuations, currency values, the state of the pound and so on) and the exploitation of radio as a high-earning advertising medium for financial services.

BRINGING THE WORLD IN – OR KEEPING IT AT BAY?

Where the audience for news was once a 'knowable' mass – it was listened to in high volume by people from all classes and walks of life – the fragmentation of radio audiences into economically or demographically defined groups has encouraged broadcasters *as a matter of deliberate policy* to target and shape the news accordingly. This has profound implications for the content of the news (and *types* of news) we hear, for the manner in which it is presented and packaged, and ultimately for general public awareness of the world beyond the front door.

Radio is not alone in this. *The Sun* and *The Times*, though owned by the same proprietor, carry news and features tailored to very different audiences with very different lifestyles, outlooks and consumer profiles. In television, different target audiences define the style and look of *Channel 4 News* (analytical, thorough, with desk-bound presenters, aimed at the returning commuter) and *Channel 5 News* (quickfire, colloquial, with presenters in standing or moving mode, aimed at young audiences with supposedly low attention spans). Even where, as in BBC radio, there is no direct commercial imperative to drive programming, it is still the delivery of an audience that justifies the funding of separate channels and stations.

It could be argued that, in this kind of market-led environment, radio news becomes a marketing tool in itself, a means of keeping the particular target audience listening. Communities become defined according to marketing objectives and consumer preferences, and news becomes just another element in the entertainment mix tailored to the tightly researched 'wants' of the target audience. This means a reductionist criterion of news selection – a sifting out of anything likely to upset or disrupt the easy-going flow, an emphasis on lightweight news and especially entertainment news. The very fact of exclusion of complex or discomforting news – or, conversely, an *over*-emphasis on sensational or scandalous news to meet a perceived demand for salaciousness – leads to an impoverishment of outlook, a dangerous ignorance, and a failure to engage with the world. Some of the most critical writers on the American talk radio boom have argued that the indulging of prejudices, the pride in partiality, the hectoring tone and brutish politics of talk radio are the inevitable outcome of the diluting of news values made possible by the deregulatory policies of the 1990s.

Yet it could also be argued that matching the news to the audience is what newspapers do all the time, and that every individual goes through a selection process of sorts in listening to or viewing the news – a process of concentrating on some items, ignoring others, and switching off if the news is boring, dull or stale. Ignorance is sometimes the preferred choice of listeners; a major aspect of the appeal of radio is precisely that it provides a temporary refuge from the harmful or upsetting.

Further reading

Bell, Martin (1993): 'Civil War in Bosnia' in *The Radio Times 1993 Yearbook*. Ravette.

Boyd, Andrew (1988): *Broadcast Journalism*. Heinemann.

Carey, Peter (1996): *Media Law*. Sweet & Maxwell.

Chantler, Paul, and Harris, Sim (1996): *Local Radio Journalism*. Focal Press.

Crook, Tim (1998): *International Radio Journalism*. Routledge.

Franklin, Bob (1997): *Newszak and News Media*. Arnold.

Gage, Linda (1999): *A Guide to Commercial Radio Journalism*. Focal Press.

Galtung, Johan, and Ruge, Mari (1973): 'Structuring and selecting news' in S. Cohen and J. Young (eds), *The Manufacture of News: Deviance, Social Problems and the Mass Media*. Constable.

Golding, Peter (1997): 'The missing dimensions – news media and the management of change' in T. O'Sullivan and Y. Jewkes (eds), *The Media Studies Reader*. Arnold.

Hall, Stuart (1986): 'Popular culture and the state' in T. Bennett et al. (eds), *Popular Culture and Social Relations*. Open University Press.

Hall, Stuart, et al. (eds) (1980): *Culture, Media, Language*. Hutchinson.

Hannan, Patrick (1999): *The Welsh Illusion*. Seren.

Hartley, John (1982): *Understanding News*. Methuen.

Hetherington, Alastair (1985): *News, Newspapers and Television*. Macmillan.

Hetherington, Alastair (1989): *News in the Regions*. Macmillan.

McLeish, Robert (1993): *The Technique of Radio Production*. Focal Press.

McNair, Brian (1993): *News and Journalism in the UK*. Routledge.

Manoff, Robert Karl, and Schudson, Michael (1987): *Reading the News*. Pantheon.

Schlesinger, Philip (1987): *Putting Reality Together*. Methuen.

Wilson, John (1996): *Understanding Journalism*. Routledge.

Activity 8.1

Gleaning your material from daily newspapers, television or radio itself, research, write and edit a four-minute radio bulletin aimed at (1) a 15–24-year-old audience, and (2) the 35-plus age group. Aim to include a lead international story, a lead national story and two lead local or regional stories. Which stories do you leave out, and which do you include? How have you prioritized your running order of news items? Write a short critique of your bulletin, making clear your reasons for exclusion and inclusion in each case. Be as objective as you can about the assumptions you have made regarding the news interests of each market. For practical guidance on constructing your bulletin, see Gage (1999) and Boyd (1988).

Actvity 8.2

Concentrating on one particular radio station, either local or national, follow a news story as it develops over a period of days. Make a note of (1) the time allotted to it and the priority given to it in bulletins and news programmes, (2) the reporters assigned to it, and (3) the main sources used in the coverage. Trace whether the angle or treatment given the story changes over days or even during the course of a day. Compare the approach that the radio station's news team takes with that of network or local news on television.

Activity 8.3

Compare the radio coverage of local news in your area with that of the local press. To what extent do both media use common sources? Pay particular note to the reporting of crime by each medium. Why are burglaries reported by local newspapers but only rarely by local radio?

Activity 8.4

Repeat the news comparison exercise tabulated in Figure 8.2, this time choosing the 7am news bulletins on a music-based station and a speech-based station within the same locality. Analyse how (or whether) the news criteria and styles of presentation differ and suggest reasons why. How would you describe the function of a news bulletin at this particular time of day, and is that function likely to vary from station to station?

9

Talk Radio

Talk radio facilitates an intriguing dynamic: audience members can feel part of a community, participate in it, and yet do so anonymously and without obligation. Callers can divulge their most confidential secrets, vent their frustrations, and launch venomous personal attacks without the responsibility of owning up to them.

Diana Owen, from *Christian Science Monitor* web site at
www.csmonitor.com, 16 March 1998

Two of the prime characteristics of radio broadcasting are its capacity for spontaneity – for immediate, unplanned reaction to events in the form of unscripted speech – and its potential for listener interaction. No genre of programming better illustrates the coalescence of these two factors than the phone-in.

Phone-in shows – those featuring telephone conversations between a studio-based presenter and listeners who call in – first became a feature of radio programming in the US in the 1950s, to fill airtime gaps during periods of low listening. The first station to feature an all-talk format, based on phone-ins and studio interviews, was KABC in Los Angeles in 1961, though a more common approach (pioneered by KGO in San Francisco) was to mix talk with news. With the growth of FM from the late 1960s onwards and the subsequent switch of music services to it, the AM waveband became increasingly dominated by news and/or talk formats. Styles of presenting varied from the inquisitive yet also quietly deferential approach of Larry King, who later transferred the format to television, and the pugnacious, self-opinionated style of Joe Pyne, whose 'shock jock' approach was heard on around 160 stations. Mostly, however, talk radio was a local affair, embracing advice shows like the influential *Feminine Forum* on KGBS Los Angeles, which was targeted at women and pioneered open and frank discussion of personal and sexual relationships. Advice shows were usually presided over by a psychologist or therapist. California, which had been the home of free-form FM radio in the late 1960s, was also the centre for radio shows inviting calls on astrological, paranormal or 'new age' matters, which by the late 1970s had counterparts in most major American cities.

Talk radio's switch from a local to a national stage came in the late 1980s, partly aided by new satellite technology which enabled much cheaper and simpler syndication of programmes, but encouraged particularly by the success of two contrasting practitioners, Larry King and Rush Limbaugh. By the 1990s, talk radio had become a major part of American broadcasting culture, inspiring several television series (*Frasier*, *Midnight Caller*) and several films (*Talk Radio*, *Straight Talk*), *Sleepless in Seattle*, and *Private Parts* starring Howard Stern as himself).

In Britain, phone-ins began as a staple of BBC local radio and, subsequently, the first legal commercial stations. As in the US, cheapness was a major factor. Most pervasive were 'swap shop' shows, in which listeners rang in to exchange items with other listeners. The one station that pioneered the phone-in format as a source of and vehicle for controversy was LBC in London – the only ILR station with a non-music-based remit – whose chief presenter was Brian Hayes, who had learned the art of interrogatory and abrasive radio in Australia. Hayes's style was argumentative and confrontational and occasionally fell foul of his employers and commercial radio's then regulator, the Independent Broadcasting Authority.

The first true national phone-in programme was Radio 4's *It's Your Line*, presented by Robin Day with more than a nod to the Larry King format of inviting callers to question a leading politician or public figure. Later phone-ins on Radio 4, such as *Tuesday Call* and *Call Nick Ross*, ploughed the same furrow by concentrating on issues in the news; interestingly, while these mid-morning programmes were accepted without much apparent criticism from listeners, a sustained attempt to build a phone-in programme into the mid-afternoon period – with *Anderson Country*, presided over by Gerry Anderson – was met with resistance and was eventually dropped. Anderson's all-embracing remit and light tone – which he perfected at Radio Foyle in Derry – were assumed to be out of place in a schedule devoted to serious matters.

The phone-in genre of programming has undergone various changes over the years, most notably in the US, where relaxation of FCC rules regarding political balance in broadcasting gave free rein to the new wave of confrontational presenters nicknamed 'shock jocks'. Today, the telephone doubles as a major tool and source of radio programming, not only in phone-in programmes *per se* but in news reportage and listener competitions and dedication slots in music radio.

ACCESSING THE AIRWAVES

The rationale behind phone-in programming is threefold. First, it is a proven ratings puller. In the US during the 1990s, the phone-in format was the fastest growing of all radio formats, continually outperforming more established music formats in major cities such as San Francisco and Dallas. Phone-ins – and particularly certain phone-in presenters – make headlines and help 'brand' the station concerned with the attractive taint of controversy, all of which ensures continued support from advertisers and programme sponsors.

Second, phone-in programming incurs little of the expense of music radio in terms of copyright fees and investment in hardware; the only fixed costs relate to the presenter's fee and the telephone line rental. For comparatively little outlay, even those phone-in programmes with a distinctly non-controversial bent – do-it-yourself advice lines or astrology readings – can attract loyal audiences and provide a strategic link between peak and off-peak periods of listening (for example, between afternoon drive time and mid-evening).

Third, it reinforces the perception of a relationship, in the form of a continuing 'conversation', between a station and its listeners. Having callers on air offers the most basic proof that the station *has* an audience; it reminds listeners that they are part of a wider listening community. It reinforces the perception that the station is involving and responsive. This is vital to the wider issue of branding a station or styling an image for it, particularly if regulators require evidence of community involvement. Phone-ins are the only real means by which 'ordinary people' (i.e. non-professional broadcasters) reach the airwaves: they give the everyday listener the opportunity to speak his or her mind and influence the opinions of others. In reality, the opportunity may be limited and subject to gatekeeping policies as fiercely enacted as those in news and music radio, but what matters to the programme producers and the radio stations they employ is the *appearance* of access. Encouraging listeners to take part in local or national debates is an important reputation-enhancer; it enables stations to underline their own participation in and commitment to the democratic process.

In Britain in the mid 1970s, when commercial radio was under the watchful eye of the public service-oriented IBA, phone-ins were one of the chief means by which stations claimed an ongoing dialogue with the community they served. This was particularly vital when the franchise was up for renewal. Brian Hayes, one of Britain's best known phone-in presenters, has criticized what he calls the 'control culture' that in his view tended to neutralize radio debate in the 70s. Drawing on his experience as a presenter and producer in Australia, he places phone-ins in a more maverick tradition of broadcasting and sees their value in their populist stance:

> The ordinary voice of the ordinary citizen is everywhere on radio, BBC, commercial and the occasional pirate. Believe it or not, there are those who think that this is a bad thing. Particularly because ordinary people do not speak very well, they play fast and loose with grammar and as for pronunciation and accent, well they set a bad example for young people, don't they . . . Never again will the voice of the public be irrelevant to the mainstream of broadcasting. The days of the listener merely providing an occasional bit of raw material to be reconstructed to fit a producer's plan

> are over. It is not that the public has taken over, but that radio has reached
> a maturity which forges a real partnership with its voice.
>   'The role of the public voice in present-day radio' in
>   Hargrave, *Radio and Audience Attitudes* (p. 41).

Hayes' comments provide a valuable insight into a phone-in presenter's perspective of his role as the audience's ambassador in a 'them and us' relationship with radio managers and regulators. But it is a disingenuous argument. Hayes' reputation is built on being argumentative not with management or even with his studio guests but with callers themselves; he is emphatically not a cipher, facilitating calls and giving no hint of his own opinions – the price callers pay for involving themselves in the cut and thrust of on-air debate is the risk of contradiction, counter-argument, impatience and even humiliation. It is not simply a matter of stating a view and signing off. There is a degree of listener empowerment, but only within certain (sometimes unspoken) rules and parameters.

Phone-ins provide the individual with the chance of access to the airwaves, but in a context that emphasizes rather than eliminates the sense of physical distance between station and audience. The presenter is a trained media professional; presenters of phone-ins on sexual or personal matters are often also trained counsellors or therapists. Ian Hutchby writes that 'public participants in current affairs phone-in broadcasts exist in a world in which *the host already has presence*, whereas for hosts callers appear at random and exist prior to their occurrence as verbal interactants only as listed names and location categories' (Hutchby, p. 122). The presenter is heard speaking from a studio, with the benefit of technically near-perfect reproduction, while the caller is heard through the crackle-ridden medium of the telephone line. All this underlines the imbalance in the relationship of presenter to caller.

The presenter controls the content, direction and flow of the conversation – and also who speaks to him or her and for how long. This control takes both overt and covert forms, and is usually operated not by the presenter working alone but in consort with a small production team who take the initial calls, vet them for suitability and brief the presenter via headphones or a computer monitor on who the caller is and what he or she has to say. This filtering process goes on unheard and is acknowledged only when a programme attracts a high level of calls. It is the presenter who sets the agenda for a phone-in programme, even if it is a general 'open line' show taking calls on anything in the news: the agenda tends to be set by the presenter's list of topics that might be discussed. If the phone-in is based around a particular issue, the calls will be selected as to their relevance to the issue or to bring different perspectives to the argument. These are editorial decisions, made on the hoof according to gatekeeping criteria that include the articulacy of the caller, the relevance of his or her argument to the subject, and the clarity or monotonic nature of the caller's voice. Equally, the length of call will be decided according to the presenter's willingness to prolong it without the risk of losing listeners. (Occasionally, a call will be abruptly cut because the caller has uttered an expletive: stations operate a seven- to ten-second delay to prevent the profanities reaching the air.) The criteria is determined primarily by topicality and relevance, but the same facets that inform gatekeeping in music radio – pace, variety, light and shade – also feature prominently in phone-ins: the producer's prime 'professional' responsibility is to create a show that is 'listenable' and entertaining, not dull or self-involved.

Some researchers and writers have gone further in their criticism of the phone-in as a spurious form of access broadcasting. Drawing particularly on Australian commercial radio, Christine Higgins and Peter Moss have identified gatekeeping values with the mediation of a dominant consumer-oriented ideology (Higgins and Moss, *Sounds Real*). The view of the world advanced by the presenters in phone-in programmes – and the conservative ideology that is implicitly conveyed by the presence of advertisements and station identifiers – becomes the benchmark by which opposing or differing views are measured. The presenter pitches himself or herself as part-arbitrator and part-judge, the voice of consensus and 'common sense'. The pursuit of consensus and the disinterested middle ground becomes particularly explicit during election campaigns, when the requirements of balance and the avoidance of bias are a matter of electoral law. At these times, phone-in programmes are mounted on the basis of giving the listener/voter an opportunity to decide between parties and policies. It is common for phone-in presenters to close their programmes with a summary of arguments over a particular issue – sometimes adding to them by quoting listener e-mails or faxes – with the sentiment that 'you've heard the arguments, the decision is yours'.

Hutchby, writing in *Broadcast Talk*, comes to a similar conclusion to that of Higgins and Moss via a different route. He focuses on a particular edition of the Brian Hayes LBC show to demonstrate the manner, language, style and attitude with which phone-in presenters handle their callers, with particular reference to how they pursue phone-in conversations. The impression is of a skilled professional conversationalist guiding not necessarily the content but the *structure* of a conversation with people who have none of the professional advantages but do implicitly understand such conventions and codes of phone-in broadcasting as the need to get to the point quickly. Hayes – in his role as interpreter on the audience's behalf – continually paraphrases, seeks explanation or confirmation of the point the caller is making, and takes issue not with the sincerity with which a view is held but with the explication of the argument itself.

The phone-in presenter is always in control: 'the invitation' to take part in his or her programme is just that – an invitation from someone who is himself empowered by the station to temporarily empower others (within given limits). The phone-in programme itself is a response mechanism (hence the familiar term 'talk*back*' radio, implying that the initiative in provoking debate lies with the broadcaster, not the listener). The nature of that response may be challenging, even gladiatorial – a crossing of swords – or much more sympathetic and consoling, but the development of the discourse lies unequivocally in the hands of the presenter.

PRESENTER POWER?

Phone-ins exist in a grey area between news presentation and entertainment, and responsibility for speech output tends to vary from department to department, depending on the broadcasting organization. Within BBC radio, phone-in programmes are produced by sports, current affairs and documentary divisions. Unlike news journalists, phone-in presenters do not work within a recognized professional code or according to any collectively agreed guidelines regarding language, topics, acceptability and so on. Even Britain's Radio Authority has no specific regulations on phone-in programmes. Unlike music presenters, phone-in presenters do not work within the comforting disciplines of a prescribed format but are hired for their ability to think on their feet. Phone-in presenters have as much or as little leeway as station heads allow them, leading to widely diverging approaches and a continual testing of the limits of tolerance.

How presenters use this power has been a major issue in American broadcasting since the late 1980s and the emergence of the new breed of 'shock jocks', hired for their ability to generate controversy (and therefore high ratings) through abusiveness and the airing of outrageous opinions. The most famous of these is Howard Stern, whose programmes were the subject of a $1.7-million fine from the FCC in 1995. His on-air persona has been characterized as 'a kind of bad-boy adolescent – willing to humiliate himself as well as humiliate and insult others, and forever fascinated by sex and bodily functions' (Scott, p. 78). Stern built his national profile through a morning show syndicated by stations affiliated to Infinity Broadcasting, in which he exchanged ribald repartee with his long-time foil Robin Quivers and introduced America to such diverse experiences as a 'dial-a-date' bestiality item, discussions on the mechanics of lesbian sex, having God read the weather and then reveal himself to be gay, and ethnic parodies of TV programmes, such as 'Hill Street Jews'.

Stern and his ilk are essentially entertainers using the radio rather than a nightclub stage as their platform. But since the dropping of the Fairness Doctrine, which since 1949 had prevented stations from airing unbalanced programming, American talk radio has also provided a platform for presenters with political (and mainly right-wing) axes to grind. Anyone broadcasting on radio or television could, after 1987, express bias without any requirement for opposing views to be heard. Increasing corporate ownership of radio stations has led to increased opportunities for syndication, giving a handful of such voices national coverage on a daily basis. The first major 'star' of syndicated talk radio was Rush Limbaugh, who made his name with a show that had no direct confrontational element – calls were kept to a minimum and there were no guest interviews – but was instead little more than an extended, improvised opinion piece. His general affability and the folksy directness of his opinions made him sponsor-friendly, while he showed a strong sense of self-marketing by encouraging 'Rush Rooms' – places in bars or cafes set aside for listeners to the show – to open all over the US, and by taking on ceaseless speaking engagements and expounding on conservative values such as patriotism and the work ethic. From 1992 onwards, he published the *Limbaugh Letter,* a newsletter devoted to core conservative issues such as maintaining family values and stopping government intervention in the economy. By 1998, Limbaugh was the author of two best-selling books, *The Way Things Ought To Be* and *See, I Told You So,* and was claiming a regular weekly audience of 20 million.

Limbaugh sees his appeal in terms of a groundswell of reaction against liberal government – personified by President Bill Clinton – and the perceived left-wing leanings of American media. His influence is feared by the Democratic Party, and the *New York Times* credited him with sweeping the Republicans to congressional victory in 1994'. As Gini Graham Scott writes in her study of talk radio:

> liberals are afraid he is offering people simplistic and distorted answers, creating a 'cadre of robots' they call 'dittoheads' because these fans call the station and agree with what Rush has said. Though Rush thinks he is doing exactly the opposite, getting listeners and now viewers to question accepted truths spread by the liberal media and government, liberals think he is dumbing down discourse, assuring his audience, for example, that if they listen to him everyday, 'they will no longer need to read newspapers or watch TV'.
>
> Scott, Can We Talk?, p. 72

Elsewhere in the same study, Scott pinpoints the appeal of Limbaugh and others like him as arising from a long period of working-class alienation from government in the US. Such hosts tap into a general feeling of betrayal of core American values that stretches back to the 1960s and the student-led protest movements that polarized America – and of which the purloining of FM radio for 'alternative' or radical content was one aspect. Conservative talk radio can therefore be seen in some ways as a reclaiming of the airwaves by the voices of hardcore Republicanism – and all in the name of freedom of speech, as protected by the American constitution. One notable talk personality, for example, is a former aide of President Nixon, G. Gordon Liddy, who was imprisoned in the mid 70s for his involvement in the Watergate conspiracy and subsequent cover-up. Liddy advised on air that, if confronted by an FBI agent, the best way to defend oneself was to shoot at unprotected areas of the body such as the groin. Instances like this have caused some critics to blame talk show hosts like Liddy and Limbaugh for encouraging an anti-establishment climate in which the growth of private militias and the 1995 bombing of a government building in Oklahoma City, at a cost of 167 lives, becomes possible.

Talk radio stations have become launching pads for political careers – and also retirement homes for figures who have left the mainstream political arena, like former New York mayor Mario Cuomo and San Diego mayor Roger Hedgecock. So successful have presenters like Rush Limbaugh become that there has been a copycat effect, with local stations seeking their own, ever more contentious presenters and sponsors preferring to fund programme formats with a proven appeal. This has in turn been blamed for the relative paucity of 'liberal' talk show hosts on the national airwaves, though there have been examples of youth-oriented advertisers like Doc Martens sponsoring programmes by avowedly 'liberal' presenters.

Britain has had its own 'shock jocks', notably James Whale (whose Radio Aire programme was simultaneously broadcast on ITV) and Caesar the Geezer, who were both in the original line-up of presenters on Talk Radio. Only Britain's second national commercial station, Talk Radio was launched in 1995 with controversy-oriented phone-ins in the American style, but its shock-jock tactics unsettled advertisers and failed to attract listeners. A reshaping of output followed within months. In late 1998, after its takeover by a consortium led by ex-*Sun* editor and Live TV boss Kelvin MacKenzie, Talk Radio switched to a programming strategy of phone-ins presented by high-profile journalists including the surprising pairing of one-time Tony Blair aide Derek Draper and right-wing columnist Peter Hitchens (from the *Daily Express*). The more controversial phone-in presenters in British radio tend to be newspaper columnists with a reputation for plain speaking and off-centre views – for example Richard Littlejohn (ex-*Sun* and *Daily Mail*), Andrew Neil (ex-*Sunday Times*) – but, Brian Hayes apart, British radio has not had the success of its American counterpart in creating stars out of the talk genre. Those political figures who have found a niche as talk show hosts (Edwina Currie, David Mellor, Charlie Whelan) have done so on the back of some minor notoriety. Mostly, however, the radio environment has been too tightly regulated to tolerate anything on the American scale of controversy and insult.

It is in tackling those aspects of life where bias is endemic and accepted and the most outrageous opinions can be the source of truly comic debate – football supporting, for example – that stations like Talk Radio and Radio 5 Live enjoy the most consistently high ratings. Peter Gibian suggests that the high profile of sport on radio is rooted in a kind of surrogate gladiatorialism – 'an urge to experience that wild crowd feeling without sacrificing the safety and comforts of the private home' (Gibian, p. 143) – and that its prevalence as a subject of radio talk reflects sport's role as a meeting point or bonding agent:

> Some people really open up only when they can meet others on the common ground of sports talk. Sports talk shows in the mass media . . . build strong bonds of intimacy as they bring trivia nuts and barroom debaters together in a new forum for which there has apparently been a great need.

A FRIEND IN NEED

> You become a kind of psychological detective, an explorer, a traveller . . . you learn to listen for when the voices changes, for the intonation in a word, and you learn to listen fast and damn hard, because that's the thing that keeps it moving, moving.
>
> Anna Raeburn

Away from the limelight of the shock jocks, one of the main characteristics of phone-in culture is the way it plays on an assumed intimacy, in both the subject matter it touches upon and the manner in which it is explored. In certain types of phone-in broadcasting, the presenter takes on the role of counsellor and confidant and personifies the preferred self-image of the station as caring and responsive.

As we have seen, the ideological strength of much radio programming is based on its ingratiation into the rhythms and routines of personal life. Radio's *raison d'être* is as a companion and friend, ever ready with information and kindly advice, and part of the presenter's responsibility is to build the semblance of an intimate relationship with the audience and thereby help to bond the station to the listener. In phone-ins, an intimacy – or at least familiarity – with individual listeners is assumed through the simple device of referring to callers by their first names (Paul from Palmers Green, Anne from Redditch, Kevin from Haywards Heath and so on). This establishes, for both presenter and audience, an immediate familiarity with the caller while also preserving his or her anonymity.

In phone-in programmes built around sexual or emotional problems – 'agony columns' of the air – these twin concerns of intimacy and the dispensing of help converge. Historically, there is another strong link with journalism here, as phone-ins of this kind began in the US in the 1970s as vehicles for some of the most established magazine 'agony aunts' such as Dr Ruth Westheimer. This was at the height of what Tom Wolfe described as 'the Me generation', an introspective period that drew Americans into a mixed bag of therapy, sexual politics and experimentation, and – in contrast to the 60s – a centring on the self rather than on the wider community. The shows moved radio into the kind of explicit programming territory that American radio had traditionally shunned, yet achieved extraordinary ratings.

The same basic idea was brought to the UK by Capital Radio in the mid 70s, with Anna Raeburn and an unnamed doctor fielding the calls and a professional presenter, Sarah Ward and subsequently Adrian Love, acting as interlocutor. (When Raeburn first took the idea to Capital, she was working for *Forum*, a 'sexual relations' magazine; Capital only launched the programme after she moved to the mass-circulation women's magazine *Woman*.) This became a model for programmes on other stations, with Raeburn's one-time *Forum* colleague Philip Hodson taking up a residency at LBC. The Capital programme, which ran for 14 years, was basically an advice line, though Raeburn has always stressed that she has no counselling training or experience as such. 'Everything I learned, I learned on the way,' she has said. 'I don't claim to counsel. I talk, and other people talk to me. I always say "this is a one-step programme, all we aim to do is get you from where you are now to the next place".'

CASE STUDY: EVERYBODY HURTS – THE DEATH OF DIANA

Talk radio tends to come into its own at moments of national crisis or soul-searching. So it was at the time of the death of Diana, Princess of Wales, in a car accident on the morning of 31 August 1997. This was a story that had an extraordinary mix of ingredients and 'angles'. The victims were the mother of the heir to the British throne and the son of an Arab millionaire, whose budding romance had been the subject of tabloid speculation throughout the summer. The circumstances were mysterious, though it appeared that the driver was drunk and the car was being chased by press photographers on motorbikes. The manner in which the royal family reacted to the events laid the monarchy open to quite unprecedented criticism from within the media who claimed to be 'representing' the British people themselves. There was a great deal for newspapers, television, radio and the public at large to talk about.

The way that radio stations reported and reacted to the death pinpointed many of the strengths and weaknesses of the medium as a vehicle for news and also illustrated one of the key dilemmas for the media student: how much did the coverage accorded to the event, both in and especially beyond the news programmes, impact upon the way that audiences responded to it? Was the laying of floral tributes by the thousand at Kensington Palace, the Mall and Buckingham Palace a spontaneous burst of public emotion or one created by the media? Who, in other words, was leading whom?

The death of Diana was not a typical news story by any means, but it is instructive because it throws light on many of the accepted practices in radio news and phone-ins, including the treatment of and attitude towards the royal family; the handling of criticism of the monarchy and discussion of its reform; how news agenda are established, followed and curtailed; how radio operates in relation to other media following the same story; the centrality of 'expert' opinion; how the communications media look at themselves; and how radio presents a staged national event – Diana's funeral – which did turn out to have a political edge to it, in the waspish oration by Earl Spencer and the supportive response to it of the crowd in the streets outside Westminster Abbey.

Later research confirmed a familiar pattern of media usage – that radio was the medium through which most people first heard news of the events in Paris (most turning on their radios between 8am and 9.30am), after which the majority turned immediately to television for information, background and explanation before turning back to the radio as the day went on, as a background to other activities. For the stations themselves, the events sent each into emergency mode, changing programming in keeping with agreed procedures in the event of the death of a member of the royal family. Except that Diana was no longer officially a member of it, due to her divorce: such questions of etiquette were to preoccupy both producers and presenters as the week went on, particularly with regard to the arrangements for a ceremony that was to be a state funeral in all but name.

Capital Radio in London took the immediate decision, after confirmation of Diana's death came at around 4am, to combine its AM and FM services and play classical music punctuated by news updates from resident newscaster Howard Hughes. Talk Radio, seeing itself (in then controller Paul Robinson's words) as 'a talking newspaper . . . a focus of debate and a focus for national grief', dropped all commercials and trailers and invited listeners to phone in with reaction and their own recollections of Diana – a pattern followed by radio stations throughout the country. BBC radio combined its Radio 3, 4 and 5 services under one frequency with a rolling news programme – part-news, part-comment, part-obituary – presented by two familiar voices of authority, James Naughtie of *Today* and Peter Allen from Radio 5 Live's breakfast programme. Radio 1 switched to a selection of low-key ballads typified by the songs which, *Music Week*'s airplay data revealed, dominated the national airwaves during the following few days – *Everybody Hurts* by REM, *You Have Been Loved* by George Michael and Elton John's original version of *Candle In The Wind*. The uniformity of music selections during that week suggested, as Radio 1 Controller Matthew Bannister later acknowledged was the case, that stations were in regular contact with each other for advice and confirmation of how they should be proceeding.

Diana's death was the first extended test of the BBC's new bi-media news department, with reporters doubling for bulletins on both TV and radio, so in terms of reportage there was little difference between the two. BBC TV news was, inevitably, heavily visual; BBC radio news was more descriptive, even lyrical at times, especially regarding the mounting flowers and the ever-growing crowds and queues. But the news agenda tended to be set by the national press, and a three-way news agenda quickly emerged. While the issue of press probing into the private lives of individuals, and Diana in particular, preoccupied TV bulletins and radio discussions, the tabloid press preferred to focus attention on the implacability of the royal family's response to the death. Between Monday and Wednesday of that week, as news broke that the chauffeur had been drunk, the focus of blame in the newspaper coverage shifted away from the paparazzi to the lack of protection given by the Al Fayed family. The spotlight then turned to outright criticism of the monarchy itself, prompting the royal family's early return to London from Balmoral, the appearance of the bereaved princes in the Mall, and the Queen's carefully stage-managed broadcast to the nation (from a Buckingham Palace balcony, with the crowds behind her) on the eve of the funeral.

The constitutional implications of the apparent public loss of faith in the monarchy – fuelled by headlines in the tabloids and vox pop interviews with 'the public' in news reports – brought a third aspect to the news agenda that became the main preoccupation of the broadsheet press, radio news programmes such as *Today* and *The World Tonight* and their TV equivalents, *Newsnight* and *Panorama*. Within days, something of a Diana industry was in place with psychologists, constitutional experts like David Starkey, Ben Pimlott and Norman St John-Stevas, newspaper editors and columnists flitting from radio studio to TV studio and then adding their own analysis in articles in the next edition of *The Times* and *The Daily Telegraph*. All this had the effect of blurring the media coverage around an almost imperceptibly self-referential agenda which had an overwhelming London bias.

We cannot know the extent to which radio phone-ins filtered out opinion that was anti-Diana or too stridently anti-monarchy, or whether the preoccupation about the events in Paris was really as obsessive among would-be callers as was suggested. Over-reaction, over-sensitivity and an unwillingness to deviate from the agreed agenda may in the end have dictated the tone and slant of the coverage as much as a genuine reflection of public opinion. Against this, to simply dismiss the week as one long, contrived media hype is to miss its complexities, subtleties and contradictions. For radio, even more than television or the press, the word was intensity. The major TV channels could lighten the mood by returning, between bulletins, to some semblance of normality – to films, soap operas and other pre-recorded material. On radio, however, because of the liveness of the output and the story's lack of resolution (until the funeral, at least), there was no escaping the Diana factor. While her death, the controversy and the circumstances mitigated against the continuous mix of light chatter and music at the heart of popular radio, the medium's coverage had a sense of personal involvement, however illusory, that neither TV nor print could fully match.

Further reading

Gibian, Peter (ed.) (1997): *Mass Culture and Everyday Life*. Routledge.

Hutchby, Ian (1991): 'The organisation of talk on talk radio' in Paddy Scannell (ed.), *Broadcast Talk*. Sage.

Keith, Michael C. (1987): *Radio Programming: Consultancy and Formatics*. Focal Press.

Limbaugh, Rush (1992): *The Way Things Ought To Be*. Pocket Books.

Scott, Gini Graham (1996): *Can We Talk? The Power and Influence of Talk Shows*. Insight.

Shingler, Martin, and Wieringa, Cindy (1998): *On Air: Methods and Meanings of Radio*. Arnold.

Activity 9.1

Try to participate in a radio phone-in and, if successful in getting on air, make a recording of it.

1. Note the steps you have to take in order to get on air – what questions are asked of you by the production assistant, whether you are called back, the length of time it takes for your initial call to be answered.
2. Without playing back the recording, assess the experience of being a caller. Were you allowed to express your view clearly and coherently? Were you treated fairly by the presenter? Did you feel you were participating in a debate or acting as a presenter's foil? Who was in control of the conversation? Did the presenter make any attempt to summarize your viewpoint?
3. Now play back the recording. How does the conversation sound from the perspective of a listener, and within the context of the whole programme?

Activity 9.2

1. Record a phone-in on a radio station of your choice. Assess whether participants are encouraged to make a contribution to a debate, or whether their function is to act as a presenter's foil. Who is in control of the conversation? Does the presenter make any attempt to summarize the callers' viewpoints? What is your overall impression of the flow, professionalism and fairness of the programme as a whole? How could it be improved?

Activity 9.3

Contact your local radio station and ask if you can sit in on a phone-in broadcast. (It may be possible to gain work experience at a station, or alternatively work as a volunteer at a hospital radio station.)

1. Observe the process of setting an outline agenda for the programme. What resources (newspapers, reference material) do the presenter and producer draw on in preparing the programme?
2. Evaluate the role of the production assistant(s) in fielding calls on the presenter's behalf. Investigate their criteria for putting a caller on air, and find out how much information regarding each caller is passed through to the presenter before the caller is put through. Who decides when a call should close, or at what point a jingle or commercial break is taken?
3. Pay special attention to any *points of surprise* in the programme – moments when a call is particularly moving or a point especially well put, or when a caller refuses to concede an argument.

Activity 9.4

Make a comparison of phone-in programmes on radio with similar programmes or features on television (for example, daytime shows such as *Richard and Judy*). What are the particular strengths of phone-ins on radio? Does the addition of a visual perspective on television phone-ins (for example, being able to see the reaction of the presenter or expert) enhance or detract from the experience of viewing?

Part Four

Practices

In the film *Groundhog Day*, a television weatherman finds himself condemned to repeat the same day, over and over again. Each day he is woken by the same radio station broadcasting exactly the same records, exactly the same news and exactly the same cheery patter. The lack of change, variety and escape from the familiar drives him to suicide – yet he still wakes up the next day, apparently doomed to a life of total predictability.

The predictability of mainstream radio programming is at once its greatest strength and its greatest weakness. Too much variation from a daily menu of proven popularity or acceptability risks alienating loyal listeners; a reluctance to vary the menu may have the same effect, especially over a period of time and in the face of new competition. At the heart of all live radio programming, therefore, is a paradoxical need for newness in the context of familiarity. The challenge for broadcasters, day after day and hour after hour, is to produce new material to slot into the familiar fixed points of radio programming – news, sport, weather, gossip, traffic, newspaper reviews, and so on. There may, in reality, be little that's novel about the material at all – no new developments in a news story, no great change in the weather, still the same roadworks at Junction 9 – but the constant challenge is to make it fresh, to stress the liveness of the moment through regularly updated topical references. For precisely the same reasons, although the basic content of music radio (usually currently available records) does not change, the choice of specific tracks and the order in which they are heard does: nothing could be more disturbing, as the anti-hero in *Groundhog Day* very quickly discovers, than to experience exactly the same musical or verbal message at the same point each day.

How radio stations create that sense of newness within the framework of repetition is the concern of this penultimate section of the book. Here we look at the practices of radio – its codes and conventions, the image that its programming and its off-air 'branding' conveys, and how the organization of the radio day informs its general message and meaning.

10

Language and Voice

Words, sounds and music are the primary codes of radio, from which listeners draw meaning. Of these, the spoken word is by far the most important: a radio station could broadcast nothing but natural sounds or non-stop music, but without the context that words bring, such sounds would relate to and represent nothing except themselves. Listening to the radio would still be an experience of sorts, but its meaning would be abstract rather than connective, forcing the listener to create his or her own context for the experience – using it as a source of uninterrupted therapeutic background sound, perhaps. On the radio as in everyday life, spoken language describes, interprets, amplifies and validates.

Language (the collation and conflation of words) communicates a literal meaning, but qualities such as tone, timbre and nuance ensure that speech communicates much more than simply words. How the message is received – the interpretation that the receiver puts on it – may be dependent, too, on factors entirely outside the broadcasters' control, such as the familiarity or otherwise of a particular voice, or listener prejudice towards certain accents or dialects. The 'professional' goal of radio talk may be clarity of meaning – achieved through straightforward vocabulary and simple syntax – but no talk, in any context, is ever unambiguously received.

The context in which radio speech is spoken is all-important: styles of delivery and discourse change depending on the kind of programming provided and the generic traditions and conventions associated with it. There is a clear difference, for example, between the dispassionate tones and language of a Radio 4 announcer reading the shipping forecast from a script and the ad-libbing of a music radio presenter filling the air between records. The major difference between these approaches is one of prescription and spontaneity, or what Ian Hutchby has defined as *institutional* and *mundane* modes of speaking. Certain institutional talk – news bulletins, weather forecasts, poetry readings, features like Radio 4's 'Thought for the Day' – is prepared, ordered and structured and broadly follows the rules of written text. The impact of the broadcast text will lie in its delivery and perhaps – in the case of, say, Alistair Cooke's *Letter from America* or of *Book at Bedtime* – the ability of the speaker to disguise or distract from its basic formality. Other

Source: Ingrid Bardua, Essex
Radio Group

Fig. 10.1 Essex FM *Drivetime*
presenter Paul Lovett at the
microphone. Voices bring a sense
of contact, colour and immediacy
to the broadcast medium

aspects of institutional talk include political interviews, parliamentary
exchanges and documentary speech, where the formality is as much in the
setting and the taking on of formal roles as in the content. Mundane talk, by
contrast, approximates far more to the conventions of everyday discourse: it
takes the form of conversation, the exchange of information or gossip, the
giving of confidences. This is not to say that there is no artificiality involved:
mundane talk sounds informal and spontaneous and therefore directly
imitative of private talk, but it is still talk that is given a public platform. The
paradox of radio talk is that it evokes intimacy yet operates on a massively
public scale.

Mundane and institutional definitions of radio talk offer a starting point
for more detailed study of how language, vocabulary and delivery differ
from programme to programme and presenter to presenter. As Hutchby
points out, much of what we hear on the radio mixes elements of both
modes and can therefore be described as 'intermediate talk ... an
approximation of mundane talk, projected somehow into a public domain,
and thus exhibiting features of institutional talk' (Hutchby, p. 120). But it is
important to reiterate here one of the major themes of this book: underlying

all forms of radio talk is the broadcaster's sense of the audience – how listeners prefer to be addressed, their limits of tolerance and understanding, the environment in which they listen, whether they really 'listen' at all. The styles and codes of radio speech have been many years developing and they are, to a great extent, the conscious product of just this kind of investigation and debate.

FINDING A LANGUAGE: HISTORICAL NOTES

One of the first challenges that the earliest broadcasters had to face was that of deciding how listeners should be talked to. Early broadcasts tended to ape the conventions of declamatory public speech – the lecture, the play, the reading – but it was quickly realized that the linguistic conventions of a public occasion were not suited to listening in a domestic environment. Scannell and Cardiff describe in detail the intensity of the debate within the BBC's Talks Department about the who, the what and (especially) the how of speech on radio. As they show, the principle of a feigned informality of delivery – giving a prepared talk in a casual, pseudo-spontaneous manner – was firmly in place by the end of the 1920s. All talkers were advised not to deliver their talk as if addressing a mass but to focus on a single listener – a one-way conversation, in effect. This accounted for the avuncular, paternalistic nature of much radio talk in the first two decades of the BBC's existence: they had the air of a senior family figure dispensing advice, homilies or the benefit of his (and it was invariably his rather than her) experience.

Some speakers had the gift of talking with clarity and focus, others did not. Ramsay MacDonald, leader of Britain's first Labour administration in 1924, was no radio natural: some English listeners complained that his Scottish accent was hard to understand, but recordings of his broadcasts show that it was the archness of his delivery and his tendency to hector that most would have found difficult. By contrast, Conservative leader Stanley Baldwin listened intently to the direct advice of John Reith and developed a confiding, intimate style of delivery that matched his portrayal in the press as a pragmatic man of the people. In the US, President Roosevelt's weekly radio addresses to the American people were nicknamed 'fireside chats' because of their folksiness and the unforced, natural style of his delivery. He was the first US president to appreciate the value of radio not only as a political tool – his chats gave a huge impetus to his promotion of an almost socialistic 'new deal' during the depression years of the 1930s – but also as a means of establishing direct contact with voters.

During 1940, when Britain appeared to be on the brink of invasion by Germany, the playwright and author J.B. Priestley made a series of evening talks which were models of quiet eloquence, each delivered in an earnest yet involving manner (and a northern accent) that accentuated the blunt 'good sense' of the content. Winston Churchill had none of Priestley's intimacy, and on paper his radio speeches can appear bombastic and linguistically overdone, but his skill was to deliver them in a rasping bulldog fashion that was entirely in keeping with the mood of the time. His unclipped and unforced accent, and indeed his lisp, accentuated the indefatigable, even contemptuous stance of the written speech. Churchill's oratory made few concessions to the intimacy of radio (and he had little time for the BBC, whose efforts he failed to mention once in war memoirs) but it has an unquestionable resonance that went beyond Baldwin's folksy plainness.

As early as 1926, Reith had set up an Advisory Committee on Spoken English with members including Rudyard Kipling and George Bernard Shaw, which recommended pronunciations of literally hundreds of words. Reith's aim was to formalize and standardize speech on BBC radio as an example for the whole nation to follow. Hilda Matheson, who headed the Talks Department between 1927 and 1932, was a critic of the policy and famously summed up 'BBC English' as 'roughly the educated speech of southern England' (Matheson, p. 66). Research eventually showed widespread dislike of (and active irreverence towards) the clipped and mannered style in which announcers and newsreaders spoke.

During wartime, a much wider policy was adopted, and there was even one regular newsreader, Wilfred Pickles, with a Yorkshire accent (albeit not a broad one). If there was a certain tokenism at work here, regional accents of many kinds were heard in comedy and light entertainment programmes, in panel games and shows like *Workers' Playtime*, where selected munitions workers were even allowed to speak for themselves on air. The thinking was that, if the BBC was to aid the war effort by reflecting it fairly and accurately across all classes and services, it had to speak and understand the same language. The legacy of the wartime BBC was a more outwardly democratic voice, ranging from the chumminess of a typical *Housewives' Choice* presenter to the mock-cockney accents of the Glum family in *Take It From Here*. Upper-class accents were even mercilessly satirised in programmes like *The Goon Show* and *Round the Horne*.

STYLES OF RADIO TALK

Most styles of radio speech carry the legacy of around 80 years of broadcasting convention, and common to all is a sense of 'liveness' – that the talk is happening *now*, even if the programme is recorded. (Programmes such as panel games are recorded in real time to give the *impression* of being live events.) Radio speech styles tend to vary according to content, context and intentionality – what the message is, the environment in which it will be broadcast (time of day, place in the schedule), how it is intended to be heard and understood by the intended audience. There are five principal forms: the *reading* of news or announcements; *narration* from a script, requiring some degree of dramatic effect; *commentary* on events as they happen; the *conversation* or interview; and *ad-libbed, spontaneous speech*. These forms do lend themselves to particular genres of programming, but they are not necessarily functions of generic differences. Different kinds of descriptive skills and different levels of knowledge are required for different kinds of commentary, for example, ranging from royal weddings and state funerals to football matches, horse races or marathons.

News reading

News reading is the most formal of all the speech forms identified above, and also the most anonymous in the sense that the identity of the newsreader has no direct relevance to an understanding of the information imparted. The classic style of news reading evolved by BBC radio involves a straight reading of a news script put together by a team of editors, reporters and writers: the skill of the newsreader lies in adopting the correct articulation and tone for each item, and keeping to time at an appropriate pace. It is, literally, a reading: the newsreader betrays little or no emotion, in keeping with the sense of dispassionate, disinterested balance and editorial neutralism which the news is meant to convey. Differences in news reading from station to station mainly relate to the style of delivery: Radio 2's on-the-hour bulletins, for example, are prefaced by a bright musical jingle and usually read by newsreaders exclusive to that station.

In commercial radio, the slightly brighter, more colourful style of presentation is mainly down to the more selective nature of the news itself. Capital FM's breakfast news bulletins, for example, are closely integrated within Chris Tarrant's programme and feature a 'personality' reader (Howard Hughes) who often makes off-the-cuff remarks about some of the more tabloid-type, showbusiness-oriented news items. Generally, however, even when news programmes are personality-led – for example, those on Radio 5 Live, where the anchorman of the programme may be a well-known news journalist such as Andrew Neil – there is still a place for the straight, unadorned bulletin given by a traditional newsreader. This is radio convention – a bulletin followed by an amplificatory magazine-type news programme was a feature of *Radio Newsreel*, which started during World War Two and was still going in the 1960s – but it serves the purpose of separating the informational aspect of news from the more discursive elements of comment, reaction and opinion.

Although female newsreaders are now familiar to listeners, news reading has traditionally been a male preserve, partly out of prejudice against the employment of women and partly because of assumptions of listener prejudice towards female voices. In the 1950s a senior management figure in BBC radio once said that it would be impossible to conceive of a female newsreader because she might weep if the news happened to be bad. Other variants on this prejudice were that women were too readily associated with gossip and rumour to be taken seriously, and that women with assertive personalities would be detected as such by the audience and disliked as the 'pushy woman' of male myth. Dyson has further pointed out a technological basis to the exclusion of women from news-reading roles, suggesting that 'not only has radio's mode of direct address developed from oratory, a traditionally masculine pursuit, but radio's fundamental technology, the microphone, was originally designed for the male vocal range' (Dyson, p. 181).

Narration from script

Aside from drama, there are three major forms of scripted speech on radio – story-telling, documentary or feature narration and the traditional radio talk. Their effectiveness – that is, the degree to which they engage the listener – depends on the skill of the speaker in keeping the listener's attention. A number of actors have established second (and very lucrative) careers for themselves not only as readers for radio but as readers of stories for commercial release in cassette form; BBC radio itself has been at the forefront of the big increase in such 'spoken word' sales during the 1990s, ironically just as the amount of broadcasting time devoted to such readings has contracted.

Factual documentaries, short 'packaged' features for inclusion in magazine programmes and educational programmes, share similar narrative characteristics, each requiring an engaging yet measured tone of delivery. As Andrew Crisell writes, the intention in any programme of educative value is that the listener should retain at least some of the information, or at least leave the programme better informed. This requires what Crisell describes as 'referential' or explanatory language, though in the case of educational programmes such as those made for schools or the Open University, it can be safe to assume a degree of pre-knowledge or basic understanding of the topic to be covered, and also that the listener will be a 'committed' listener and stay with the programme throughout. Programmes of the factual kind have traditionally tended to favour low, masculine voices to convey some notional sense of authority and credibility, and Radio 4 – which broadcasts by far the largest number of documentary programmes by any station – uses a small core of presenters including Paul Vaughan (the long-running *Kaleidoscope*) and Derek Cooper (*The Food Programme*).

Radio talks are, again, mainly a feature of Radios 3 and 4, and a hangover from the days when radio was the prime entertainment medium. The avuncular chats of the BBC's wartime 'Radio Doctor' Charles Hill (later a Chairman of the BBC) are echoed in the homespun homilies of Rabbi Lionel Blue, one of the regular speakers on the *Today* programme's five-minute talk spot, 'Thought for the Day'. Blue has the ability to switch from artful self-deprecation to absolute seriousness without breaking his stride, but again it is his skill in engaging the listener that accounts for his popularity. His talks, like those of Alistair Cooke in his long-running *Letter from America*, are superb examples of a marriage of theme, structure and clarity of language, tightly scripted but put over in a slightly halting 'natural' style (which may or may not be feigned). Both *Letter from America* and 'Thought for the Day' are examples of a well-trodden radio format in action. In both Blue's and Cooke's talks, for example, there is a clear sense of being led towards a dénouement or conclusion, which brings the listener right back to the thematic point at which the talk began.

Live commentary

To bring national events into the home – live, as they happened – was one of Reith's first objectives for the BBC. Radio offered a means of accessibility for the public to events of state, together with a kind of surrogate participation in them. But 'outside broadcasting', as all relaying of material from outside the studio was called, was one of the few forms of programming that could not be scripted, though enormous effort went into planning what would be said at certain points in the proceedings (say, of a royal wedding or state visit) and the inevitable policy committee deliberated long and hard about the kind of tone and language that the commentator should adopt. Early live commentaries tended to be reverential, wordy and colourful in the extreme, but a kind of template of conventions was established during the 1930s that was followed by both radio and television right through to the 1980s.

For many years, the BBC's Outside Broadcasting department covered both live occasions and sporting events; commentators on the latter were often news journalists with an interest in particular sports. There have been many occasions since in which the boundaries between commentary and reportage have become blurred – for example, the demonstrations against the South African rugby tour of England and Wales in 1969, the taking of the Israeli team as hostages by Palestinian terrorists during the 1972 Olympic Games in Munich, and the disaster at Sheffield's Hillsborough stadium in April 1989, when nearly 100 spectators were killed, which was relayed live on Radio 2.

Commentary styles vary according to the sport – hushed and leisurely for golf, measured and reflective for cricket, excitable and high-pitched for football – but the function of commentary in each case is to describe and explain (or 'read') the game or sport on the listener's behalf. Conventionally, commentary is a double-act comprising a senior commentator and an 'expert' summarizer (perhaps a player or manager), who adds analysis, background and a sense of authority. The commentator's skill lies in improvising, often for the duration of a match, but he (or she – although sport is still a male preserve, more female commentators are emerging) has to balance description, analysis and narrative colour with a strong sense of drama. Again, it is tone and delivery as much as the content that determines the level of listener engagement. A commentator may see it as his responsibility to make a dull game seem interesting, but a more familiar approach – characterized by that of Alan Green, BBC radio's senior football commentator – is to describe dull or negative play in highly critical, even withering terms: one of the quirks of Green's commentary is his rising level of impatience with players at what he sees as their tactical naivety.

Green is an example of the more critical, less sycophantic sports commentators to emerge in the 1990s. The breaking of the BBC's radio monopoly on sports coverage has led to the recruitment of commentators with backgrounds in sport or entertainment rather than news journalism, and to the personality and quirkiness of the commentator emerging as the centre of a complete programming package created with ratings in mind. An example is Jonathan Pearce, who developed a particularly impassioned and frenetic style of delivery at Capital Radio. Pearce sees himself as a champion of the ordinary football fan and styles his language accordingly – direct, critical and involved.

Occasionally, commentators do transcend their particular sports to become national icons: the commentary team behind *Test Match Special* – a blend of bluff West Countryman John Arlott and blunt Yorkshireman Fred Trueman with the public school tones and humour of Brian Johnston – became famous as much for their comic interplay and private language as for their descriptive abilities. In *Understanding Radio*, Andrew Crisell deconstructs a test match commentary by the late John Arlott to point up how a commentator's skills can successfully blend improvisation with genuinely literary skill – particularly his use of metaphor and simile – though it is of course impossible to convey on the printed page how much the sound and grain of Arlott's voice contributed to conveying the tension of the particular occasion. One of Arlott's most legendary broadcasts was not in fact a commentary on play at all but an improvised and wholly unprepared monologue on the removal of the protective covers at Lord's cricket ground. Arlott's talent was to turn a sporting event into a radio experience on its own merits.

Conversation

On the radio, as in life, monologue and dialogue are the two primary modes of speech. Outwardly, conversation is the most naturalistic of radio speech forms, in that it replicates the spontaneous to and fro of everyday speech. However, radio programmes do not simply reproduce or eavesdrop on conversation, they create an environment in which conversation or discussion can be generated – usually in the form of an interview – according to an agenda that is in many cases predetermined:

> The interview, far from being a neutral conduit for the transmission of information and opinion, is in fact a strongly institutionalised genre of discourse that exerts a pervasive influence on the conduit of journalists and public figures, and on the manner in which they form their talk with one another.
>
> Clayman, 'News interview openings', p. 49

Conversation in broadcasting is never genuinely two-way: the very term 'interview' underlines the artificial, inquisitorial and perhaps adversarial nature of the relationship between interviewer and interviewee – a relationship in which the former is firmly in control.

Even in broadcasting situations where the conversation is non-contentious, the presenter remains the focus of control. In the 'zoo' format that was popularized in Britain by Steve Wright at Radio 1 and is now a feature of many radio shows, the core content is the conversation – often ribald banter –

between the presenter and his or her production team. The role of the team is to act as comic feeds. Even given the 90s fashion for teaming presenters – Zoë Ball and Kevin Greening at Radio 1, Russ and Jono at Heart 106, Mark Radcliffe and Mark Riley on afternoon Radio 1 – it is customary to find one of the team acting as straight man, the other as comic foil.

Phone-in programmes offer an opportunity for the public to converse with a presenter or guest over a chosen topic, but again the conversation is weighted in favour of the presenter, who can cut off a caller at the touch of a button. Such conversation does replicate the informality (and, occasionally, the formality) of everyday conversation. One of the least engaging facets of phone-in programmes, for example, is the meaningless exchange of 'how are you's' between presenter and caller that often precedes the conversation proper. The convention of introducing callers by their first name smacks of forced informality and a spurious intimacy and equality between caller and called.

Intimacy is another characteristic of radio conversation. Some of this sense of privacy is technologically enhanced: the environment of the radio studio obliterates all noise except that picked up by the microphones, forcing an aural focus on what is being said. It is notable that the prime source of two-way chat on television – the chat show format – has never worked well on radio, because the laughter or applause of a studio audience sounds like an intrusion. Some of

Source: Heart 106.2FM

Fig. 10.2 Jonathan Coleman (Jono) and the Heart 106.2FM team on location in a London store. In contrast to the hyperactive Chris Evans, who took over Coleman's previous breakfast show on Virgin, Coleman's style rests on a mischievous but easy-going informality

the most compelling radio broadcasting occurs when the intimacy of the studio setting enhances the confessional nature of the conversation, as in Anthony Clare's probing *In the Psychiatrist's Chair* or some of the calls to the 'agony' phone-ins. The former programme emulates the ambience of a psychoanalyst's consulting room, the latter the ambience of a doctor's surgery. Here, the presenter demonstrates what are basically counselling skills – the initial, delicate probing to distinguish the subject's perception of the problem from the reality; the questioning to pinpoint the source of anxiety or depression; the advice as to how the subject can help himself or herself, often by getting appropriate help from other sources. This confessional form of programming is often criticized for being exhibitionist and voyeuristic.

Spontaneous speech

In the comparatively regulated days of the late 1970s, radio in Britain was criticized by a government-sponsored committee of inquiry, the Annan Committee, for being too heavily preoccupied with 'pop and prattle'. When the IBA subsequently issued directives to existing stations or laid down requirements for new stations to follow, the phrase 'meaningful speech' was frequently used. While, with deregulation, there are no longer any such requirements on stations to avoid the prattle of what we might call *meaningless* speech, much of the output of music radio in particular remains centred on the ad-libbed, stream-of-consciousness remarks of the daytime DJ. Presenters at news- or talk-based stations have the advantage of providing a service – in most cases backed up by strong editorial teams – that is basically information-led, even if delivered with the gloss of entertainment. Music radio presenters are there to provide pure entertainment and companionship, and the scope for spontaneous speech that does not centre on the trivial or inconsequential is limited. So what is the substance and style of ad-libbing on music radio?

Presenters do not always have free rein. The disciplines of the station's format regarding placing and timing of links, trailers, advertisements and the music itself tend to ensure that talk is kept to a minimum anyway. Some stations even set a time limit on talk between tracks. This tends to subordinate the presenter to the position of linkman, which is a far cry from the traditional image of the egocentric, smooth-voiced DJ who can talk on tap on any subject yet say nothing of consequence.

Generally, the larger the station, the bigger the name, the freer the rein that the presenter enjoys. But what makes the spontaneous speech of a Chris Evans or a Steve Wright arresting is the way it reacts *against* the norms of restrictive daytime programming. What the station is doing is giving these personalities – who are performance artists or stand-up comics as much as presenters – licence to deviate. Evans, for example, continually undermines listener expectations by playing unusual selections and often going for as long as 20 minutes without even playing music. This suggests a high level of confidence, arrogance and an ego to match, and Evans can reel from brilliant on-the-hoof

Source: Essex Radio Group

Fig. 10.3 Presenters at stations owned by the Essex Radio group. The function of presenters is to form a bond with listeners that will encourage them to return to the station again and again. Further discussion of the nature of the presenter's role can be found in Chapter 13

improvisation to self-indulgent, even spiteful diatribes against people who have upset him, in the course of a single show.

For all of the spontaneous, ad-libbed nature of radio speech, it has a strong core of routine and repetition. There are, most obviously, the continual references back and forward – to the programme just gone or the item to come, reminders of telephone numbers or addresses – but there is routine, too, in the very phrases used and the pitch and tone adopted. Goffman suggests that a radio presenter 'has a limited resource of formulaic remarks out of which to build a line of patter. A DJ's talk may be heard as unscripted, but it tends to be built up out of a relatively small number of set comments' (Goffman, p. 324).

This is the central paradox of contemporary radio broadcasting: the need to routinely recreate the same programme on a day-to-day basis, making programming sound fresh yet familiar, the same but different. In daily life, it is the familiarity of language as much as the substance of what is said that matters: the stock phrases of a friend or colleague, the pleasantries of greeting or goodbye, the mental switching-off on hearing a tale told before or the switching-on at a new piece of gossip or news. Ultimately, the to and fro of radio talk provides a sense of location, a reassuring sense that the world still *sounds* the same.

Further reading

Boyd, Andrew (1988): *Broadcast Journalism*. Heinemann.
Clayman, Steven E. (1991): 'News interview openings: aspects of sequential organisation' in Paddy Scannell (ed.), *Broadcast Talk*. Sage.
Crisell, Andrew (1986): *Understanding Radio*. Methuen.
Donovan, Paul (1998): *All Our Todays: 40 Years of the Today Programme*. Arrow.
Dyson, F. (1994): 'The genealogy of the radio voice' in D. Augaitis and D. Lander (eds), *Radio Rethink: Art, Sound and Transformation*. Walter Phillips Gallery.
Goffman, Erving (1981): *Forms of Talk*. Blackwell.
Hutchby, Ian (1991): 'The Organisation of talk on talk radio' in Paddy Scannell (ed.), *Broadcast Talk*. Sage.
Matheson, Hilda (1933): *Broadcasting*. Thornton Butterworth.
Pickles, Wilfred (1949): *Between You and Me*. Werner Laurie.
Scannell, Paddy, and Cardiff, David (1986): '"Good luck war workers!": Class, politics and entertainment in wartime broadcasting' in T. Bennett et al. (eds), *Popular Culture and Social Relations*. Open University Press.
Shingler, Martin, and Wieringa, Cindy (1998): *On Air: Methods and Meanings of Radio*. Arnold.

Activity 10.1

Record 30 minutes of a speech-based magazine programme (for example, *Woman's Hour* on Radio 4 or *The Jimmy Young Show* on Radio 2). Analyse the speech content according to the modes of talk identified by Ian Hutchby and described in this chapter.

Activity 10.2

1. Prepare, record and edit a five-minute radio talk on any subject of your choice for an early-morning 'opinion' slot on a radio station geared to a 35-plus age group. Keep in mind the time of day and the characteristics, profile and likely receptivity of the audience.
2. Amend your talk as an opinion piece for a programme tailored to a student audience. List and account for the changes that you thought necessary to make to the content of the talk, the style and pace of presentation, and the formality or otherwise of the language you used.
3. Play your recording to a group of friends or fellow students and note their feedback. How might your talk be improved?

Activity 10.3

Record and transcribe a radio interview between a presenter and a government minister or representative. Highlight the transcription at the point where the direction of speech changes from introductory remarks made for the listener's benefit to questions aimed at the interviewee. What techniques does the interviewer use (such as mode of address, interjection, reference to the listener) to keep the dialogue in the public rather than conversational sphere?

Activity 10.4

This is an exercise in mixing preparation with improvisation, a skill at the heart of all sporting commentary. With a friend or colleague, produce your own outside broadcast from a sporting event. Divide it into three sections – scene-setting, commentary and a post-match report or summary – and record each in real time, as if you were broadcasting live. In preparing for the 'broadcast', consider the moods you will need to convey in each section, research whatever facts or statistical material you wish to have at hand, and decide between you who is to play the role of commentator and who the role of summarizer. Analyse your efforts and assess your performance in terms of the smoothness of your delivery, the quality of the information imparted and the interaction between commentator and summarizer. Repeat the exercise, reversing the commentator/summarizer roles.

11

Sequence and Flow

Live radio is a voracious medium which, during any given day, consumes and regurgitates an enormous amount of information and material. All this has to be not only pre-selected but organized and presented in a broadcastable manner; and it has to be placed and timed within some kind of coherent framework, be it an individual programme, a sequence of programmes running successively, or what is commonly called 'stripped' programming – the mixing of news, music and talk and other programming elements across blocks of time. The theme of this chapter is the role that sequencing plays in radio broadcasting, and particularly how it is related to what was explored in Chapter 5 – perceived audience uses of the radio medium, especially at either end of the working day. Only from an understanding of the content of radio *in relation to how it is structured to be received* can we begin to take note of the medium's ideological thrust.

Writing in 1974 with reference to commercial television in the US, Raymond Williams was the first to identify what he called 'sequence or flow' as the 'characteristic experience' of all developed broadcasting systems (Williams, p. 86). The flow of messages, programmes, commercials, trailers and continuity announcements broadcast by television stations is, Williams argued, the key to broadcasting's impact. Klaus Bruhn Jensen took the concept further by defining 'flow' as a 'sequence of program segments, commercials and pre-announcements that is designed by the individual station to engage as many viewers as possible for as long as possible' (Jensen, p. 111). The effect is to blur programme boundaries and so give the viewer no opportunity or excuse to tune out.

We can see proof of Jensen's point in the programme schedules of any TV station and the attention paid to matching viewing predilections or habits at particular times of day. Scheduling is itself a prized skill within broadcasting circles, requiring an astute awareness of the susceptibilities of the market and acute judgement of how and what to schedule against a competitor's fare. In recent years, the timing and placing of soap operas within the television schedules has been a prime battleground, not only because of the 'achievement' of winning a high-profile ratings battle against a rival but because viewers are known to stay with the channel in question once the particular programme is over. In other words, key programmes like soap operas can *build* the audience.

These factors are prevalent in radio, too, where the concept of flow programming applies both to the scheduling of discrete programmes – especially in the context of a station like Radio 4 – and to the far more widespread use of a flow of programming *items* woven together. Flow programming is, if not listener-*driven* then listener-*focused*: it is so structured because the radio consumer is assumed to be giving less than full attention because he or she is listening on a secondary (background) or even tertiary (unaware) level. His or her receptivity is low or at best uneven and fragmented, and listening is sporadic; consumers dip in and out, switching off and on according to mood or circumstance. Programming is therefore geared to short, easily assimilated segments of speech or music, with fixed 'anchor' points across the schedule to encourage continuous listening. The task for the producer or programme controller in planning this kind of sequenced output is therefore to create programming that moulds to the needs of a very mobile and volatile audience yet discourages that audience from crossing over to another provider. The aim is not to keep the fingers from the off-switch but from the dial.

Others have developed Williams' theme in a radio context. In *On Air*, Martin Shingler and Cindy Wieringa draw together the arguments of Canadian writer Jody Berland and the Australian writers Christine Higgins and Peter Moss. Berland writes of the 'carefully managed rapidity and predictability of pattern' that she found to be a characteristic of mainstream radio, pointing up its orchestrated nature and its lulling, accepting impact on the listener (Berland, p. 211). Higgins and Moss interpret 'flow' not simply as a sequence of items but as a flow of cultural meanings across continuous programming. They suggest, with reference to specific examples from a study of phone-in programmes on Australian commercial radio, that the cumulative effect of these items of programming – and the juxtaposition of downbeat or argumentative calls against the positive, superficially resolving message of the commercials – is to 'coalesce to produce a flow of compatible consumer messages' (Higgins and Moss, p. 37).

This tends to suggest that the whole function of programming in commercial radio is to provide an appropriate environment and context for a repetitive stream of advertising messages, though this assumes a degree of calculation and prescription (not to mention outright manipulation) that is perhaps beyond the wit and capability of even the shrewdest of programme controllers. What we are talking about here are patterns and tendencies rather than strictly defined processes, and patterns that are often just as evident in non-commercial broadcasting. Radio broadcasters themselves prefer to stress – perhaps disingenuously – the practical need to hold the listener's interest by balancing serious and light features, and to strike the right balance between continuity and change of pace, repetition and novelty.

CASE STUDY: BREAKFAST-TIME RADIO

A good starting point for studying how 'flow' works in radio – in terms of both its internal mechanics and its context within the whole radio day – is to look at a particular broadcasting hour in detail across competing stations. This enables the student to point up differences and commonalities between genres of radio and between publicly funded and commercial services; to focus on the formulaic nature of the flow of output; to point up contrasting or similar treatments of the same story; and to draw some conclusions regarding the sources of programming – how the same sources supply travel news across several stations, for example, or how reliant presenters are on other media for their on-air material.

Breakfast time is a rich source of study because it represents for radio stations a key battleground for audiences. This is when radio attracts its highest volume of listeners and when it achieves its highest profile. Presenter Chris Evans, recruited to Radio 1 from Channel 4 TV's *The Big Breakfast* show in 1995, was widely credited with arresting Radio 1's declining audience figures through an innovative breakfast-time show centred around his outlandish personality. When he in turn left the station in 1997 and soon after joined Radio 1's major commercial rival, Virgin Radio, the stage was set for what the tabloid press called 'the breakfast-time wars' between his new show and the team recruited by Radio 1 to take over from him – Zoë Ball (a former Evans researcher on *The Big Breakfast*) and Kevin Greening (a one-time contemporary of Evans at Greater London Radio). The story became even more high-profile when Evans' company, Ginger Media, bought Virgin and the former occupiers of the station's breakfast spot, Russ and Jono, were dismissed. They in turn decamped to another London station, Heart 106.2FM, to host its breakfast-time show.

There is more to this than simply good newspaper copy. Breakfast-time radio acts as a shop window for the station, enabling the rest of the station's wares to be trailed. As with soap operas on television, the ratings that breakfast shows achieve help build the audience for the rest of the day. The stakes are therefore high, as the fees paid to the presenters illustrate. Chris Tarrant, long-time presenter of Capital FM's top-rated London breakfast-time show, was persuaded to accept a new contract worth a reported £3 million during 1997 – this against a background of Capital's aborted attempt to buy Virgin Radio. Talk Radio's revamp during 1997 was spearheaded by the high-cost recruitment of Kirsty Young, presenter of Channel 5 News, to its breakfast slot. Radio 4's major revision of its schedules during 1998 was built on a fine-tuning of the 7am–9am *Today* programme to prevent the haemorrhage of listeners after 8.30am – listeners who, BBC research appeared to indicate, then deserted the station altogether.

Figures 11.2 and 11.3 depict the output of two of these rival shows – Chris Tarrant on Capital FM and Zoë Ball on Radio 1 – between 7am and 8am on a day chosen at random, 6 October 1998. They list the main editorial elements in sequence. In Chris Tarrant's case, music takes up just under half the hour,

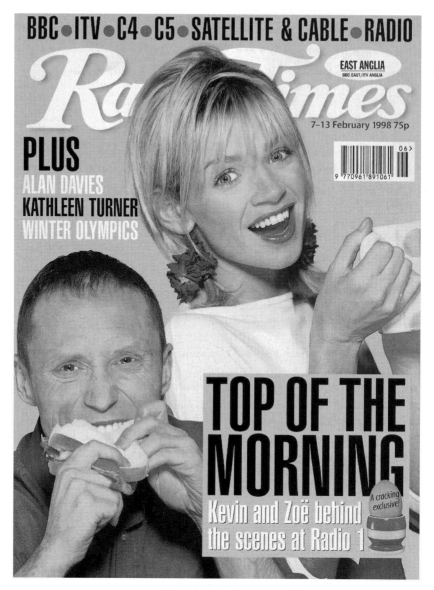

Source: Radio Times

Fig. 11.1 In 1997, Radio 1's choice of Zoë Ball and Kevin Greening as co-presenters of the flagship breakfast show signalled a new era of ratings rivalry between the station and its commercial competitors

with four of the tracks taken from the current chart, one a recent hit, and the other two comprising tracks that at the time were not yet commercially available but had been playlisted by Capital. In the case of three of the selections, Tarrant used the inclusion to link back or link forward to the station itself: Bryan Adams was mentioned as a previous guest, Boyzone as the subject of a

Fig. 11.2 Chris Tarrant's breakfast programme on Capital FM: sequence and timing of programme items, 6 October 1998

Key to Figs 11.2 and 11.3

CT: Chris Tarrant
ZB: Zoë Ball
HH: Howard Hughes (newscaster)
FE: Flying Eye (small aircraft reporting travel news)
ID (live): live station identification
ID (rec): station identification in recorded (jingle) form
TRAIL (live): live mention trailing later item
TRAIL (rec): recorded trailer for later item
WTHR: weather update
TRAV: travel update
TC: time-check
ADV: advertisement
MUS: music
CALL (live): live telephone call
CALL (rec): taped answerphone message

7.00–7.04
ID (rec): 'your Birthday Bonanza station, 95.8 Capital FM'
NEWS: 11 items + sport headlines + weather
ADV: Channel 4 *Dispatches* programme on Chinese nuclear tests

7.04–7.05
CT: It's Chris Tarrant, good morning London.
(under music track) Showbiz news headlines (3)
WTHR

7.05–7.09
ID (rec): Capital FM
MUS: *Be My Baby*, Savage Garden
CT: New 24-hour hotline has gone berserk. Very strange people out there.
CALLS (rec): George from Ealing with Flintstones Bedrock joke.
Michael from North Circular with scaffolding erection joke.
Jill from Egham: which is the London roundabout that directs traffic the wrong way?
CT: Hotline number.

7.09–7.14
MUS: *Each Time*, E-17
TC
CT: 'Madwoman from Surrey' says the roundabout is in Hemel Hempstead.
CALL (live): Jim on M23: the roundabout is in Hatton Cross.
CT: Traffic is bad every morning, might as well give same bulletin.
TRAIL (live): Birthday Bonanza

continued

Fig. 11.2 *continued*

___

7.14–7.15
CT: Travel update from RAC Travel.
TRAV
WTHR

7.15–7.23
ID (live)
TRAIL (live): for Mick Hucknall, Harry Hill and San Francisco competition on drive-time show
MUS: *Day Like Today*, Bryan Adams
CT: Mick Hucknall coming in later.
ID (live)
CT: Man declared dead on Tube regains consciousness.
TRAV: James Farrell reporting from car at Elephant and Castle, suggests roundabout may be the
    entrance to Savoy Hotel
ID (rec): Meat Loaf parody 'a DJ like Christ Tarrant'.
TRAIL (rec): Birthday Bonanza
ID (rec)
ADV: Channel 4 *Dispatches* programme on Chinese nuclear tests
ADV: P&O Stena Lines price promise
ADV: One-to-One phone package for business
ADV: Premier Points at Argos

7.23–7.26
TC
ID (rec)
CT: Had call from Richard from Hemel Hempstead. The roundabout is there and called 'the
    magic roundabout' by locals.
ID (live)
WTHR
MUS: *No Matter What*, Boyzone

7.26–7.31
ID (live)
CT: TC
TRAIL (live): Boyzone ticket competition with Clearasil; Boyzone's Ronan Keating talking to
    James Cannon tonight; Mick Hucknall mention
CT: Flying Eye in a couple of minutes . . .
TRAIL (live): Birthday Bonanza
ID (rec)
ADV: P&O Stena
ADV: Harrods
ADV: PC World
ADV: P&O Stena
FE + Cellnet mention – can't fly today because of poor weather.

continued

Fig. 11.2 *continued*

Banter between CT and reporter on roundabout and Monday's Birthday Bonanza.
TRAV
'Flying Eye with Cellnet at 7.31'

7.31–7.34
HH: NEWS update – seven items
Banter between CT and HH on proposals for three types of marriage contract
    (CT: Consummate and leave . . . it works for tigers.).
HH: WTHR, TC

7.34–7.37
CT: showbiz news update
ID (live) + date
MUS: *Outside*, George Michael
ID (live)
TC (given as '23 to 8')

7.37–7.38
WTHR
ID (live) + date
TRAIL (live): Birthday Bonanza
CT: Fun story from Munich: a midget bites fat man's bottom.
ID (rec)
TC (given as '22 to 8')

7.38–7.42
MUS: *All Around the World*, Oasis
TC (given as '19 to 8) + ID (live)
TRAIL (live): Birthday Bonanza
CT: reminder of hotline number
TC (given as '18 to 8')

7.42–7.50
CALL (live): Sarah in Leatherhead spotted CT's double in Redhill pub.
MUS: *What Can I Do*, The Corrs
TRAIL (live): Birthday Bonanza
CT: Birthday for today is 20 July – ring now.
ID (live)
WTHR
FE report + sponsor mention (Cellnet)
Banter: CT + FE

7.50–7.53
CT: Showbiz news item – Sylvester Stallone buying house next to ex-wife.
ID (rec)
TRAIL (rec): Birthday Bonanza

continued

Fig. 11.2 *continued*

ADV: PC World
ADV: Toyota Corolla
ADV: *Time Out*
ADV: Channel 4 *Dispatches*
ID (rec): 'Tarrant in the morning'
TC: (given as '7 to 8')

7.53–7.58
TRAIL (live): Mick Hucknall on drive-time show, Celine Dion on last night's show.
MUS: *You Are My Hero*, Celine Dion and R. Kelly
TRAIL (live): for Dion's Capital-sponsored concert at Wembley.
TC (given as '2 to 8')

7.58–7.59
WTHR
ID (rec)

7.59–8.00
TRAIL (rec): Birthday Bonanza
ADV: Mercedes Benz

Source: Logged by the author

Fig. 11.3 Zoë Ball's breakfast programme on Radio 1: sequence and timing of programme items, 6 October 1998

7.00–7.09
NEWS: 12 items + sport (2 items: both football)
WTHR
ZB: Today's mission – get me a job on *Blue Peter*
MUS: *Millennium*, Robbie Williams
Newspaper review: yo-yo craze (now £110 in Hamleys).
ZB: If you could bring something back from childhood, like Spangles sweets, what would it be?

7.09–7.20
TC
MUS: *Bitter Sweet Symphony*, The Verve
ZB: Remember deely-boppers? The *Dr Who* Tardis up for sale (news story).
MUS: *Rockefeller Skank*, Fat Boy Slim
ZB: Calls coming in suggesting Golden Nuggets.
CALL (live): Andy – your weather forecast is wrong.
TRAV
WTHR

continued

Fig. 11.3 *continued*

7.20–7.24
TRAIL (rec): New daytime schedule starts 20 October
ID (rec)
MUS: *Here's Where the Story Ends*, Tin Tin Out

7.24–7.27
TC
Live link to Palisades, Birmingham
MUS: *Game On*, Catatonia

7.27–7.32
TC
ZB: Can't get hold of Piers in Birmingham
TRAIL (live): 'How low can you go' after 8am
Live link from Birmingham
TRAIL (live): coming up – Battle of Britain competition + Sweatbox, Oasis, Supergrass

7.32–7.39
NEWS: seven headlines + sport + WTHR
ID: Zoë Ball's breakfast show
MUS: *Late in the Day*, Supergrass

7.39–7.41
ZB: Happy Birthday, Blue Peter.
Bring back Texan bars.
Confess to vandalizing *Blue Peter* garden.
Live link to Birmingham.
Live vox pop.
TRAIL (rec): Come to Paris with Zoë.

7.41–7.45
TC
MUS: *Raincloud*, Lighthouse Family

7.45–7.54
TC
'Battle of Britain' competition to win Nintendo 64:
Lee from Nottingham ('bring back *Magic Roundabout*').
Tracy from Waterlooville ('bring back Golden Nuggets').
Four questions – no correct answers from either contestant.
Tracy wins.
MUS: *All Around the World*, Oasis

7.54–7.55
TC
TRAV
WTHR

continued

Fig. 11.3 *continued*

7.55–8:00
TC
TRAIL (rec): New daytime schedule from 20 October
ID (rec)
MUS: *Everything's Gonna Be Alright,* Sweatbox
Recap of calls: suggestions to bring back Sugar Puffs, Pitkin, Hartley the Hare.

Source: Logged by the author

competition that evening (with a quick soundbite from a Boyzone member), and Celine Dion as a guest on the drive-time afternoon show the previous evening. He took the major 7.14am traffic report as an opportunity to suggest that, because the hold-ups mentioned always related to the same places, he might as well just repeat the same report every day; and both he and the Flying Eye reporter used the 7.29 traffic report as a vehicle for discussing the Birthday Bonanza competition to be held the following Monday – would the reporter be in for work that day or would he be ringing in to try his luck himself? The continual references to the station, amplified by a total of 15 station identifiers and jingles across the hour, offer a constant reminder to the listener of the station's presence and character. For all Tarrant's 'personality', it is the station itself that is the star of the hour: only one jingle even mentioned Tarrant himself, and that a slightly mocking homily on 'a DJ like Chris Tarrant' before the 7.22 commercial break.

The main emphases in Tarrant's programme are on 'nowness' – the continual time-checks (19 within the hour), six references to the date and day of the week, a total of 10 weather mentions – and on newsiness in the form of brief headlines centring on bizarre events or on the entertainment world (a new TV series inspired by the film *Titanic,* Michael Jackson's parents being sued again). The phone-in element is brief but significant, offering an opportunity to listeners to phone in with on-the-spot traffic news and offer answers to the main query of the day – in this case, the location of the worst roundabout in London, a query that itself came from a message left on Capital's 24-hour hotline the day before. The flow of programme items from 7am onwards is punctuated by jingles continually plugging the Birthday Bonanza of £100,000 – such a jingle, describing Capital as 'your Birthday Bonanza station', prefaces the main news at 7am – and held together by Tarrant's sense of calm spontaneity. Most of the news stories Tarrant quotes are in fact 'timeless' items provided by researchers and serve as an opportunity for a well-timed joke – for example, the doctor's mis-diagnosis is blamed on the fact that every Tube passenger looks lifeless and stares straight ahead. The total effect is a curious mixture of the breathless and the measured: Tarrant's delivery is so quick-fire that it is difficult sometimes, even with the advantage of having taped the show, to fully catch what he says, yet there is no sense of anarchy or of the show veering out of control. If the flow is repetitive, it is created in the knowledge that listeners dip in and out: time-checks and stations 'idents' give the listener an immediate sense of time and place, and even the advertisements are mainly confined to three two-minute blocks at 7.21, 7.29 and 7.51.

THE RADIO DAY

In radio, the flow of programming carries the listener from one item to the next, from one programme or strip of programming to the next, on a 24-hour basis, in real time. The structures are such (and so widely familiar) that, even if a listener opts out through necessity or choice, he or she can pick up the threads at any point in the day. In this sense, radio is a tap to be turned on and off as required – a domestic utility taken for granted but missed if unavailable. But what are the parameters that guide radio flow, and what determines them?

The prime determinant is time: the radio day runs parallel to the flow of daily life itself. The medium's liveness, its sense of living in the 'now' of the present moment, is consistently brought home by the battery of time-checks, news bulletins and verbal references to what is going on in the world on that particular day, but these are essentially no more than accentuation points. The radio day does not reflect on or mimic the passage of time, *it lives within it*. Filling time on radio does not simply mean plugging a gap – it means bringing organization, coherence and meaning to it, in a manner that the listener understands and relates and responds to.

For the early broadcasters, this meant replicating some of the time-specific cultural conventions of the period – the late-afternoon tea dance, the theatrical presentation or concert at 7.30pm, the Sunday-morning church service – but the process of structuring the radio day has become infinitely more sophisticated, complex and problematic as the radio day itself has expanded and the means by which radio can be heard have broadened, and as competition grows for the listener's time from other media, from home entertainment, from increased mobility and socialization.

Paddy Scannell points out that, however familiar and predictable radio programming may be, every day and every programme is an 'event': it is something conceived, planned and executed to be received. Organizing the radio day in the holistic sense – like organizing any event – means creating and sustaining a flow of items (essentially, *mini*-events) that is understandable, logical and implicitly if covertly directive. *Understandable* in the sense of being located in common experience; *logical* in the sense of being both time-appropriate and sequentially non-disruptive; and *directive* in the sense of guiding the listener from one point to another. The key principle underlying all these factors is listener use, shaping the flow of programming according to the reception context (time, place, circumstances) in which it will be heard, and matching the *pace* of that flow to the rhythms of daily life – quick at breakfast

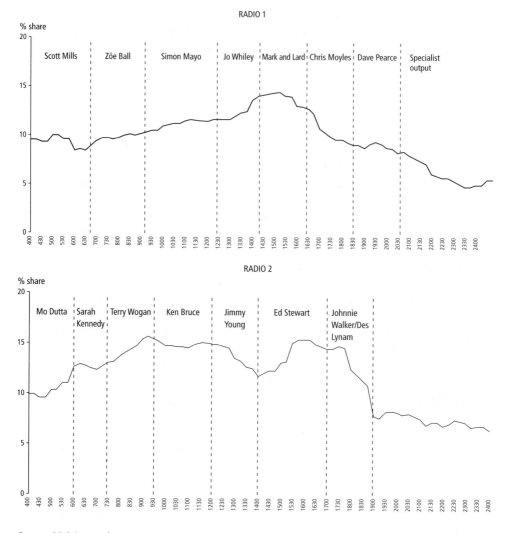

Source: BBC Research

Fig. 11.4 BBC Radio 1 and Radio 2 shares by daypart (weekdays, 1998)

time, more mellow after 9am as the audience settles into the routines of work, livelier once more as the rush for home begins. This does, of course, involve making a huge number of assumptions about what the mass of listeners are doing at any particular time; it suggests a level of ingratiation that has implications for the tone of programming and especially the manner in which audiences are addressed. Yet while radio programming matches life, runs in tandem to it and even frames certain aspects of it – notably the process of getting up and ready for work – it does not impose upon it. It polices daily routine, but unobtrusively. The radio day is seamless, and the seams should not be noticeable.

Seamless does not mean unsegmented. Typically, the radio day is broken up into segments, partly to reflect changing patterns of listening, partly to enable advertising to be charged at different levels according to peaks and troughs of listening. The art of scheduling is partly to allow a smooth transition between segments so as not to lose listeners.

THE MECHANICS OF FLOW

'Flow' functions as an audience-builder and retainer, but it generally works within a formulaic structure that allows repetition or even rotation of items. This is especially true in the case of music radio, where commercially available singles are programmed to be played at a predetermined frequency. That frequency of play may be decided by a single's placing in the current Top 40, by its newness, by its popularity as evinced by sample polling of listeners by telephone, or even by a station's association with a particular artist or event – for example, a concert that it might be sponsoring. The rationale is that listeners are constantly tuning in and out and so will rarely hear a sequence of programming for long enough to confront this kind of repetition – yet, for the amount of time that they do listen in, they will expect to hear at least some of the currently popular sounds that they like. It is the continuous flow of familiar music, its *structuring* in a familiar yet lightly varied pattern – which will be different from station to station, according to music policy and target age group – that gives music radio its distinct character. Part of that structure may even be 'segueing', to use the terminology – the programming of tracks in a tight sequence, without a presenter to link them.

Repeated speech may be tolerated in the case of advertising, but not as the main focus in programming: the thrust in news radio, as in its television equivalents (BBC News 24, Sky News, CNN) is to treat news stories as ongoing and running, mixing regular live coverage of some 'developing' story with discussion with experts. The aim is to persuade the listener to stay with the station for fear of missing the latest development. LBC in London currently offers a familiar news/phone-in service on its FM frequency and a rotation of news, sport, travel and weather in 20-minute segments on its AM waveband. The AM programming attracts Londoners wishing to tune in specifically for up-to-the-minute information, but it is deliberately not conducive to ongoing listening.

THE PITFALLS OF PREDICTABILITY

Like any routine, radio programming has its comforts and its irritations, but its pre-packaged and time-governed nature also carry an implicit tyranny. This is especially so in commercial radio, where all programming must of necessity be constructed around one- or two-minute sequences of advertising. In music radio, the break-up of each broadcasting hour into segments and sweeps of music restricts the scope of what can be played to what fits with the format; it makes programme preparation itself the subject of routine, a processing of codes and numbers (literally, as most music radio stations use computer systems to select and programme music tracks) rather than a creative sequencing that mixes listener expectations with the occasional surprise.

In news radio, the brevity of reports and interviews or, conversely, the dwelling on subjects to fill the allotted time, determines the level and parameters of what is discussed, while the primacy of the format ensures that nothing must interfere with the weather and traffic reports on the quarter hour or the trudge through the sports news for two minutes after each extended bulletin. In the name of short attention spans and an assumption of a promiscuity and casualness in listening, is radio programming more often driven by the disciplines of flow, sequence and format – by its mechanics – than by its content?

The sequenced pattern of programming not only assumes that there are common, universal patterns to how people use radio, it suggests and draws its dynamics from reinforcing assumptions of common ideological bonds – that we belong to a community sharing certain common tastes, interests and perspectives, that there are certain ways in which we as individuals *should* be spending our weekdays (in work) and evenings and weekends (having fun or improving ourselves). The radio day is defined by the working day, and in its scheduling as much as the content of its programmes radio acts in tandem with the work experience – framing the day according to the physical process of preparing for and returning from work, and providing a daytime soundtrack for a consensus of employees and houseworkers magically united by Elton John and titbits from today's newspapers.

Further reading

Berland, Jody (1993): 'Contradicting media: towards a political phenomenology of listening' in Neil Strauss (ed.), *Radiotext(e)*. Semiotext(e).

Higgins, Christine, and Moss, Peter (1982): *Sounds Real: Radio in Everyday Life*. University of Queensland Press.

Jensen, Klaus Bruhn (1995): *The Social Semiotics of Mass Communication*. Sage.

Shingler, Martin, and Wieringa, Cindy (1998): *On Air: Methods and Meanings of Radio*. Arnold.

Williams, Raymond (1974): *Television, Technology and Cultural Form*. Fontana.

Activity 11.1

Using Figures 11.2 and 11.3 as a template, construct a chart of your own depicting an hour of drive-time output (say, 5pm to 6pm) on a station on consecutive days. Highlight the continuities and differences in speech content, music, advertising (if applicable), jingles and traffic and weather reports. What advantages does the format of the hour have for the listener and for the station? How do listeners and stations use the hour?

Activity 11.2

Compare the 6am–7am early-morning output of a station with the programming broadcast between 11pm and midnight. Note differences in pace, choice of tracks (if the programmes are music-oriented), tone of presentation and over-all ambience. How might the target audiences for these hours differ?

12

Branding and Marketing

In a medium as competitive as radio, how a station *sounds* – the sense of style and personality that it conveys on-air, on a daily basis – is all important. The question of why people listen to one particular station over another may come down, very simply, to one of personality and identification – the very same factors that may determine consumer preferences for a particular newspaper, supermarket, or make of car. The differences are subtle, not always completely rational and not always to do with the content of what is offered. As in

Source: Ingrid Bardua

Fig. 12.1 Essex Radio advertises itself by taking to the road

conventional consumer marketing, the difference may relate to issues of lifestyle or age identification, attitude, sentiment or reputation. How stations pitch themselves on- and off-air is therefore vital in establishing a relationship with listeners (and, ideally, *long-term* loyalty) and achieving leverage over a competitor.

Branding gives an added value to the product – a sense that the customer is buying more than simply the item itself. Usually, branding gives identity in visual and verbal terms – for example, the Midland Bank's 1980s gryphon symbol and the slogan 'the listening bank' – but in the case of radio it takes a more diffuse form, as a kind of aural typography (jingles, station identifications or 'idents', trailers) and also through the kind of listening experience that the station offers:

> In a culture dominated by visual icons, radio operates on an experiential rather than tangible plane … for a marketing consultant this may constitute radio's unique selling point. For the purposes of branding a radio station, it points to the creation and reinforcement of an image that relates to listeners' self-image, sense of identity and deeply held values rather than what they can do with the product.
>
> Wilby and Conroy, *The Radio Handbook*, p. 37

In commercial radio, the brand may not just be a single station but a series of stations under the same ownership: the stations may share some programming, but the branding generally signifies a common format, target audience and listening style. Examples in Britain include Kiss, which started as a pirate station in the 1980s and encompassed stations in Manchester, Leeds and London before being bought up by the Chrysalis Group, owners of the Galaxy branded stations. Capital Radio's Gold brand is another example, its unique selling point (USP in marketing parlance) a format aimed at the 44-plus age group and built wholly around records from the 60s, 70s and 80s. Gold stations operate in London, Birmingham, Kent and Hampshire. In 1997, EMAP Radio relaunched its group of similarly pitched 'oldies' stations in Yorkshire under the umbrella name Magic, targeted at a 35–44-year-old market and playing what its managing director Dee Ford described in *Broadcast* as 'contemporary adult music'. The launch was preceded by a £1-million TV and poster advertising campaign based around the copy line 'as if by Magic'. Here, the USP is not so much the content – many other stations offer a similar mix of hit tracks from the 1970s to date – as the low-key nature of the presentation. During drive time, Magic stations (of which there are now a number beyond Yorkshire) feature long sweeps of records punctuated only by idents, advertisements and traffic news.

Commercial radio also brands *itself* to its prime sources of income – advertisers and sponsors – via the Radio Advertising Bureau. (Identically named and similarly functioning bodies exist in both the US and UK.) Britain's RAB is funded by a levy payment from all Radio Authority-licensed stations, based on a percentage of revenue raised from national advertising. It acts as an information point for the industry, collating and commissioning qualitative

Source: Stephen Barnard

Fig. 12.2 The simplest form of station promotion: a bus advertises South Devon's Pirate FM with its on-air slogan, 'the world's greatest music'

and quantitative research into the effectiveness of radio as an advertising medium; it runs training courses and promotes the advantages of radio as an advertising medium to agencies and business.

Branding is not confined to commercial radio. One of the most instantly recognizable 'brands' in the media world – and indeed in the world generally – is the BBC itself. The very initials BBC carry all manner of associations related to history, tradition, high cultural standards and concepts of truth and fairness. Anything that has the BBC's name attached to it capitalizes on these brand values, from magazines like *Radio Times* and *BBC Wildlife* to concert promotions and commercially produced spoken-word cassettes. The BBC's marketing efforts have intensified since the 1980s, when its commercial arm (BBC Enterprises, which published *Radio Times*) was privatized. As part of internal restructuring of the BBC during 1994, BBC Worldwide was formed to co-ordinate and exploit the Corporation's commercial activities at home and abroad. The BBC also has a team of marketing strategists working under the Director of Marketing and Communication, as well as a head of corporate marketing.

The former team was responsible for the relaunch of the poorly performing Radio 5 as Radio 5 Live in 1994 and for the billboard and press advertising campaign that helped reposition Radio 1 in 1995. One of their most spectacular successes was a promotional video designed to build awareness of the BBC's commitment to music, which included a string of artists (each appearing for only a nominal fee) each singing a line of the Lou Reed song

'Perfect Day'. It was released as a single with all proceeds going to the BBC's adopted charity, Children in Need. Commercial stations found that, by playing the record, they were effectively promoting their most serious competitor; they also argued that the BBC had no business putting licence payers' money into an advertising vehicle which it could then play over and over again on its own radio stations.

'Perfect Day' conveyed BBC music as contemporary, diverse and accessible, and it skilfully made some of the less commonly publicised aspects of BBC music – Radio 3, for example – appear undaunting and worth exploring. The message was that the BBC could cater for all while giving space to minority taste and culture, that it could be simultaneously populist and elitist – and even a bridge between the two. (The song was also brilliantly chosen: its lyrics dwelt on the pleasures of being with someone you love throughout the day – which is precisely how the BBC's music radio services would wish their relationship with the listener to be seen.)

The BBC has a political interest in marketing itself: by exploiting the brand – particularly internationally – it can supplement the licence fee, plough more into programming and prove its cost-effectiveness to the politicians who control its purse strings. (During 1998, the BBC commissioned accountants Ernst & Young to study the value of the BBC brand.) In a competitive radio market, the higher profile that its stations receive and the more distinct an identity that they can promote, the more likely is the BBC to keep ahead of the opposition. With the coming of digital services on TV and radio, high-profile marketing on the BBC's own stations helped establish not only the availability and range of the new services but also the BBC's own position at the cutting edge of new technology. In other words, the marketing effectively reinforced the BBC's self-proclaimed primacy in television and radio – something that the ITV and the independent radio networks, because of the number of different providers, could not compete with in the same way. One aspect of the BBC's marketing drive in the 1990s was the brazen way in which all the Corporation's broadcasting outlets – two TV networks, five national radio networks and 39 local radio stations – promoted one another. Not even the parochial world of BBC local radio has been immune from the touch of integrated marketing: in 1998, so-called 'Trailblazer' units were introduced to co-ordinate and produce promotional campaigns across all 39 stations.

ON-AIR BRANDING

Wilby and Conroy define style in a radio context as a 'holistic concept of voice, music, language and topic which fit together in a coherent and inter-related way to create the station's own distinctive sound or signature' (Wilby and Conroy, p. 40). The station's aural identity is usually articulated by means of guidelines to presenters and producers (even to the point of setting time limits on the amount of talk between music), and policed by regular monitoring of output. In some of the more fiercely formatted stations, the programme controller's key task is to work out a programming formula in which all the necessary elements can be smoothly and strategically interpolated, including the points at which a presenter should talk:

> The key thing is that we're a radio station, not a collection of programmes . . . our programming is clinical and disciplined, and the way you do things in radio is actually more important than what you do, it's a 'how' medium. Style is paramount, it's more crucial to sound professional. Style must come before content if you're starting a radio station, because otherwise it will lack a recognisable identity. Style is what matters, the typography of a station comes before anything else, and I don't believe people in my job in other stations are clinical enough or technical enough about what they're doing.
>
> (Bob Snyder, Programme Controller, Radio Trent,
> 1975–78, quoted in Barnard, p. 78)

Likening the fashioning of radio style to typography – the arrangement and appearance of printed matter – is useful. Typography makes the printed word acceptable to the eye but also adds meaning to the text: the selection of a particular typeface can layer the text with connotations – say, a Gothic face for a horror story – and the integration of the text with illustrative material (perhaps a backcloth of graphics, or an arrangement of photographs) can create a holistic effect that is pleasing or possibly deliberately disconcerting. Line and paragraph spacing, indentation, type size, the presentation and positioning of headlines on the printed page all contribute to a text on a stylistic rather than simply decorative level. Just as the printed text in a magazine, newspaper or book gains, through the integration of typography and design, an aesthetic added value, so in radio audio material can be organized to create an experience of listening that goes beyond the simple imparting and receiving of information.

Links, trailers, jingles, sound effects and cyclical features like traffic and weather reports, sports and news bulletins, share-price checks and so on have been likened to the 'punctuation points' of radio, and in purely functional terms they are. Like commas, semi-colons and full stops (periods), jingles and trailers break up the radio 'text' into easily assimilated sections. A jingle identifying the station, programme or presenter will ease the way from one piece of music to the next; it aids continuity, by closing an item and literally clearing the air for the next; it may frame the start and end of commercial breaks; it can indicate a change of mood.

But punctuation is a function of form, not of style: the real value of jingles and all the other punctuation points of radio is that they also double as means of on-air branding. In message and execution, jingles should not only identify the station to the listener – vital in a crowded market – but also exemplify the station's style: as one American radio consultant has put it, jingles are essentially 'image orchestrations' for the station (Keith, p. 30). Jingle packages are usually provided by specialist companies with a range of technical, copywriting and composing skills to draw upon, who work in tandem with the station's marketing department to produce packages that complement and enhance the whole promotional effort, off-air as well as on-air. Jingles can become over-familiar, and it takes an astute programme controller to recognize that it is time for a change; equally, a new jingle package is always at the forefront of any repositioning or major schedule change that a station undergoes.

In radio, music, news items, phone-ins, weather checks are collectively important but individually subservient to the sound of the station, to its aural identity or signature. What matters is the manner in which these elements are framed and presented, and whether the placing and scheduling of these individual items persuades the public to listen and keep listening. Even news can be subject to manipulation in the interests of programme continuity: Virgin Radio, for example, gives a breathless on-the-hour summary with the noise of a busy office in the background, to give a sense of up-to-the-minuteness and, like other stations, limits the summary to just two minutes to discourage listeners from turning their dial in search of music. Even elements that seem to have a purely functional value, such as traffic reports and weather forecasts, have an essentially cosmetic use: they create an impression of pace, mobility and activity which suits the station's self-image and gives the listener an illusion of service.

The one component in the sound package over which programme controllers have no control is also the station's prime revenue source, the commercial: attracting advertisers to the station and the buying in and scheduling of advertisements is the responsibility of the sales department or the sales house of the group to which the station belongs. There have been instances of stations turning down advertising because its style does not tune in with the station's image, or because the music in a commercial blatantly jars with the station's musical emphasis. This can be overcome at a local level by the hiring of in-house staff to conceive and produce commercials for clients (using the station's own facilities) which do the required selling job while taking into account the station's style.

On-air branding need not be wholly dependent on jingles or a strictly policed format, or any of the battery of devices just described. Neither BBC Radios 3 or 4, for example, carry any kind of station identification beyond the spoken 'You're listening to . . .' before each programme. As Wilby and Conroy suggest, even the short silences preceding Radio 4 programmes are eloquent: they add to the slightly imperious and unruffled style that has been a feature of BBC speech programming since the 1920s.

OFF-AIR BRANDING

Radio stations also require a tangible visual identity – especially so at local level, and particularly so at the time of launch. Only through the visual media – press and TV – can the station announce itself, whether through advertising

Source: Stephen Barnard

Fig. 12.3 Capital Radio has a strong visibility throughout central London, thanks to an ongoing billboard advertising campaign and its sponsorship of Leicester Square tube station, the nearest station to its studios

or a concerted public-relations effort. Only by presenting a pictorial equivalent of the station's projected aural style can the station persuade listeners to at least give it a try. This is why almost as much money and energy can be spent on the design of a station logo and developing a promotional strategy as on the programme budget itself.

A logo is the visual means by which a station will be recognized: the most effective and memorable logos incorporate the station name, wavelength and some aspect of the character it wishes to convey. Classic FM's logo features its name in a classic Roman face, to suggest class and a sense of history; LBC features its initials in large quotation marks, to underline its identity as a talk station; Kestrel FM in Basingstoke features a kestrel's head in its logo; Ocean FM in Portsmouth has a fish to underline its coastal connection; The Wolf in Wolverhampton features a wolf howling against the moon. The logo should demand instant recognition, whether seen in advertising, on buses or on car stickers, or at any roadshow event.

Naming, too, can be crucial, as it creates expectations in the listener's mind. Traditionally, radio stations have named themselves after the locality they serve – if not the county or city itself, then some place or geographical feature within it – Essex Radio, Piccadilly Radio (Manchester), Radio Aire (Leeds), Swansea Sound, Plymouth Sound, Devonair, Radio Clyde, Radio Forth, Mercia and so on. Expansion and greater competition – and the ending of

Source: Classic FM Magazine

Fig. 12.4 Classic FM publicizes itself not only by traditional means of branding such as on-air promotions but also through its own magazine, which builds on listener loyalty and generates additional advertising revenue

Source: Essex Radio Group

Fig. 12.5 Station logos give a sense of visual identity to radio stations

simultaneous broadcasting on AM and FM, leaving established stations free to offer differing services – led to different priorities in naming. FM services in particular were renamed with short, snappy titles to emphasize their contemporariness, while new services adopted one-word names to achieve a similar effect (Kiss, Power, Pulse, Spirit, Vibe, Wish, Surf, Mix, Crash). Animal names have been in fashion – Fox FM in Oxford, The Wolf in Wolverhampton, The Bear in Stratford, Ram FM in Derby. There remain stations whose names give no real clues to their programming approach (Liberty, Heart, Gemini, Century, Oasis, Lite, Galaxy, Horizon, Delta) but which are memorable and distinct enough to register in their particular localities.

Publicity and promotion are part of the fabric of radio: they are the means by which stations maintain their visibility in the marketplace. The most visible means of off-air branding are live outside broadcasts from local shopping centres, factories, colleges or schools. Most stations have a roadshow unit –

Source: Heart 106.2FM

Fig. 12.6 Radio hits the road. 'Roadshows' were the invention of former Radio 1 Controller Johnny Beerling in the early 1970s. They can range from visits to local fêtes or festivals to full-scale, heavily promoted ventures such as Capital's Party in the Park and this open-air concert by the Corrs, sponsored by Heart 106.2FM

effectively, a studio on a trailer – which in summer will make a tour of local fêtes, fairs, air shows and so on, with the objective of increasing the profile of the station and helping build a relationship – a point of association – with the audience. The same applies to promotion or sponsorship of local concerts, whether by amateur choral groups or orchestras, or concerts featuring major stars. The former tend to be prestige events, designed to give the station local credibility and prestige; the latter provide opportunities for ticket promotions and competitions.

For its Party in the Park in July 1998, Capital Radio brought together over 30 major pop acts for a line-up designed to appeal to both the young pop fans who make up Capital FM's audience and to their parents. The concert, in Hyde Park, was one of the best attended open-air concerts ever. It illustrated the skilful mix of marketing, self-interest and altruism that often goes into promotions of this kind. The concert was a charity event (in aid of the Prince's Trust), so guaranteed the appearance of high-profile stars at relatively low cost; it was attended by royalty (Princes Charles and Harry) and so became a news event of national interest; it became the major source of programming on Capital FM and its sister stations up and down the country for that day – and the sessions were played on the stations for weeks afterwards. The subsequent (edited) TV coverage and its release on video brought in further revenue. The concert gave endless opportunities for the stars themselves to endorse Capital; and it enabled Capital to highlight a handful of acts (including Conner Reeves and Lutricia MacNeal) who were signed to the station's own record company, Wildstar. Most of all, the concert enhanced Capital's image as London's most aware, most responsive and most popular radio station – and this at a time when Capital's main rival in London, BBC Radio 1, had just devoted much time and energy to covering the Glastonbury Festival, which had taken place in a quagmire and had featured bands that may have fitted the station's 'cutting edge' profile but had none of the immediate resonance of the acts in Party in the Park. In short, Party in the Park demonstrated Capital's *inclusiveness* in action.

PRESENTERS

Branding is a marketing matter, which is why, in many radio stations, the promotions manager has a status comparable with that of the programme controller. But the people with the main responsibility for ensuring that the station's style is maintained, amplified and exemplified on a daily basis are the presenters. They are the voice and the public face of the station: what they say, how they conduct themselves, and their attitude to the listeners is all-important in establishing the personality and approachability of a station.

Stations recruit presenters primarily on the basis of how well they suit the station's audience profile and fit the station's brand image. A DJ with a club background is unlikely to fit well with a 'golden oldies' format; a small community-based station in the Welsh valleys or the Scottish highlands is likely to favour local accents over those from the English home counties. It is the policy of some stations not to recruit on a 'personality' basis at all, but to favour virtually anonymous presenters who keep to a prescribed style of minimal talk; others have a policy of recruiting nationally known names for key slots in the schedule – former Radio 1 DJs, for example, find a natural retirement home on Gold stations, where they play much of the same music they were associated with during their BBC prime. Radio 2 has long had a policy of hiring presenters with little or no radio experience at all – ex-*Daily Express* editor Derek Jameson, TV game show host Sarah Kennedy, BBC TV gardener Alan Titchmarsh – on the basis that personalities with an established appeal to the over-35s always attract good audiences. Talk stations such as Radio 5 Live and Talk Radio itself favour ex-DJs with a populist and slightly abrasive edge – Nicky Campbell, Chris Ashley – who can hold their own in an argument. Radio 1 has always been a personality-led station, from the 'Smashey and Nicey' era of the 70s and 80s so skilfully parodied by Harry Enfield and Paul Whitehouse – an era when DJs lived for opening supermarkets and talked endlessly of their work for 'charidy' – to the days of Chris Evans and Zoë Ball, each of whom were well known as TV personalities before working for the station.

Presenters are the cheery, matey voice of local radio in particular – the

Source: Talk Radio

Fig. 12.7 Talk Radio's breezy tabloid-style promotions are an extension of the station's personality. This 1998 competition was promoted by means of a national newspaper insert

important personal link between station and audience, their role (depending on the station) often combining that of entertainer, counsellor, professional Everyman, permanent PR man, interviewer of the great and the good, expert on the day's news, fascinated questioner on everything from antiques to veterinary bills, and source of perpetual good humour and repartee. Mixing elements of straightforward announcing, reporting, news reading and stand-up comedy, the radio presenter is (especially at local level) a broadcasting jack-of-all-trades floating uneasily between the two worlds of show business and journalism.

Presenters shoulder the main responsibility for the success of music radio as entertainment, and like any entertainers they fall prey to delusions of grandeur and an exaggerated view of their own importance. The most overbearing tends

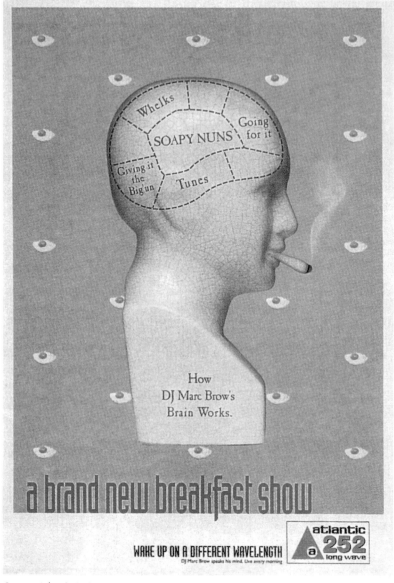

Source: Atlantic 252

Fig. 12.8 Atlantic 252's relaunch in 1999 was promoted by means of a series of cryptic, offbeat posters and press advertisements aimed at a young, hip listenership

to see his audience as a community united around him, and the tell-tale signs are an over-defensiveness in interviews, a cultivated anti-intellectualism and an inordinate stress on the size of his programme's postbag. But if disc jockeys are entertainers, they are also sales reps. DJs sell themselves and their station; they record voiceovers for radio and television commercials. One of the most important training grounds for DJs are the in-shop studios to be found at stores like Top Shop, where they nudge customers towards bargain offers or new-to-store lines between custom-made jingles and bursts of Simply Red.

CASE STUDY: BRANDING AT XFM

The tone and content of the promotional work undertaken in the station's name can provide telling insights into the station's personality, style and ambience, and how it perceives itself and its audience. The launch of the London station Xfm in September 1997 is a good case in point. Xfm won a licence on the basis of catering for an audience which the Radio Authority decided was overlooked by daytime radio in London – consumers of 'indie' music, a problematic term usually applied to rock music pitched as an alternative to mainstream music. ('Indie' is an abbreviation of 'independent' and once referred to the music produced and distributed by independently-run record companies.) Xfm was in fact conceived as a distinctive 'brand' of radio – in its own description, 'of cutting-edge alternative music' – and plans were announced, well before the station's start date, to spread the brand by bidding for licences in central Scotland, north-east England and urban areas such as Greater Manchester.

The estimated media spend on the launch was £1 million. This included the cost of branding all seats, escalators and passageways at Camden tube station with the Xfm logo for a 12-month period; TV advertising on Channel 4 and MTV over a two-week period; and funding numerous promotional concerts around the city. The nature of the branding was significant: Channel 4 and MTV attracted a profile of the kind of young, aware media consumers that Xfm wished to pull in, while Camden – home of the Gallagher brothers from the rock band Oasis – was at the time the acknowledged heart of trendy, streetwise London.

That advertisements were placed in *The Guardian*'s weekend section reveals something about the perceived target listenership – hip, media-aware, pleasure-seeking but discriminating. On a simple denotative level, the advertisements informed the reader of Xfm's existence and how to find it (its wavelength), but they also worked on a connotative level: the muddied graphics suggested something off-centre, unconventional and contemporary, while the copy line ('If other stations are middle of the road, we're lying drunk in a ditch') used established terminology from the radio and music industries – 'middle of the road' meaning conventional and inoffensive – to connote a whiff of disrepute, challenge and non-sobriety. It was an advertisement that risked impressing a minority by excluding a majority, but risk-taking is part of the brand's values that is implicitly hinted at here. The advertisement promised difference and alternativism, but also assumed readers' identification with those values. Literally, it talked their language.

The advertisement 'worked' in the sense that it immediately made clear where the brand stood in relation to its competitors (although the competitors

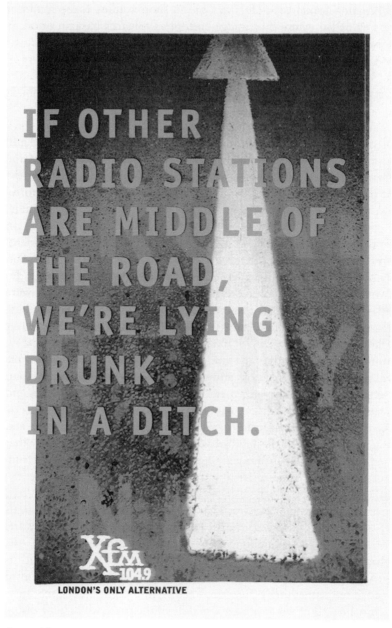

Source: Xfm

Fig. 12.9 Pre-launch advertisement for Xfm placed in *The Guardian* and *Time Out*, August 1997

were all tarred with the same brush), and it had an element of 'attitude' which is a familiar feature of advertising to the teenage and student market. But Xfm had an unfortunate history. It began broadcasting on 1 September 1997, the day after Diana, Princess of Wales, was killed – a day when every station in the country amended its programming to reflect a sombre, reflective mood. Its initial listening figures were poor, it was criticized heavily at a radio industry conference, and losses stood at £1.7 million by the end of December 1997. Within a year it was taken over by Capital Radio and transformed into a supposedly more inclusive kind of 'indie' station. Part of its problem, according to some industry observers, was that the station failed to deliver the promise of its advertising, not so much in the music it played (though its music policies were criticized) as in its absence of a truly attitudinal style. Its presentation was too low-key compared to that of stations which traded on a different kind of alternativism, notably dance music stations like Kiss FM, which recreated a club ambience on radio and featured clubland DJs. In the end, for all the shrewdness of its promotional work, it lacked an identifiable personality or, to put it another way, a really distinct aural style. When Capital re-launched the station, one of its first acts was to bring in one of the most voluble and opinionated personalities on the rock scene (albeit somebody with limited presenting experience), Bob Geldof, to present the weekday drive-time sequence. A well organized and concerted campaign by some of Xfm's original hard core of listeners failed to change Capital's strategy and by mid-1999 the new owners were announcing plans to introduce live football commentary on Saturday and some Sunday afternoons in tandem with similar coverage on Capital's AM station, Capital Gold. The issue now was not that Xfm listeners would no longer be able to hear alternative music for a significant part of each weekend – they would no longer be able to hear music at all.

Further reading

Barnard, Stephen (1989): *On the Radio: Music Radio in Britain*. Open University Press.
Keith, Michael C. (1987): *Radio Programming: Consultancy and Formatics*. Focal Press.
Rider, David (1977): *Happy Birthday Radio 1*. Everest.
Wilby, Pete, and Conroy, Andy (1994): *The Radio Handbook*. Routledge.

Activity 12.1

Assess the public 'visibility' of a radio station in your area. Over a period of a week, keep a record of where and in what circumstances you come across (1) advertisements for the station (for example, posters on buses or taxis, concert promotions), (2) mentions of the station in the local press, (3) sponsorship of local events, and (4) involvement in local events by means of roadshows or live outside broadcasts. What kind of public image of the station does all this add up to?

Activity 12.2

Study the promotional flyer for Talk Radio reproduced on page 213.

1. What impression does the flyer give you of Talk Radio as a whole? Does it reinforce or confront your expectations of what Talk Radio is like?
2. What is the purpose of the flyer and the competition that it promotes? How might the station judge its effectiveness?
3. In which newspapers or magazines would you expect the flyer to be inserted? Justify your reasons in terms of the readership profile of the publications concerned.
4. How else does Talk Radio promote itself?

Activity 12.3

The advertisement reproduced on page 214 was part of a re-branding exercise carried out by Atlantic 252 during 1999.

1. Consider the brand values which the advertisement conveys. At which age and social group is the re-branding pitched? What sense of the station does the design and copy give you? What would you expect the station's music policy to be?
2. In what kind of advertising environment would you expect the advertisement to be placed?
3. Sketch out three or four ideas for follow-up advertisements that build on the brand values you have identified.

Activity 12.4

Make a study of the programmes of one particular presenter on any radio station of your choice. Who is the focal point of the shows – the station, the listener or the presenter? What sense of personality do you derive from the kind of language he or she uses and the references he or she makes?

13

Ideology and Representations

In previous chapters, our concern has been with the content and manner of broadcast output, how it is programmed and the prevalence of certain modes of presentation. Now we can turn to the cumulative impact of all this – the attitudes and ideologies encapsulated by radio programming. What kind of perspective on life, on relationships, on the world around us, has the medium of radio traditionally offered the listener? How far is radio's view of the world a reliable one? What, finally, is the underlying message that radio mediates to its listenership – and can it be reshaped or challenged?

Throughout literature, film and popular culture in general, radio has traditionally been seen as a repressive influence, controlling thought processes and inspiring either mindless compliance or apathy. George Orwell's *1984* (published in 1949) remains one of the most chilling accounts of thought manipulation in all literature: much of the raw material for the book, its depiction of the stifling effect of bureaucracy on the individual, drew on Orwell's experiences working for the propaganda-led foreign service of the BBC in London during World War Two. Aldous Huxley's *Brave New World* (1932) depicts radio as having a more insidious impact, as a purveyor of sweet, pacifying music and relentless good cheer. The experience of totalitarianism, whether observed at close quarters or from afar, gave popular culture a perhaps clichéd view of radio as a disingenuously friendly and manipulative medium.

Orwell and Huxley were writing at a time when broadcasting was truly a mass medium, limited to a single provider. It is less easy to articulate certainties about the ideology of broadcasting when the broadcasting map is itself much more fragmented, when the pressures of the marketplace dictate different perceptions of the audience, and when the availability of broadcast media as a whole – terrestrial TV, cable, satellite, the Internet and so on – is growing.

RADIO'S WORLD VIEW

Any medium acts as a filter of information; all media activity is selective. Within radio, certain messages, stories, musical styles, tones of voice predominate – sometimes as a deliberate act of policy, sometimes unconsciously. Much of radio programming is based on an *assumed shared recognition* of certain perceptions of the world. These meanings, however, are never wholly fixed but are constantly shifting.

Ideology refers to a set of values drawn from a partial, selective view of reality. Radio has been wilfully and artfully used down the years, especially by totalitarian states, to inculcate the dominant ideology of the state and its politics. In late 20th-century western societies, however, a much more subtle process has been at work, complicated by a multiplicity of media owners and 'gatekeepers'. Marxist theory offers the straightforward paradigm that those with money naturally exert the most power and influence, and that those in control of the media wish to protect their own interests – i.e. the status quo – through the media itself. Put simplistically, in a capitalist society, television, radio and the press act to legitimize political systems. So the inequalities of daily life, the struggles of class, are portrayed as natural, unchallengeable; entertainment itself, Marxism suggests, is a means of neutralizing that struggle by encouraging passivity and a cult of bread and circuses.

Against this, one must place the conventional, disingenuous view that the media as a whole – and radio in particular, because of the regulatory battery surrounding it and the enshrinement of political neutrality in law – is simply reflective of the way things are. The mirror theory denies the selectivity and gatekeeping processes at work in defining what is heard, seen and written about. What is *not* featured on radio is as much a clue to the medium's ideology as what *is* featured. Gramsci's hegemonic model refines this perspective still further, and in a manner that underlines the subtleties and complexities of the relationship between media ownership, the state and the audience. According to Gramsci, the success of many western societies in avoiding the kind of outright revolutionary struggles witnessed in more 'backward' societies can be put down to the forging of a common ground between the ruling class and the populace, in other words by the skill of the ruling class in ingratiating itself with 'common' values. The media has been a prime force in this success, and certain key moments in history illuminate the point – the BBC's supposed neutrality at the time of the General Strike in 1926, and the endorsement of Margaret Thatcher by the Murdoch press in the 1980s. The forging of national identity is a prime product of hegemony, repeated and continually *reinforced* as a received wisdom, as a set of defined values handed down like a birthright – which is what nationhood is. Today's agenda-setters, the hegemonic argument goes, have no need to create a new ideological framework: it exists as myth already.

To attempt to define a single ideology within radio would be mistaken: of more concern is how radio, both independently and in consort with other media, reinforces (and at times challenges, because these values are never wholly fixed) dominant ideologies. What one can identify – certainly in British radio – are tendencies towards a conservatism of outlook, primarily rooted in the domestic context of the medium; radio's relationship, generally junior and subordinate, to other media; the pressure for immediacy in news and reaction; the traditional institutional conservatism of radio, through the BBC and an actively regulatory Radio Authority; pressure from advertisers to provide programming that acts as a vehicle and setting for advertising; increasingly refined evaluation of audiences; the mobility of the workforce within stations and media owners, including the BBC; the pressure to deliver an audience quickly, and in numbers, which discourages experimentation and the pursuit of diversity. The ideological impact of radio must be traced through the kind of values its programmes and presenters – collectively, over a period of time – predominantly convey.

THE DOMESTIC DAY

Radio's values have traditionally been domestic, family-based and built on a belief in the primacy of work. One can see in the very pattern of daytime programming from the 1930s to date a reflection of the prevalent ideology of man as breadwinner, woman as housewife. This was disrupted by the war and the conscription of women for war work, but the post-war Light Programme implicitly reflected government objectives to encourage women to vacate the factories and return to a domestic role while their menfolk resumed their own 'natural' role. The pattern of programmes began with light music, continued with *Housewives' Choice* (record requests from home-based women), featured *Music While You Work* (ostensibly for the factories, but equally a 15-minute section of uninterrupted music as a background to housework) and *Listen With Mother* (as its title suggested, a programme for pre-school children) and also included *Woman's Hour*. By the 1960s, embellishments included a half hour of music for teenagers at lunchtime, with drama and documentaries generally left to the weekends or weekday evenings. Each day, and indeed each programme, was built on routine: *Housewives' Choice*, for example, had an air of free and easy gentility but was ruthlessly scripted and policed, so that each selection of records reflected a similar pattern. Every listener knew that the classical request could always be heard as the last item on the programme.

The pattern is not so different in the closing years of the century. Breakfast-time programmes ease the way to work, whether offering news, music, interviews or a mixture of all three. After 9am, there is a noticeable change of tone, reflecting an assumption that more women are listening; around lunchtime, a concentration on news; during drive-time (4pm onwards), a switch back to a faster-paced programming, punctuated by travel reports to ease the way back home. Radio punctuates the routine and in some ways even polices it. How many listeners time their leaving of the home according to particular points in the breakfast show of their choice?

The working day is, implicitly, held out as the norm – even one to which those not fortunate to have a job are encouraged to aspire to, via joblines and reports on the latest vacancies from local job centres. Radio *frames* the working day as no other medium does, as it can provide a constant accompaniment. In so doing, it acts to *validate* the working experience, offering a means by which to tolerate it, a soundtrack to escape from it, and also a constant reminder that – in effect – one is not alone. Going to work becomes a shared experience, work itself an inclusive experience. The weekend, too, looms large in radio talk, especially as the week goes on: the weekend is traditionally a time of designated leisure, offering escape, reward and replenishment after a week of work.

REPRESENTATIONS AND STEREOTYPES

A major concern of media studies is how the various mass communications media represent their audience. Representation has a double meaning: it implies that the medium or its 'representatives' speak and act on behalf of their viewers, readers or listeners, but it also means 're-presentation' in the sense of presenting to the audience a picture of itself. But neither radio nor any other medium can accurately and faithfully reproduce the world as it is: however benign or objective is the medium's agenda, it can only select, pinpoint and highlight. Everything we see, hear and read is an interpretation from one of an infinite number of possible perspectives. The issue for the mass media is how they can interpret, select and arbitrate with the maximum fairness and objectivity towards their audiences as communities and as individuals. In the end, do the communities that radio serves recognize themselves in how they are portrayed and addressed on the air?

A familiar theme in media studies is how different media perpetuate constructions that have strong ideological foundations, such as nationhood and the family unit – constructions that have a basis in the human need for social connection. Such constructions have complex historical, even mythical roots and the role of the BBC, during the first three decades of its existence at least, was to reify and legitimize them as a matter of deliberate, proactive policy. For example, it was the BBC under Reith that was largely responsible for popularizing the concept of the royal family as a symbolic family around which the nation and the empire could rally.

Much has been written about how media texts such as advertisements, news bulletins and television dramas draw on stereotypes in their depiction of people. Stereotypes offer an easy shortcut to comprehension, in that they play on exaggerated representations of familiar and commonly held perspectives. Stereotyping is endemic to radio research and the categorization of listeners (actual and potential) according to social class, gender and age. It is the *interpretation* of this data and the catalogue of assumptions made on the basis of it regarding tastes, interests and propensities that drives the content of programmes and how people are represented (and addressed) within them.

Television programmes and press coverage have been frequently criticized for being too ready to resort to stereotypes in representing gender, age and race. Examples include the depiction of women as submissive and passive, men as football-obsessed and insensitive to women's feelings, youth as a 'problem', and blacks as lazy or criminally inclined or both. That such constructions prevail has sometimes been related to the lack (or at least the lack of visibility) of women, young people and blacks in decision-making positions in the respective media. As a medium that draws heavily on television and press for programme material, a similar stereotyping is perhaps inevitable on radio, though it is obviously an *aural* depiction that radio conveys – mediated through language and nuance rather than visual codes. The absence of visual representation might suggest that issues of racism and ageism are less contentious in radio than in other media, because the skin colour and age of the speaker is invisible to the audience. What matters, however, is how gender, social class, age and race are represented in the daily routine of radio content.

Regarding age, previous chapters indicated how music policies can be fashioned to appeal to particular age groups. Within commercial radio, the reasons are primarily economic: the stations create programming to match the tastes of age groups at which advertisers aim their products. BBC radio took a strategic decision in the early 1990s to redefine Radio 1 in age terms by switching from an all-inclusive teens-to-40s appeal to a much narrower 15–25-year-old base – not out of any economic considerations but to strengthen its credibility and identity as a youth music station. Even though the station lost literally millions of listeners over a period of years, that loss was deemed not only acceptable but necessary, as it made a positive impact on the numbers listening to Radio 2, which repositioned itself as a station with a core age base of 25–45.

But the creation of age-specific programming is rife with difficulty. It entails making gross assumptions about the tastes of particular age groups, especially in relation to music. The strategy in relation to Radio 1 in the early to mid 1990s was conceived and enacted by management and presenters who were themselves a good deal older than the audience they assumed to speak for. The resulting music policy was in fact heavily criticized for being too biased towards 'indie' music and 'Britpop', with too little account taken either of dance music culture or the traditional Top 40-oriented pop music of boy bands like Boyzone and Take That. Radio 1's representation of youth was itself selective and partial.

Most curious of all is British radio's attitude to children and the elderly. Commercial radio has traditionally fought shy of catering for either age range, but this hasn't stopped Capital Radio from applying for a franchise to operate a children's station (Fun Radio) or Saga – a company specializing in holidays and products for the over-50 market – from applying to run an over-50s station. Capital's model is the network of children's stations run in the US by Disney, while Saga's argument rests with the growing affluence of senior citizens with a high level of disposable income. BBC radio programmes for children, meanwhile, are now limited to just a programme on children's books and an occasional Sunday evening serial.

The perceived shortcomings of BBC and commercial stations with regard to black and Asian audiences was a major push behind the impetus for community radio in Britain during the 1980s – particularly the sense that these audiences were being ghettoized into the low-funded 'minority' slots of mid-evening and weekends. Funding for ethnic minority programmes within BBC local radio comes from the station's education budget and responsibility for them has traditionally rested with education producers, some seconded from teaching positions at local colleges. There remains an unmistakable sense of dispensed liberal favour about the programmes that result, although the BBC's Asian Network, networked across BBC stations in the Midlands, is comparatively well resourced and has a high penetration among Asian communities. It is the lack of black and Asian voices on mainstream daytime radio that reflects least kindly on British radio's representation of non-white listeners.

'LOOK AFTER YOURSELF': THE SELF AS CENTRE

The language of daytime radio is the language of individualism. The conversational tone emphasizes the intimate nature of the relationship between listener and presenter or radio station. The message is 'you are not alone', and is exemplified by three particular stereotypes of listener on which stations like to draw – the lone female at home, the male traveller in his car, and the student in his or her bedroom.

Individualism also finds its most potent expression in radio programming through a focus on aspiration and achievement, on solving problems (or at least finding a temporary resolution to them) and making things better. In commercial radio, this can be related partly to the fact that advertisements are never more than a few minutes away: advertisements sell products or services by appealing to individual 'needs' (for gratification, love, comfort, influence, power and so on), and the most effective radio advertisements dramatize those needs in a personal way – through contrived conversations, for example. But even in non-commercial radio, a similar emphasis on consumption is evident, though weighted more towards consumerism – obtaining redress for consumers from manufacturers or retailers, highlighting listeners' complaints regarding shoddy goods or failure to give refunds, and advising on consumer law. Radio 4 has a weekday programme, *You and Yours*, focusing solely on consumer issues, and a daily segment of Jimmy Young's Radio 2 show does the same. Local radio stations have phone-in programmes featuring representatives from the local Citizens Advice Bureau or the Consumers' Association.

So complementing the message 'you are not alone' is a parallel message, 'we are here to help'. Radio 4's speech output includes what are basically advice programmes – *Money Box*, *The Food Programme*, *In Touch* (for visually impaired listeners), *Gardeners' Question Time*. *Woman's Hour* has a strong advice element, running features and interviews on issues such as women's health or nursery provision. Radio 1 went through a period in the late 1980s of concentration on what was termed 'social action' broadcasting – running documentaries and phone-ins around issues such as safe sex, drug abuse and teenage runaways.

Phone-ins on consumer and money matters, legal affairs, crime prevention, employment issues and benefit entitlements are common features of the local radio landscape. They are often tied in with promotional events devised by organizations such as the Law Society or government ministries or quangos – for example, a 'write your will' week devised to promote the services of solicitors, or a national 'leave your car at home' day designed to focus attention on reducing pollution. Each August, when A-level results are issued, national and local stations operate advice lines for would-be students in search of a college place.

There is a classic liberal middle-class agenda at work here – a transference of the culture of the caring professions (social work, teaching, medicine) to a broadcasting context. It reflects a certain nannyism – that the broadcasters know what's best for us – that has always been a part of the BBC's paternalistic values, but it also has a strongly individualistic edge: the programmes, advice features, phone lines and back-up literature are designed to be *enabling,* to give the individual the means or incentive to improve his or her lot. It helps the station present itself as a dispenser of advice and care, paralleling television and popular journalism. Matters of physical and emotional health, for example, have been a strong feature of women's magazine journalism since the 1940s: phone-in programmes are in some ways a radio counterpart of the traditional 'agony' column, to which people write in search of a resolution to personal dilemmas. Two of the most familiar 'agony aunts' and 'uncles' of contemporary radio are Anna Raeburn and Philip Hodson, who came to radio from writing just these type of columns for magazines such as *Woman* and *Forum.*

A culture of self-improvement is a feature of daytime television, from keeping fit and healthy eating to more blatantly playful programmes of the *Can't Cook, Won't Cook* kind. There has been a noticeable shift since the early 90s from straightforward programmes of tips and advice on such pursuits as cookery, gardening and do-it-yourself to more obviously aspirational programmes based on the concept of holding the perfect party (Ainsley Harriot's *Having a Party*) or decorating a house in a particularly individualistic way *(Changing Rooms).* Radio, too, has its fair share of local cooks (usually restaurant owners), gardeners (often garden centre managers), builders, astrologers and tarot card readers who advise listeners on a regular basis. A chef and a clairvoyant may seem worlds apart, but they earn their place on the air for the same reasons – because they represent expertise in a field of 'professional' mystique; because the listener can enjoy, for snatches at a time, the benefit of their professional advice; and because their perspective is one of help.

All this can be a fairly inexpensive way of filling airtime, relying on the often unpaid contributions of local 'experts' from law or accountancy firms, the local branch of the DHSS, the police and so on, who shoulder listener enquiries while the presenter acts as host and intermediary. Such programmes enable the station to claim a direct role in bettering the lives of its listeners, and one clothed in a personal language – the one-to-one conversation of a phone-call, heard by a third party in the privacy of their own personal space. Whether or not he or she actually takes part in the programme, the listener is invited to *share* in the experience and gain direct personal benefit from it, on the principle that a trouble shared is a trouble halved.

The presenter's role in all this is to keep a 'professional' eye on the proceedings by interpolating the usual battery of time-checks, trailers and station identifiers when required, and also to act as a kind of layman's representative – seeking explanation of technical terminology, perhaps, or steering the discussion in (or away from) a particular direction. The presenter and his or her production team (if applicable) will take the 'professional' decisions as to which calls to feature, how long to give the caller and when to end the call. The presenter remains unequivocally in charge throughout, mediating in a literal sense between expert (a figure of authority and knowledge) and listener. The relationship is in fact a near-perfect example of radio's role as mediator, in that it illustrates the limitations and something of the illusion of the medium: the impression given is of instant access to a figure of authority, of the laying bare of a problem and the shared discovery of a potential resolution to it, while simulating the confidentiality of a doctor's surgery or psychotherapist's consulting room. The reality is that there is – obviously – no confidentiality at all, that only a handful of perhaps scores of callers will have their problems aired, and that the resolution is at best temporary. The editorial priorities of such programmes perhaps relate more to what problems make 'good radio' than to the real needs of listeners. But whatever the real motivations of the broadcasters, the *image* that radio conveys – its outward ideology and culture – is tied in with notions of support, comfort, advice and resolution.

CASE STUDY: HOUSEWIVES' CHOICE?

Anne Karpf has been forthright in her criticism of what she sees as an institutionalizd sexism within British radio. Writing in 1979, she pointed to the almost complete lack of women as phone-in hosts, quizmasters [*sic*] and daytime radio presenters and to the fantasy world that male DJs convey (Karpf, pp. 41–53). Women's voices, she suggested, tended to be restricted to women's 'issue' programmes such as *Woman's Hour* and to women seeking advice on medical or child-rearing matters on phone-ins – where the advice-giver was invariably a trained male doctor or paediatrician. Rosalind Coward, Dorothy Hobson and the Women's Media Group developed similar theses during the 1980s, with Coward making a particularly telling connection between daytime radio and the loneliness of house-tied mothers in her book *Female Desire*. She showed how the features of a typical Capital Radio daytime show – the dedications of records to loved ones, the romantic bias in pop music itself, even the horoscopes that only half-jokingly promise romantic encounters – are all geared to the emotional lives of women. 'Daytime radio works to validate the choices which women have made,' she wrote. 'The phase of their lives when they went to parties, experienced their carnival of emotions, is treated nostalgically as part of a comfortable personal history ... [it] tells women who are isolated and at home, and possibly very fed up, that the choices which they made were OK' (Coward, p. 145).

Coward identifies an assumption that the rooting of musical meaning in memory or evocative value, not in straight musical appreciation, is an intrinsically 'feminine' concern. Conversely, valuing the music *as* music – and actively pursuing a passionate interest in it – is seen as a masculine interest, of which collecting records is one aspect. During the 80s, Simon Bates interpolated a daily slot called 'Our Tune' into his mid-morning show, for which listeners were invited to pick a track associated with particularly strong memories of an event, person or time. A piece of lush orchestral music, played gently under Bates's voice, would set the tone for a story of personal upset or tragedy – a child born to a father shortly to die of cancer, a marriage that both sets of parents said would never work and didn't – that acted as a prelude for the song in question. 'Our Tune' was hugely popular, attracting the biggest postbag of any feature or programme on BBC radio and also the highest listening figures, and it exemplified many of the ideological characteristics

'Sometimes, the search for a real mother doesn't bring the happiness people hope it will. Nicola, from Lancashire, shows how.' December 1986 ('A Different Corner', George Michael)

'When couples find love the second time around, there are often terrible pressures – especially when children are concerned. Melanie and Nigel found out just how terrible the pressures can be.' January 1987 ('Bright Eyes', Art Garfunkel)

'There is nothing worse than truly not knowing what you want in life. And if you can't make a decision, then you could end up a loser all round. Michael has found that out the hard way.' January 1989 ('I Knew You Were Waiting', Aretha Franklin and George Michael)

'People will sometimes endure the most terrible torture – mental and physical – in the belief that they love someone. And they will endure it for many, many years until finally they can take no more. But Clare's story proves that after the pain and the hurt can come true happiness.' April 1989 ('Suddenly', Billy Ocean)

'The hardest part about relationships is talking to each other. Many people write to tell me that they think they'd still be with their loved ones if they had talked more. Pete found out the hard way.' April 1990 ('Temptation', Wet Wet Wet)

Source: Simon Bates, *Our Tune* (Arrow)

Fig. 13.1 Extracts from 'Our Tune', the Simon Bates Show, BBC Radio 1

discussed in this chapter. The letters themselves were never read directly to microphone but consisted of Bates' extemporization – in effect, his own interpretation – of what the letter said. It thereby foregrounded Bates as mediator between audience/listener and problem, enhancing his status as star, and drawing out some implicit moral or message – always let your loved ones know where you are, don't leave things hanging, don't take people for granted, time is a great healer, we only have one life. As Martin Montgomery points out, in a detailed analysis of the structure, narrative and meaning of 'Our Tune', the feature's main ideological focus was the family: 'although the family may be destabilised by various life crises in the course of the 'Our Tune' narrative, the narrative trajectory is one which reinstates the equilibrium of the family at the end, so that basically it reproduced in narrative terms the family as a normative order . . . "the family" as a potent narrative seems to survive within our culture precisely because it is the most generally and perhaps the only available way of imagining the small community and so mediating between the individual and society' (Montgomery, pp. 172–3).

Central to the idealization of the family is the depiction of the woman as wife, mother and home-maker, and the 'housewife' has long been a prime focus of BBC radio mythology. The idea of a diligent, houseproud, housebound wife running a household and taking on the day-to-day responsibility of bringing up children originated in the immediate post-war period and was for many years encapsulated in the Light Programme's *Housewives' Choice*, heard on every working day (including Saturdays) between 9am (later 8.30am) and 9.55am. Sandwiched neatly between taking the children to school and going shopping, the programme was designed as a reward to the female populace for giving up their wartime occupations in the munitions factories and service industries and returning to an almost wholly domestic role. *Woman's Hour* began in 1946, its arrival paralleling the growth of women's magazines like *Woman's Mirror* and *Housewife*, which gave a similar mixture of consumer advice, romantic fiction, practical items such as recipes and cleaning suggestions, human-interest features and advice on personal matters. Their ideological strength came from the fact that they were edited and written largely by women, so did not have the air of a dispensed sexism.

But radio offers more than just a commentary on or practical guide to domestic tasks: looking beyond the factual content of broadcasting, it is the message inherent in daytime radio – the seemingly inconsequential chat, the lyrics of the music played, the relationship of the (mainly male) presenter to the audience, and the depiction of women in the commercials – that reveals radio's true perception of and attitude towards the female listener.

The daytime presenter is in the front line of the maintenance of radio's domestic ideology, and the sexism at work in the patter of 1970s and 80s disc jockeys such as David Hamilton and Tony Blackburn has passed into legend. Many of the presenters who found their way into commercial radio at this time came via industrial stations such as UBN (United Biscuits Network), which trained their presenters in the art of speaking to a captive, mainly female workforce – jollying them along, reassuring them of the value of their work, making great play of being a male in an all-female world. A number of UBN-trained presenters later moved into management positions within ILR.

It might be argued that this kind of reading of radio programmes perpetuates an image of female listeners as passive recipients of a dominant and manipulative ideology – a variation on the familiar depiction of women as victims. It is also a reading rooted very much in its time – the 70s and 80s, the days of 'Our Tune', when Radio 1's listening figures were at their height – while the 90s have seen women move into major presenting positions in music and talk radio, and there is less of a tendency to target women as the sole daytime listening audience. The two presenters who most represent Radio 1's reconstructed self-image in the late 1990s are women with very different public personas – Zoë Ball, the fun-loving, swear-word-dropping, Manchester United-supporting, tabloid-reading ladette and drinking pal of the stars, who has the third most listened to breakfast show in Britain (after Terry Wogan and the *Today* programme); and Jo Whiley, knowledgeable rock fan and mother, late-night Channel 4 host and champion of indie music. Profiled in lifestyle magazines and recruited for voiceovers, commercials and product endorsements, do they each in their way represent a new kind of stereotype?

Further reading

Baehr, Helen, and Ryan, Michele (1984): *Shut Up and Listen! Women and Local Radio*. Comedia.

Bates, Simon (1990): *Our Tune*. Arrow.

Coward, Rosalind (1984): *Female Desire: Women's Sexuality Today*. Paladin.

Garfield, Simon (1998): *The Nation's Favourite: The True Adventures of Radio 1*. Faber & Faber.

Gramsci, Antonio (1985): *Selections from Cultural Writings*. Lawrence & Wishart.

Hobson, Dorothy (1980): 'Housewives and the mass media' in Stuart Hall et al. (eds), *Culture, Media, Language*. Hutchinson.

Karpf, Anne (1980): 'Women and radio' in Helen Baehr (ed.), *Women and Media*. Pergamon Press.

Montgomery, Martin (1991): '"Our Tune": a study of a discourse genre' in Paddy Scannell (ed.), *Broadcast Talk*. Sage.

Scannell, Paddy (1996): *Radio, Television and Modern Life*. Blackwell.

Activity 13.1

Make a special study of the weekend output of a chosen radio station. How does it differ from weekday daytime output in terms of timing, pace, style, content and approach? What differences are there between Saturday and Sunday programmes? Who is the programming aimed at, and what assumptions regarding people's leisure time underlie it?

Activity 13.2

From a day of broadcasting on any commercial radio station, analyse how women are represented in terms of (1) the broadcasting functions that women perform – as presenters, reporters, interviewers, etc.; (2) the number of stories or items featuring women as the main subject; and (3) the frequency or otherwise with which women appear in advertisements. On the basis of your research, what general conclusions might be drawn about the 'visible' role of women in commercial radio?

Activity 13.3

Test the points made in this chapter about the emphasis on self-improvement and individualism in phone-in programmes by listening to as many such programmes as possible over a period of seven days. Note the range of topics covered – possibly anything from gardening and do-it-yourself to astrology or self-defence – and, in the case of commercial radio, the advertising and sponsorship that the programming attracts. What assumptions are made about listeners' aspirations and attitudes? Where are the 'experts' drawn from, and how is their credibility emphasized? Assess the kind of advice given and the professionalism and expert knowledge (or otherwise) of the voices dispensing it.

Activity 13.4

'Our Tune' was a long-running feature on Simon Bates' Radio 1 programme during the 1980s and early 90s. Study the extracts reproduced in Figure 13.1. All are framing references designed to draw the listener into the story and make him or her want to hear more, and all were originally broadcast at 11am on a weekday.

1. What kind of narrative conventions are at work here, and to which other radio forms is 'Our Tune' most analagous? See Bates' own comments about the feature in Bates (1990) and Garfield (1998), and Martin Montgomery's analysis of the feature (1991).
2. Attempts to revive 'Our Tune' on other stations have not been particularly successful. Consider whether the feature was a product of its time, and the extent to which such a feature disrupts the flow of music radio.

Part Five

Perspectives

Nation shall speak peace unto nation.

BBC motto, 1927

Everyone has the right . . . to seek, receive and impart information and ideas through any media and regardless of frontiers

Universal Declaration of Human Rights

Radio is a medium of global penetration. Wavelengths are subject to international negotiation and allocation, while bodies such as the European Union develop policies on regulation and technological convergence that impact significantly on the broadcasting ecology of member states. Every country in the world has its own radio services, and the technology of radio enables the same services – and those specifically targeted at expatriates or citizens of former colonies – to be heard way beyond political boundaries. At the start of the 21st century as much as during World War Two or the subsequent Cold War, radio remains a weapon in the psychological and ideological battleground between hostile nations.

Although the commercial and public service models established by American radio and the BBC in Britain have had a profound influence on the development of national broadcasting services throughout the world, radio on a world scale remains a multiplicity of formats and systems. To map these systems is beyond the scope of this book, but by looking at the international aspects of sound broadcasting – especially the economic and cultural relationships between broadcast institutions across different territories and the propaganda uses of radio in undermining political systems – we can gain a perspective on the medium that goes beyond the domestic and parochial. It also helps delineate radio's future within a media culture that is not only global in scale but is also in the process of being transformed by new technologies that make the 'global village', famously envisaged by Marshall McLuhan in the 1960s, a reality.

14

Global Radio

> Local radio is the most powerful way of reaching people in the Congo. The road system is in a poor state and of course television is not widespread. Freddy gave us an example of radio's effectiveness in getting results. A farmer's cow wandered one day. A description was given on one local radio station. Three hours later, the cow was brought to the station to be picked up by its grateful owner.
>
> Richard Thompson, 'Radio for peace in Kinshasa', *The Friend*, 20 November 1998

Radio's global dimension takes a number of forms, including its role as an agent of cultural imperialism – the infiltration of new and alien cultural modes and products into established local cultures – and the increasingly international (and concentrated) nature of media ownership. In the field of media studies, these are familiar concepts: the impact of American television imports on British popular culture, for example, is well-trodden ground, as is the role of international concerns like Rupert Murdoch's News International in the broadcasting and print media of countries across the globe. Radio's global dimension has clear parallels with that of television, but the very parochialism of radio – its localness and the absence from it of programmes drawn from American or other international sources – make the issues more complex. If television has been a vehicle all over the world for American values, embodied or represented in specific cultural products from situation comedies to crime thrillers, radio has taken on aspects of Americanization in much more insidious ways: we are talking here formats, voices, styles and promotional gimmickry rather than programmes and personalities. It is not even a question of US content, as the British version of American 'pop radio' became as much a vehicle for British-made popular music as for its American counterpart.

We should note at this point that assumptions are being made here which reflect all too easily the western-centric (and especially Anglo-American) nature of cultural studies. The equation of Americanization with globalization, for example, has historical justification but is too pat an explanation for a media world in which Australian, Japanese and German companies are key players – in the latter two cases, in manufacturing technology in particular. English is not the world's most spoken language. Neither can we assume that the function of radio as a secondary medium in relation to television is anything other than a western perspective: in some African countries, for example, radio sets outnumber TV sets by something like ten to one. One of the most ingenious developments in radio technology in recent years has been the clockwork Freeplay radio, devised to enable reception without batteries specifically for the African market.

There can be an overriding tendency, too, to stress the impact of cultural imperialism via television, radio or popular music in negative terms of swamping or cultural distortion, rather than point up the consequent adaptation or creation of new cultural forms. British pop music, for example, began as a slavish imitator of American sounds and styles but developed its own voice, not by rejecting the model but by refining, absorbing and reinventing it. Much of this happened as a positive consequence of the *lack* of pop music on BBC radio in the late 1950s and early 60s – and the implicit encouragement which that paucity gave to young people to make their own music.

Two other points to consider are political and technological change. The collapse of communist governments in Eastern Europe from 1989 onwards, and that of the Soviet Union itself in 1991, precipitated massive changes in the ownership, funding, operation and content of national broadcasting services. In Poland, for example, broadcasting was removed from direct government interference by legislation in 1993, with ownership of the broadcast media placed in stock companies owned by the state and new regulations introduced regarding impartiality of content. The radio airwaves were also opened up to independent, commercially run stations such as Zet, Fun and RFM. In 1998, Poland had the largest radio advertising spend of the former communist bloc at $66 million, with Hungary and the Czech Republic not far behind. Wholesale changes from centralized, state-controlled broadcasting to a free-market model have created opportunities for investment on the part of international companies, besides uncovering a whole new set of tensions regarding programming – how to fully reflect Eastern Europe's potentially explosive multiplicity of ethnic cultures, for example.

Radio, too, has a part to play in television's satellite age, with the convergence of means of communication – the digitalization of both media, the cross-border availability of services, and the diminution of international regulatory control. Trans-continental, even global, television already exists in the form of 24-hour cable and satellite stations; the equivalent in radio terms is at present much more limited, basically to the World Service of the BBC, Voice of America and World Radio Network, though the potential has existed since the development of short-wave radio in the 1920s. The opening up of radio via new means of contact and dissemination such as the Internet automatically redefines radio's notion of 'territory' and, with it, changes the very concept of a listening community from the parochial and domestic into something much more powerful and challenging.

■ MESSAGES TO THE WORLD

It seems all you need to make a government these days is a radio station and a declaration that you have made a government.

The Imam of Yemen, quoted in *New York Times*, 1962

Traditionally, governments have used external broadcasting as a weapon in times of war and as a means of securing or maintaining political and economic hegemony in times of peace. The value of radio as a propaganda instrument and a vehicle for (often undeclared) warfare between nations has been demonstrated throughout the medium's history. Radio broadcasts can sow dissent, undermine morale, and spread disinformation and panic; they can also – as the above quotation suggests – give instant credibility to an organization bidding for power or influence. World War Two was a battleground for minds as well as territories, between two different schools of propaganda for which radio was the primary vehicle – one based on manipulation by unnerving and relentlessly repetitive hectoring, exaggeration and lies, the other by a more subtle blending of truth, half-truth, omission and inference in coverage that was partisan yet measured in tone and temper. In the end it was the believability of the BBC's external broadcasts in particular, made credible by a selective acknowledgement of setbacks and failures as well as victories, that won this particular theatre of war in Europe. One of its legacies, for better or worse, was an unprecedented practical understanding on the part of a hard core of skilled, experienced clandestine broadcasters of the manipulative potential of radio. Many moved into high-powered positions in government, broadcasting and especially advertising.

In his book *Radio Power*, Julian Hale lists numerous pre-war and wartime examples of clandestine broadcasting operations, including Soviet Russian broadcasts to German workers in the early 1920s and a 1930s IRA station broadcasting from deep in the heart of rural Ireland. During World War Two, William Joyce gave nightly broadcasts from Berlin (via the Radio Luxembourg transmitter) aimed at feeding dissension and doubt among the British populace, at the same time that the Nazi regime in Germany outlawed listening to equivalent broadcasts from foreign sources. His broadcasts, though palpably propaganda, always contained enough credible material – descriptions of air-raid damage on English towns the night before, for example – to make them at least partly believable. As well as Joyce (who was nicknamed 'Lord Haw Haw' because of his exaggerated upper-class accent), celebrities of clandestine radio included 'Axis Sally' and 'Tokyo Rose', who broadcast seductively from Japan to US servicemen in the Pacific. All the major countries involved in the war developed their own forms of so-called 'white' or overt propaganda and 'black' or covert propaganda – the latter including broadcasts to enemy territory in the guise of genuinely local programming. Latter-day clandestine stations tend to fall in one or other of these categories, and there are also 'grey' propaganda stations, which operate in territories with the unacknowledged backing and funding of foreign governments.

At the height of the Cold War, the US and USSR invested heavily in stations aimed at each other's territories and those within each other's sphere of influence. Soviet jamming of Voice of America broadcasts to the USSR began in 1948, just three years after the end of World War Two, and of those of the BBC World Service a year later. Programming techniques varied from operator to operator, Voice of America tending towards a generally chauvinistic tone while the World Service – having resisted attempts to turn it into a voice of NATO – took a more subtle tone, which a writer in the Russian communist party newspaper *Pravda* acknowledged as particularly pernicious:

> The foundation of BBC propaganda is the latest news, broadcast with emphatic objectivity. It should be noted that in selecting material for broadcasting to the USSR, the BBC does not draw any conclusion of its own but leaves this to the listeners, who sometimes, through lack of experience or lack of knowledge, are hooked by those who for years have made it their practice to fish in troubled waters – 'White' propaganda is straightforward propaganda. It is waged by the enemies of communism quite openly, even though under the mantle of 'impartiality' and 'objectivity'. But this does not lessen its hostile nature.
>
> Quoted in Mansell, *Let Truth Be Told*, p. 220

The US later funded stations broadcasting to Cuba (Radio Americas, Radio Caiman and Radio Marti), Sudan, Iran, Libya and Afghanistan as part of a policy of undeclared psychological warfare against what it regarded as 'rogue' regimes. Both Radio Free Europe and Radio Liberty were run covertly by the Central Intelligence Agency until the 1970s, when unmasking by the press obliged them to become overt operations. Funding had purported to come from 'groups of private American citizens through funds raised by appeals within the United States. This "cover story" both absolved the State Department of public responsibility for what the stations said, and protected the "private" stations from Congressional committee scrutiny' (Tunstall, p. 226). Some sources credit these two stations with a crucial role in the fall of communist regimes in Eastern Europe at the close of the 1980s. It was this perceived success that led the Clinton administration to begin a new phase of overseas broadcasting in 1994, with the creation of the International Broadcasting Bureau under the terms of a new International Broadcasting Act. This combined all America's overseas broadcasting operations under one body overseen by a bi-partisan Broadcasting Board of Governors. This included the long-established Voice of America, a new service called Radio Free Asia, and Worldnet Television.

In 1998, these were joined by a pan-African service called Radio Democracy for Africa aimed (in President Clinton's words) 'directly at encouraging progress towards freedom and democracy, respect for human rights, and an independent and objective media'. The station received $5 million in funding in its first year, directed via the Voice of America; programmes are carried in nine different languages and aimed at 19 African states. The Clinton administration also acted on a proposal, made by the conservative think tank called the Heritage Foundation, to create a station aimed at channelling subversive material at Saddam Hussein's regime in Iraq and promote support for the exiled opposition party, the Iraqi National Congress. Radio Free Iraq became a reality in late 1998, with an editorial base in Prague and a reported budget of $4 million over two years.

Even in post-Cold War Europe, cross-border radio broadcasting can still be a contentious political issue. In 1998 an ongoing dispute between Belarus, the former Soviet republic, and member states of the European Union over visa restrictions became the catalyst for the establishment of a station, Radio Free Belarus, in Bialystok in Poland. Reportedly funded by the US and EU, the station was aimed at encouraging democracy in what was seen in the west to be an increasingly authoritarian Belarus – this at a time when the Belarussian authorities were themselves increasing their own broadcasts to Russia itself and the ground was being laid for a possible political reunification of Belarus with Russia.

THE WORLD'S REFERENCE POINT?

The main arm of America's propaganda effort overseas – though the word 'propaganda' is never officially used – has traditionally been the Voice of America (VOA), which was established under the control of the Office of War Information shortly after the US entered World War Two. Since 1953 VOA has been part of the US Information Agency, operating under a charter drafted in 1960 and signed into law in 1976. Over the years, the function and focus of VOA has changed from outright propaganda to a more subtle and varied form of positive cultural projection, exemplified by the charter's specification that the VOA should broadcast news that is 'accurate, objective and reliable', that its programmes as a whole should 'present a balanced and comprehensive projection of significant American thought and institutions', and that the station should 'present the policies of the United States clearly and effectively – [and broadcast] responsible discussions and opinion on those policies'. Today, VOA employs around 1,200 staff, broadcasts in 52 languages to 86 million listeners, and originates around 700 hours of programming every week. It receives around $100 million in funds from the US Congress each year.

VOA is effectively a US government agency and for this reason has never quite shaken off its image as a basically political operation. The BBC's World Service has traditionally enjoyed a greater reputation for impartiality because of its nominal detachment from the British state – though it is part-funded by the Foreign Office – and its historical commitment to at least the appearance of objectivity in its representation of global political issues. It began as the Empire Service in 1932, as a means of linking the colonies with the mother country. Aimed at expatriates rather than the colonized, its programmes were heavy on sentiment and nostalgia. The threat to empire posed by the rise of Fascism in the 1930s, and particularly the setting up of powerful short-wave stations by Germany and Mussolini's Italy, changed BBC thinking and turned the Empire

Service into more of an English-language service for the world. In addition, between 1938 and 1942 the service massively expanded its foreign-language services, with a carefully considered policy of creating different programmes to suit different national milieu. Its North American Service, whose programmes were taken by many US stations, played a significant role in swaying American opinion towards Britain in the months before the US entered the war.

The war cemented the BBC's reputation as the world's most respected and trusted broadcaster, and today's BBC World Service remains an embodiment of that legacy. But there are particular responsibilities and expectations arising from this that have created their own moments of crisis, to the point that even in the late 1990s the World Service's role is not wholly clear nor its continuing status guaranteed. Although independent editorially, it has always received its funding on the basis of government assessments as to the necessity, value and cost-effectiveness of its services – and particularly its foreign-language services, which inevitably depend on specialist staff and a high level of sustained technical investment. Changing political situations and unanticipated events such as the redrawing of the political map of Central and Eastern Europe between 1989 and 1992 mean switches in policy and a whole set of new priorities, which are externally defined yet have to be mediated by professional broadcasters working within a particular World Service tradition. The World Service remains the BBC's most massive undertaking in terms of reach and ambition, if not in actual cost, and it has to operate in a global media context populated by commercial operators competing not only for audiences but also for a similar degree of hegemonic influence. While the activities of the Voice of America and its ancillary services have become more defined in a political and cultural sense, the World Service has become rather less focused. The arguments as to its future rest on what, and more importantly *who*, the World Service is for.

That it is a service with formidable reach is unquestionable. It broadcasts in 44 languages, with output organized into geographical divisions and comprising a total of 1,036 hours per week; its total audience was calculated in early 1999 at 143 million. Its news bulletins and a selection of other programmes are re-broadcast by over 1,000 radio stations in 90 countries. Radio 4 carries World Service programming during the night after its own programmes close down. Yet it could be said that the World Service's place in world broadcasting increasingly mirrors that of Britain's in the political world – a vocal, visible and respected presence founded in history but disproportionate to its actual economic and political influence. Its status even within the BBC seemed questioned in 1991, when BBC World Service Television was launched (later to be remodelled as BBC World and joined in 1995 by BBC Prime, cable and satellite channels aimed at European audiences). Attempts by BBC management to steer the World Service towards a 1990s focus began in 1996 with the reorganization of BBC radio into one directorate (see page 36). The World Service remained responsible for commissioning and scheduling its programmes but would no longer produce its own English-language programmes (now the responsibility of BBC Production) nor have its own

Source: On Air

Fig. 14.1 The BBC's World Service activities include production of a magazine aimed at an international listening audience

independent technical and support services. The World Service news team – albeit still working from their own headquarters at Bush House – were placed under the combined television and radio news operation. All this was part of an overall cost-trimming exercise that reflected cuts in government funding in real terms of around 7 per cent. The reorganization was not well received within the BBC or by the parliamentary Foreign Affairs Committee. Director-General John Birt, the main butt of the complaints, insisted that 'People talk of the World Service like a statue in the garden that needs preserving. It is not an appropriate image: the needs of the audience are changing and it is focusing on audiences in a way it has not done in the past.'

But which audiences? In 1999, the BBC's German service – the last remaining western European language service – was closed down just two weeks after services to the Balkan countries were massively increased with the start of NATO bombing raids on Yugoslavia. Stories ran in the industry press of unpublished plans to turn the World Service into a rolling news service, and it was suggested that the new focus on being 'audience-led' was an

Source: On Air

Fig. 14.2 BBC World Service programme schedule

acknowledgement of the new commercial reality – that its future lay in becoming a major player in news distribution, via arrangements such as that struck between the North American English division and US broadcasters to provide continuous news to stations as a sustaining overnight service. A comprehensive 're-branding' was undertaken in 1998 by consultants Lambie-Nairn that resulted in the World Service being relaunched under the banner of 'the world's reference point'.

Both Voice of America and the BBC World Service fulfil functions of cultural diplomacy rooted in different kinds of imperial pasts. As such, however well preserved or adaptable they may prove to be, they do not represent the future of global radio. That lies in two intricately related directions, each encouraged by technological convergence – deregulation of media within national and trans-continental territories, and commercial expansion of broadcasting on a global scale. The impact of convergence is discussed in the next chapter, but here it is worthwhile to trace the route that commercial expansionism has taken from radio's beginnings in nationally structured broadcasting systems – and particularly the US – to its growing concentration in the hands of globally connected media corporations.

COMMERCIALIZATION AND GLOBAL MEDIA

As noted in Part One, national broadcasting systems developed either under some degree of direct or indirect state control or under an openly capitalist structure relatively free of government involvement. When the former systems began opening up to commercial competition in the post-war period – for example, in the UK in 1955 – American broadcasting and advertising interests were particularly well placed to exploit it, with the consequence that television in Europe, South America and Australasia became heavily exposed to American products and advertising methods. This was abetted by the American-led reconstruction of broadcasting in Italy, Germany and Japan after the war, often along new, non-centralized (and therefore politically neutralizing) lines. In West Germany, for example,

> The Americans (and the French in their zones) deliberately organized radio at the *Land* (regional government) level and then embedded it into the power structure – by including representatives of all the political parties and the main religious, economic, social and cultural pressure groups in the region . . . well into the 1950s a pattern of local media continued, leaving a vacuum at national level.
>
> Tunstall, *The Media Are American*, p. 158

America's post-war economic dynamism alarmed both old and new friends: fear of (and resistance to) an Americanization of programming became one of the key policy platforms of the BBC in the 1950s, while Canadian broadcasting – pluralistic, but with an established commercially funded sector – was particularly vulnerable to US influence because of its proximity. After World

War Two, the Canadian government introduced restrictive quotas on overseas content that are still partly intact. But the battle mainly centred on television. In radio, the American influence was more insidious, driven by stations which adopted American models (notably variations of the Top 40 format) and by the huge global popularity of rock'n'roll – a form which became the focus of intense debate on the 'debasement' of culture within the US itself. American radio institutions never established themselves as a world force because their units of programming were not exportable (with some exceptions, such as their inclusion on Radio Luxembourg and the American Forces Network) in the way that TV programmes were.

Nevertheless, investment by some maverick American radio operators helped fuel the offshore (pirate) broadcasting boom in Europe in the 1960s, notably the launch of Radio London (owned by the Marine Investment Company Inc. of Freeport in the Bahamas, which registered Radio London's ship in land-locked Liechtenstein, a small independent principality between Switzerland and Austria). With such backing came expertise: Gordon McLendon, a one-time associate of Top 40 architect Todd Storz, helped launch Radio Nord off Sweden in 1961, while Radio London's managerial staff included Philip Birch, who had worked on radio accounts with the J. Walter Thompson advertising agency in New York. American influence therefore reached radio in other territories by the back door, its impact (via the pirates) being to act as catalyst for the introduction of a national music radio station (BBC Radio 1) and legal commercial radio, though strict controls exercised by the Independent Broadcasting Authority on overseas ownership prevented any great US-led incursion into the latter. In the mid 80s, Laser 558, a pirate station with mainly American disc jockeys and mysterious American funding, drew large audiences and again forced a rethink on programming within both Radio 1 and Independent Local Radio.

Although Radio Luxembourg ceased operation in 1991, its owners CLT-UFA still carry on the tradition of broadcasting an American-style format of pop music to Europe via Atlantic 252, a long-wave station transmitting from the Irish Republic since 1989. CLT-UFA itself is a good example of trans-continental cross-media ownership in action, with shares in Channel 5 TV and interests in 21 television stations and 22 radio stations across Europe. In 1997 the original CLT merged with UFA, a German company specializing in film and television production and rights acquisition. Until 1998 CLT-UFA had a controlling share in Talk Radio, as well as interests in Xfm, RTL Country 1035, Radio 106 and Thames FM. However, despite being the largest single radio company in Europe, CLT-UFA only claims 7 per cent of the total European market – a sign of the traditional domination of national radio markets by indigenous companies. This domination is already being challenged throughout Europe by progressive deregulation on the part of individual countries and the removal of restrictions on overseas ownership.

UK radio, for example, was opened up to foreign investors from the late 1980s onwards, including the IBA-ratified acquisition by the Australian media concern Darling Downs TV of interests in LBC, Marcher Sound, Beacon

Radio, Radio Forth and 50 per cent of the sales house Independent Radio Sales. In 1987, over two thirds of ILR stations were estimated to have some degree of Australian interest at board level. Once the Broadcasting Act of 1990 was in force, allowing station groups to expand and diversify, the emphasis shifted to British expansion abroad, with Classic FM and Virgin vying for an FM licence in South Africa and DMG investing in stations in Hungary. GWR, which took control of Classic FM in 1996, eventually took the latter format to Finland, Austria, Holland, Italy and Poland. (In the space of six months during 1996 it also bought and sold, at a £5.4-million profit, the New Zealand radio company Prospect.)

For GWR, as for all radio-centred groups seeking to grow in foreign territories, the strategy with Classic FM is to adapt a proven, tested format for localized use – especially in those territories whose communications markets have been freshly liberalized, such as Eastern European countries. A *Financial Times* report on European radio in 1996 noted the increasing activity in Eastern Europe of the French company Europe Développement. Critics of globalization fear a cloning effect, rather like the proliferation of McDonald's, the Body Shop and Benetton stores in shopping malls and retail centres in the world's major cities – a replication of format that will eventually make genre-driven stations across the globe virtually indistinguishable.

Meanwhile, in the US, one of the effects of the 1996 Telecommunications Act was to so boost the internal market for stations that a shortage resulted in the number of major market stations available for sale. It was this that prompted Clear Channel Communications, one of the largest radio owners in the US, to launch an aggressive new policy of buying stations in Australia, New Zealand, China and the Czech Republic – and, in 1999, to ally with Talk Radio and the Ginger Media Group to prepare bids for any planned UK regional digital radio licences, and to take a minority shareholding in Golden Rose Communications, owners of Jazz FM. Time will tell if this signifies the start of a concerted American entry into British commercial radio.

Further reading

Hale, Julian (1972): *Radio Power: Propaganda and International Broadcasting*. Paul Elek.

Laing, Dave, and Tyler, Bob (1996): *The European Radio Market*. Financial Times Business Publications.

McLuhan, Marshall (1964): *Understanding Media*. Routledge & Kegan Paul.

Mansell, Gerard (1982): *Let Truth Be Told: 50 Years of BBC External Broadcasting*. Weidenfeld & Nicolson.

Tunstall, Jeremy (1977): *The Media Are American*. Constable.

Walker, Andrew (1992): *A Skyful of Freedom: 60 Years of the BBC World Service*. Broadside Books.

Wallis, Roger, and Malm, Krister (1984): *Big Sounds from Small Peoples: The Music Industry in Small Countries*. Constable.

Activity 14.1

Record a BBC World Service news programme and a Voice of America news programme on the same day (Radio 4 goes over to the World Service after normal transmission hours. Check the VOA web site – www.voa.gov/allsked.html – for frequencies and schedules.) What kind of news agenda is at work on each, and are there significant differences in approach between the two services? How oriented are the programmes to British and American interests respectively? Note and account for those news stories which are included or discussed in only one of the programmes. Are there any significant differences in the kind of experts used on the news programme to analyse the day's events and issues?

Activity 14.2

Using Internet sites as your prime source of information, research how deregulation has so far affected radio broadcasting – both in programming and organizational terms – in a country other than Britain or the US. Identify any threat that further deregulation may continue to pose during the next decade.

Activity 14.3

Investigate the historical role of radio in an African country of your choice, particularly in relation to print media and television. Use Internet sites as a source of information, together with the books listed under *Further reading* at the end of this chapter. How far are its institutional structures of broadcasting based on colonial or imperial models? What are the threats and opportunities that broadcasting in Africa faces in the new century?

Activity 14.4

According to Jeremy Tunstall, 'the media are American' – in the sense of cultural influence as well as ownership and investment. Discuss this assertion in the light of your own reading, research and listening. How 'American' is radio in Europe in terms of style and content? How do you account for differences in the level of American influence and investment between individual European countries?

15

Futures

The form that sound broadcasting took from the 1920s onwards was constrained by its technological limitations. Subsequent developments in technology – transistors, FM transmission, and latterly the digital multiplex – have opened up new means of delivery, while radio production has been revolutionized by computerization of the kind described in Chapter 7 and particularly the advent of the ISDN (integrated subscriber digital network) system and new recording technologies such as DAT and mini disc, which allow stations to conduct and edit interviews or relay outside broadcasts with crystal-clear clarity and with comparatively less effort, cost and labour. This simultaneous cost-saving and technical improvement means that a small-scale station can emulate the big 'sound' and professionalism of a larger station at very little cost, while the bigger stations or groups can produce and deliver cost-effective localized programming by networking and automation that may have the effect of squeezing out the genuine local operators.

This final chapter takes a necessarily tentative look into radio's future in the new technological context. New modes of transmission like digital broadcasting open up new commercial opportunities and reshape the balance of power and influence within the existing patterns of control and ownership; they demand policy decisions on the part of governments regarding regulation of content and limits on ownership; and they raise questions as to what will happen to the existing analogue spectrum. In some cases, new technology has the potential to redefine the broadcaster's relationship with the listener, in that it can allow far greater scope for interactivity than ever before.

THE CONVERGENCE ISSUE

The biggest challenge facing broadcast media at the start of the 21st century is that of convergence – meaning the converging of traditional and new communications services that digital technology allows. The advantage of convergence to the consumer is that it has the potential to combine personal computing, the Internet, telecommunication and television and radio reception via a single piece of hardware, but it also has profound implications for the business of providing communications services and for popular culture and personal lifestyles in general. All this continues the process started in the 1980s with the convergence between telecommunications and computing, where technological convergence gave rise to market convergence and the rethinking of regulatory philosophies – the telecommunications sector being highly regulated throughout Europe in particular, while the computing industry had expanded within a free-market environment.

A prime example of convergence in action is cable technology. This enables the delivery direct into the home of numerous services which are available independently, by other delivery means. These services include telephone, Internet access and e-mail, television channels (terrestrial, satellite and cable-only channels) and radio stations. To encourage consumers to make a switch from conventional telephony (as provided by British Telecom, for instance) to cable-delivered telephone services, a cable company has to offer the consumer added value in the form of, say, additional TV channels or Internet access – in other words, to offer a complete *package* of communications services at a premium price.

While offering such a combination of services is, technologically speaking, fairly straightforward, it involves negotiation and resolution of complex financial, legal and copyright issues relating to the content and ownership of the material that the technology delivers – and, most important of all, its cost. It radically undermines the traditional infrastructures of the tele-communications, information technology/computing and broadcasting industries by blurring the distinctions between them. It also raises issues of regulation and public policy – why, for example, should someone watching cable TV exclusively (but including BBC channels as part of the package) have to pay a compulsory fee for a licence to receive television and radio signals by traditional means? If the technology of broadcasting shifts from an analogue to a digital basis, should the basis of regulation similarly shift from a broadcasting to a (traditonally less prescribed) telecommunications model? Can the BBC itself any longer be regarded as a *broadcaster* in the strict meaning of the term, when the actual means of transmission are no longer analogue-exclusive and are owned by other agencies?

Most significantly, the exploitation and marketing of new technologies like the Internet and the development of new delivery systems like cable has encouraged communications companies to move beyond what were once seen as distinct core businesses and diversify, notably by means of alliance, acquisition and merger. This may include 'horizontal' partnerships (enabling complementary skills to be shared and the level of financial risk reduced) or 'vertical' deals in which leaders of one particular market field extend their interests into other, related markets. In so doing, companies consolidate their economic base, minimize the effect of competition and keep costs down. Between 1995 and 1999, around 15 per cent of the total value of global mergers and acquisitions was generated by communications-related industries. New market structures emerge along with new power players, the classic example in recent years being the Microsoft Corporation. Microsoft began as a software manufacturer, diversified into production of computer hardware and subsequently into cable TV in the US (via the Comcast cable network, in which it has an 11.5 per cent stake, and the news channel MSNBC, a joint venture with NBC) and an Internet-on-TV service, WebTV Networks.

For radio, convergence has a number of specific ramifications. Computer technology has itself revolutionized radio production at many levels, from news gathering and selection, programming and delivery of music to complete automation of programme output. This has enabled programme budgets to be cut to the point that it is perfectly possible for a station broadcasting to a small-scale area to run with a staff of two. Digitalized transmission, when applied to broadcasting networks, also expands the available capacity, eliminating the problem of scarcity of spectrum that limited radio's growth in its early years and defined the regulatory pattern in which the medium would develop. As with television, it opens the way for subscription services to particular radio channels, and for the provision of complementary services such as graphics and text alongside sound.

The downside of convergence is that, unregulated, it concentrates control of broadcasting output in the hands of a small number of players with global rather than national or regional priorities. The cost involved in launching digital services is such that normally competing companies have to pool their resources in a common interest, while smaller, newer operators are excluded. For example, an alliance of Talk Radio and the Ginger Media Group (owners of Virgin Radio) joined forces with US group Clear Channel Communications in February 1999 to bid for all British regional DAB (Digital Audio Broadcasting) licences as advertised by the Radio Authority.

On the other hand, the issue of regulation is problematic, as the converging technologies have very different historical traditions of governmental involvement in their affairs. In some countries, for example, radio and television stations are prohibited from releasing the results of opinion polls immediately prior to an election, while web sites run by the same stations are not. Definitions of 'public interest' vary from country to country, and one of the main aims of the European Commission's involvement in encouraging convergence has been to balance the interests and broadcasting traditions of member countries against the stated aim of promoting a pan-European policy of low-level regulation. In Britain, technological convergence has forced a reappraisal of the need for the three existing regulatory bodies – the Radio Authority, the Independent Television Commission and Oftel (which supervises telecommunications). In the long term, these three bodies may themselves be converged into one (possibly titled Ofcom and possibly covering the presently self-governed BBC as well) with responsibilities equivalent to that of the FCC in the US. The Commercial Radio Companies Association (CRCA) in Britain fears that such a move may result in a diminution of radio's 'voice' within the political sphere.

Overall, convergence offers the radio industry flexibility of operation, new means of delivery, raised production values and improved sound quality. The trade-off is the integration of radio into multimedia as a whole and the loss of control and distinctiveness that this implies, together with the opening up of radio to competition from new forms of broadcasting such as 'webcasting' (broadcasting via the Internet). There is also the need to persuade radio's core audience of the value to them of the benefits of convergence, involving as it does investment on their part in new hardware and a certain re-education as to how radio can be used.

DIGITAL RADIO

Digital radio – or the broadcasting of digitized signals – is a transmission system promising better sound quality and greater ease of use to the listener and a more efficient management of the broadcasting spectrum than the current AM, FM and long wave systems. It was first developed in the 1970s by BBC research engineers, initially using NICAM stereo signals; working with European partners, they established a standard called Eureka 147 or Digital Audio Broadcasting (DAB) which was also adopted by Canada, Mexico, South Africa and Australia. This system requires the exclusive use of new, high-frequency bands and the 'bundling' of groups of services into 'multiplexes' or collections of frequencies. In the US, several alternative systems were trialled, including what rapidly emerged as the front runner – IBOC (In Band On Channel).

By international agreement, Britain has seven multiplexes to be divided between BBC and commercial operators. The BBC began its own digital radio services as early as September 1995, simulcasting its existing services and adding coverage of sport and parliamentary sessions. Meanwhile, the Radio Authority licensed experimental London-based DAB services that were supported by stations including Virgin, Talk Radio and Kiss FM. The first multiplex to be offered to commercial operators in Britain, in 1998, went to the only consortium to bid for it, Digital One, comprising the GWR radio group, National Transcommunications Ltd (NTL, which runs the transmitter network for commercial stations) and Talk Radio. By mid 1998, the BBC and Digital One were sharing 27 DAB transmitter sites with a collective potential coverage of 60 per cent of the British population. Digital One's multiplex became fully operational in late 1999.

Unlike AM and FM, DAB is almost completely immune from interference (such as hiss and crackle), fading and the 'flutter' effect that occurs in urban areas. While AM and FM transmitters can only broadcast one service on one frequency, DAB transmitters can broadcast up to six in stereo or 12 in mono (or any mixed configuration): with more space available, there is room for more stations. DAB also allows text or graphics such as telephone numbers or stock market prices to be transmitted simultaneously, giving additional or complementary advertising opportunities.

If only at the level of increasing the number of available services, DAB has the potential to impact heavily on the existing ecology of radio. However, like all technologies, its impact will be minimized or maximized according to political decisions regarding how the technology should be regulated, which operators should be granted the spectrum and at what level of cost, what requirements on programme content should be put in place, and so on. In Britain, government policy (for Labour as for the previous Conservative administration) is to let the Radio Authority oversee DAB but with rather looser criteria for programming than it imposes over analogue radio. 'The regulator will take an interest in matters of taste, decency and politics, but not format,' Radio Authority chief Tony Stoller has stated. 'It's the same basis on which we regulate radio on cable and satellite, with new programme services available more or less on demand.' Simple replication of existing analogue services is not seen, by manufacturers, government or regulators, as enough of an incentive to consumers for them to buy digital receivers.

The commercial radio industry in Britain, where DAB has been pioneered, has been largely lukewarm about investing in digital radio, because of the high start-up costs involved and doubts about consumer resistance to switching from traditional analogue radio to digital. The only radio group to show real confidence in DAB's future has been GWR, which owns the majority shareholding in Digital One. The value for GWR of such an investment is control of up to 10 stations with national coverage – a position analogous with Sky TV, which invested heavily in satellite TV at a time when potential competitors were fighting shy of it and as a result achieved almost unassailable market leadership. The CRCA has estimated the cost to its members of launching into digital at £35 million per year, and most of the UK's major radio players (including Capital and EMAP) were conspicuously absent from bidding for the first commercial multiplex licence. Normally competitive operators have been forced to pool resources and forge alliances by forming consortia to bid for available multiplexes, as the cost of solo investment is prohibitive. To make involvement in DAB more attractive to the operators, the government has offered to grant – through the Radio Authority – an automatic extension of existing analogue licences to any company winning a DAB franchise. It has so far stopped short of what would be a politically unpopular decision to set a date for switching off analogue services altogether, although there has been lobbying from manufacturers in favour of this.

Even DAB's most enthusiastic proponents predict that it may take until the end of the 21st century's first decade for the new system to reach even 40 per cent market penetration. The major growth area is likely to be in-car DAB, echoing the success of the RDS system (which allows the driver instant access to travel bulletins on local radio, whichever station he or she happens to be listening to) in the late 1980s. The first in-car DAB radios (priced around £500) were unveiled by manufacturers Kenwood, Grundig, Clarion, Blaupunkt and Pioneer in July 1998.

It is ironic that, if DAB does become established in Britain, the commercial radio industry will have the BBC to thank for smoothing the path and increasing public awareness of its potential. The BBC has undertaken exhaustive research into audience understanding and expectation of DAB and has characterized the first wave of likely consumers of digital radio (what it calls 'early adopters') as:

> Affluent gadget enthusiasts earning £25,000 plus and owning appliances such as
> - Surround sound TV, DCC, a mobile phone and PC
> - Hi-Fi buffs having spent at least £750 on a hi-fi in the last year
> - Serious music fans – readers of top music/hi-fi magazines
> - Car CD owners and PC owners with Internet
>
> BBC Research, 1997

Just as the BBC created an ecology of broadcasting into which commercial radio had to integrate in the 1970s, so the Corporation is again in a position to profoundly influence the commercial sector in the digital era. DAB is just one plank in the BBC's digital strategy, which also embraces digital television (BBC Choice, BBCs 1 and 2 in widescreen format, a planned educational channel) and an Internet web site, www.bbc.co.uk, which is one of the most visited in Europe. Taken together, this investment represents around 10 per cent of the licence fee. More than its commercial competitors, the BBC has clear programming strategies to underpin its investment, taking digital radio as an opportunity to add to its existing activities, rather than replicate them, through new specialist channels (news, sport, parliament, comedy, music, and an Asian channel) which will all have national coverage.

In the end, it is consumer reaction to the kind of programming offered that will determine digital radio's future, whoever the provider happens to be, though radio's ability to compete technologically with television in particular will also be vital. As David Vick of the Radio Authority suggests: 'Where digital is definitely important is in making sure that radio does not lose ground to other broadcast systems. If in, say, ten years' time, radio were the only medium not to be broadcasting digitally, it would look insignificant in the overall scheme of things' (*Q Sheet*, issue 176, July 1997).

INTERNET RADIO

The last decade of the 20th century has seen a massive expansion of, and commercial investment in, the Internet. The Internet was started by the US Defense Department in the late 1960s and grew to comprise thousands of networks (collections of computers connected to share information) around the world. It is now a means of exchanging electronic mail, accessing information and entertainment, and shopping online. Connection to the Internet is available only via a computer modem connected to an Internet Service Provider (ISP) such as America Online (AOL) or CompuServe. The only cost incurred in using the Internet, apart from a subscription to an ISP, is that of a phone call. The World Wide Web is part of the Internet, offering literally millions of web sites and pages (hypertext documents) which can be found by means of search engines such as Yahoo or Altavista.

The Internet is unregulated and uncontrolled; literally anyone or any organization can set up a web site, with no bar on content or language. It can be interactive, providing the web user with a means of instant electronic communication with the site. Radio stations have developed their web sites as information points to bring added value to their services, as well as offering permanent online access to the station's output. Many stations have web sites – the US was estimated to have 800 station-related sites during 1998, the UK 35 – and most broadcast their output live. They can be accessed individually or via what are called 'portal' sites with links to available stations. Web sites open up new opportunities for sponsorship, advertising and promotion of the station's off-air activities. Few such sites are profitable in their own right, but as with all commercial web sites, they have value in building brand loyalty and customer confidence, generating information about the product, and selling merchandise direct to the consumer (and increasing revenue by eliminating the 'middle man'). Part of the challenge is to keep users coming back to the site by creating an expectation of new information every time.

The Internet enables the output of even the smallest, most localized station to achieve literally worldwide reach – and at relatively little cost. It breaks down the territorial boundaries that have historically restricted a station to a particular catchment area, thus disrupting regulatory controls on scope of operation and content; and it adds value to the station as an advertising vehicle. It also lays radio stations open to charges of infringing music copyrights, by broadcasting recorded music beyond agreed boundaries, and of undermining sales and encouraging music piracy: any audio material broadcast on the web can be recorded and downloaded on to CD for future use.

But Internet radio is not confined to established stations outputting on their own web sites. Some 'stations' exist only as web sites. AOL has its own music and news service available by audio; sports sites offer commentaries on high-profile football or cricket games; businesses broadcast company statements live over the Internet to shareholders and employees; record companies allow fans exclusive previews of new releases via Internet broadcasts. Pirate radio operators have found that they can broadcast freely, without interruption or the threat of prosecution, via the Internet. In restrictive political regimes, radio stations that are forced off the air can recreate themselves as Internet stations, with the advantage of spreading their message internationally while operating without the continual threat of having equipment confiscated and offices raided – the precise geographical source of an Internet 'station' is almost impossible to trace.

For its advocates, the great potential of Internet radio is that it has a democratizing effect on the business of broadcasting. Just as anyone, anywhere, can launch a web site, so anyone, anywhere, can start their own radio 'station' and broadcast to the world – without prohibitively high start-up costs or investment in state-of-the-art equipment. For some, this is a return to the pioneer spirit of unregulated, experimental 1920s radio. In practical terms, however, there are obvious drawbacks. Sound quality is variable, according to

How radio uses the Net to enhance the listening experience

Radio stations have begun to use the Internet to build a strong relationship with listeners, Mairi Clark says

If the "killer app" of digital TV is interactivity, then what will digitalisation bring to radio? There are many who believe CD-quality sound and a host of new frequencies do not a revolution make.

They should look elsewhere for signs of radio's brave new future. Until recently, radio had limited ambitions on the Net. But over the past few months, Britain's leading stations have gone beyond simply airing their programmes over the Net, and have begun to use the medium in the preparation and the presentation of shows. As the stations wake up to the opportunity to build relationships with listeners, radio and the Internet could share a rosy future.

Radio 1 has already put live video on its Website with a broadcast of Simon Mayo's morning show, which hosted its first Internet party in July last year. Listeners were invited to call the station if they could read the message on a blackboard behind Mayo, a live feed of whom was put on the site.

Jason Wilburn, Radio 1's Website manager, believes this venture was successful because offline listeners weren't isolated from thos listening over the Net. "The idea was to take listeners on to the Net but bring them back on to the radio and vice-versa," he says.

On another occasion, Radio 1 benefited from the global reach afforded it by the Net when its presenter, Mary-Ann Hobbs, was heard by the Beastie Boys in the US. The band contacted Radio 1, said they loved the show, and eventually came over to the UK to perform a live set.

However, Radio 1's Website doesn't broadcast continuous live audio, preferring to allow users to download individual shows on their PCs. This restriction is imposed because the service is funded by UK licence-payers and the BBC feels British users should benefit more than global users. "We offer radio on demand because nobody is going to listen to a four-hour live audio feed. We're not trying to make the site identical to the station because merely rehashing what you have on air doesn't work," Wilburn says.

Plans are afoot to introduce listeners' top tens (voted for online), city guides and live chat. Users can already win tickets for gigs on the condition that they write a review for the site. But Wilbourn is wary of the barriers to radio on the Net, especially the cost. "Going online to listen to the radio is costly. A Website for a radio station has to add extra value."

No-one recognises this more than John Ousby, the head of new media at Virgin Radio. "We're trying to see how we can use the Internet to increase the relationship between the station and the audience. The Internet is very good at interactivity and cutting out the middle man," he says.

While Radio 1 has based its Website around its reputation as a purveyor of dance music, Virgin has harnessed the popularity of Chris Evans, its maverick owner and breakfast show presenter. While its site broadcasts continuous live audio, Ousby is a pioneer of archived radio feed and has also signed Virgin up to the push-channel provider, BackWeb. The Virgin channel has been promoted on air and subscriptions have topped 30,000 since mid-November. The station is also looking at selling records online.

Ousby believes the link with Evans' breakfast show is the biggest thing for Virgin's site, and Evans is supportive of the Website. He mentions it frequently on air and listeners can enter competitions online. They also send in jokes, ideas and reactions to the breakfast show over the Net. Most famously, Evans' quest to make his assistant, Holly Samos, the star of an ad campaign last autumn was championed online.

Capital has also identified the need for users to get something back from its site, which carries cinema listings and archived shows, as well as the obligatory DJ profiles. Extracts are themed around features, such as Steve Penk's wind-ups, instead of shows. Stuart Ledden, marketing executive at Capital Interactive, is a firm believer in building relationships with listeners. "If we concentrate on audience participation we can build a sense of community. Enabling users to interact with each other is on the agenda," he says.

While all the stations recognise the limitations of the Web, particularly in terms of sound quality, its ability to add to the listening experience is clear. Ousby's vision is typical. "Virgin is never going to try to be everything to everyone," he says. "We'll focus on what we do best, reinforcing brand values, excitement and innovation."

But he allows himself a flight of fancy: "I'd like to see a time when you can search for a song by word association, listen to a clip and, oncy you've identified the song you want, purchase it online. You could download the song on to your hard disk and press it on to a CD. A site that did that would make the best use of the Net."

Source: Campaign

Fig. 15.1 A commentary on radio usage of the Internet, from *Campaign* 20 February 1998. Reproduced with the permission of the copyright owner, Haymarket Business Publications Ltd

how busy the Internet is at any particular time. Although speed and accessibility to the Internet are improving all the time, it is still a cumbersome and not always user-friendly medium to access. Being PC-driven, it has none of traditional radio's portability. It cannot be accessed at the press of a button or the flick of a dial; the very process demands some degree of diligence and persistence. It demands a dedicated rather than casual listener. In this sense, Internet broadcasting returns radio to its status as a primary medium – one in which information and entertainment are pursued rather than simply accepted.

Nevertheless, sound quality and ease of use are likely to improve with developments in technology. Web literacy and penetration are increasing year on year. A further challenge may be provided by Internet connections of the kind offered by PointCast and yoyo.com, which runs in the background of a computer and provides what is effectively a user-tailored radio service for as long as the computer is switched on.

▮ SATELLITE RADIO

Globalization has another aspect – global or trans-continental radio, broadcast via satellite. A satellite may carry up to 16 transponders which receive TV and radio signals beamed up from the ground. They boost the signal and return it back to earth, to be picked up by domestic satellite dish. Most are relays of stations that broadcast terrestrially: all five BBC radio networks and the BBC World Service can be accessed via the Astra satellite. Made-for-satellite radio services include Country Music Radio; the almost wholly automated European Klassik Rock; and World Radio Network (WRN), which delivers selected programming from national services such as Radio Australia and Channel Africa to a worldwide audience. Sky Music Choice was launched as a joint venture between BSkyB and Music Choice Europe (part-owned by the Warner Music Group and Sony) in early 1998; subscribers to Sky TV can receive up to 44 channels of music per day. Most satellite services operate in English, but the music stations are most notable for keeping talk to a minimum. Sky Radio, for example, is nominally a Dutch station but is virtually presenter-free: the only speech it carries is advertising and news.

Satellite radio can offer CD-quality sound, but it is a domestically static medium, to be accessed via a TV or radio set connected to a dish. At present, it lacks the advantage of portability. One of the major technological developments in radio, which may yet dwarf digital audio broadcasting in its impact, is a satellite-based system targeted at car drivers that was launched by a Washington DC-based company, CD Radio, after winning a national satellite broadcast licence from the FCC in 1997. The start-up cost, including satellite construction, was a reported $425 million. A miniature receiver, 2-inch aerial and radio card, which is inserted into the car's audio player, will give the listener access to 50 channels of music programming and 50 channels of news and sport for a cost of $9.95 a month.

Apart from the direct-to-car advantage, CD Radio has two other novel selling propositions – a choice of channels that build on internal distinctions between styles of music (between contemporary jazz, classic jazz and big band swing, for example), and a commercial-free environment made possible by subscription sales. 'A significant number of consumers attempt to avoid car radio advertising by switching stations early in a string of advertisements,' CD Radio's chief executive David Margolese has explained. 'The majority of our music formats represent 27 per cent of recorded music purchases, yet are absent from radio stations in virtually every market throughout the country. This is due to the economics that force commercial broadcasters to serve advertisers and chase market share. We, on the other hand, can aggregate our listeners nationally and serve them regardless of where they happen to live.' CD Radio has promised a national launch in the US by the end of the year 2000.

▮ THE FUTURE OF ANALOGUE RADIO

The history of technological development gives us no real indication as to whether new enhancements, inventions or means of delivery will become accepted. Massive investment failed to secure either the future of quadrophonic sound (a successor to stereophonic sound) in the early 1970s, or the Video 2000 or Betamax video formats in the 1980s. FM technology was first developed in the 1930s but took more than 40 years to become the prime medium of radio transmission. When competing formats emerge, much depends on which will be accepted as an industry standard and to what extent the technology represents a genuinely new consumer benefit. Even this can vary from territory to territory: US television operates a 525-line system, while the rest of the world broadcasts on 625 lines; the PAL system is used by videocassette manufacturers throughout the world except the US. A similar divergence is occurring over digital radio in the US, where the IBOC system is being introduced rather than European DAB because the radio industry corporately sees digitalization in terms of enhancing the existing AM and FM wavelength structure rather than creating opportunities for completely new services.

In spite of (and perhaps because of) digitalization, the future of AM and FM in the US seems secure. Elsewhere, the long-term future of analogue radio is less certain. In Britain, some predict its demise by 2010, but this will require a government decision on a date for literally switching off the transmitters. Prior to this, there will have to have been a long period of transition in which consumers are encouraged to buy digital sets.

Any abandonment of AM and FM will have implications for existing operators. Access to the digital multiplex is currently guaranteed for national broadcasters and available to regional and local stations, but for the smaller commercial stations the cost of entry may be prohibitive and also compromise their independence if it means allying with larger stations or consortia. While the Radio Authority is, in 1999, pressing ahead with plans for yet more regional and local AM and FM licences, it is difficult to see how the current system of awarding short-term Restricted Service Licences could be accommodated within a digital system. Abandoning AM and FM would probably have to be co-ordinated internationally, too, to avoid the prospect of AM or FM stations in neighbouring countries reshaping their programming for a possibly more lucrative AM/FM-less territory. In the midst of all the talk of the benefits to listeners of improved sound quality, it should be remembered that Atlantic 252, broadcasting chart music from Ireland on the technically variable long wave, continues to attract around 4 per cent of listeners in Britain.

There are a number of possible scenarios for the fate of analogue services. One is that DAB and AM/FM continue to co-exist, with the latter spectrum given over to small-scale and community-based broadcasters – even a whole new tier of radio equivalent to microradio in the US (see Chapter 4). Another is that the frequencies will be auctioned off to providers of mobile communications services. This would be in the context of increasing convergence between fixed or cabled telephony (wired) and mobile telephony (wireless). In time this may in turn lead to the full integration of wired and wireless technologies via digital mobile communications systems. Could it be that, at the very point that conventional ether-based broadcasting stands in apparent danger of being superseded by a new digital transmission system, wireless communication will be returned to what some of its pioneers originally intended it for – as a means of one-to-one communication?

Further reading

Boyd-Barrett, Oliver, and Newbold, Chris (1995): *Approaches to Media: A Reader*. Arnold.

Crisell, Andrew (1997): *An Introductory History of British Broadcasting*. Routledge.

Euromedia Research Group (1997): *The Media in Western Europe*. Sage.

Franklin, Bob (1997): *Newszak and News Media*. Arnold.

Kaye, Michael, and Popperwell, Andrew (1992): *Making Radio: A Guide to Basic Radio Techniques*. Broadside Books.

O'Sullivan, Tim, et al. (eds) (1997): *The Media Studies Reader*. Arnold.

Woodyear, Clive (1999): *Radio Listener's Guide*. PAQ Publishing.

Activity 15.1

Research the appropriate consumer magazines (for example, *What Hi Fi*) and visit your local electrical store to ascertain the current cost and level of availability of digital radio hardware. At what rate are costs coming down, and what kind of projection do retailers make of consumer take-up of digital radio over the next few years?

Activity 15.2

Conduct a survey of customers at your local electrical store to find out the level of public awareness about, and knowledge of, digital radio. Prepare a list of questions asking how much customers would be prepared to pay for digital hardware. Repeat the exercise at a local car accessories store, or wherever car radios are sold, or among car owners in a supermarket car park. Assess to what degrees the future take-up of digital radio may depend on links with car manufacturers.

Activity 15.3

Opponents and critics of the BBC have suggested that it should switch from a licence fee basis of funding to a voluntary subscription basis, along the lines of satellite television. Assess what kind of impact such a move would have on the BBC itself, on the type of radio programmes and services it offers, and on competitive and complementary services in the commercial sector. Based on your reading and research, is there a future for subscription radio of any kind?

Activity 15.4

Using Internet sources in particular, research the history, development and potential of digital radio broadcasting in a country (other than Britain) with an established duopoly of public service and commercial broadcasting – for example, Canada, South Africa or Australia. Which digital system is the country adopting, and why?

Activity 15.5

Map out the implications for broadcasters, consumers, hardware manufacturers, regulators and government if analogue radio broadcasting was to be switched off officially in favour of a digital system in, say, the year 2010. How would you advocate the retention of the analogue system from the point of view of a small-scale operator unable or reluctant to invest in digital?

Bibliography

1. Histories of radio and related industries

Barnouw, Erik (1966–68): *The History of Broadcasting in the United States*, vols 1–3. Oxford University Press.

Barnouw, Erik (1975): *The Evolution of American Television*. Oxford University Press.

Baron, Mike (1975): *Independent Radio: The Story of Commercial Radio in the United Kingdom*. Terence Dalton.

Black, Peter (1972): *The Biggest Aspidistra in the World*. BBC.

Briggs, Asa (1965–79): *The History of Broadcasting in the United Kingdom*, vols 1–5. Oxford University Press.

Briggs, Asa (1979): *The BBC: The First Fifty Years*. Oxford University Press.

Briggs, Susan (1981): *Those Radio Times*. Weidenfeld & Nicolson.

Crisell, Andrew (1997): *An Introductory History of British Broadcasting*. Routledge.

Davies, John (1994): *Broadcasting and the BBC in Wales*. University of Wales Press.

Denisoff, R. Serge (1975): *Solid Gold: The Popular Record Industry*. Transaction.

Harris, Paul (1968): *When Pirates Ruled the Waves*. Impulse.

Harris, Paul (1971): *To Be a Pirate King*. Impulse.

Hilmes, Michele (1997): *Radio Voices: American Broadcasting, 1922–1952*. University of Minnesota Press.

Keith, Michael C. (1997): *Voices in the Purple Haze: Underground Radio and the Sixties*. Praeger.

Ladd, Jim (1991): *Radio Waves: Life and Revolution on the FM Dial*. St Martin's Press.

Lucas, Rowland (1981): *The Voice of a Nation?* Gomer Press.

MacDonald, J. Fred (1979): *Don't Touch That Dial! Radio Programming in American Life from 1920 to 1960*. Nelson-Hall.

Madge, Tim (1989): *Beyond the BBC: Broadcasters and the Public in the 1980s*. Macmillan.

Mansell, Gerard (1982): *Let Truth Be Told: 50 Years of BBC External Broadcasting*. Weidenfeld & Nicolson.

Parker, Derek (1977): *Radio: The Great Years*. David & Charles.

Scannell, Paddy, and Cardiff, David (1991): *A Social History of British Broadcasting*, vol. 1. Blackwell.

Smith, Anthony (1976): *The Shadow in the Cave: The Broadcaster, the Audience and the State*. Quartet.

Snagge, John, and Barsley, Michael (1972): *Those Vintage Years of Radio*. Pitman.

Waller, Judith C. (1946): *Radio – The Fifth Estate*. Houghton Mifflin.

2. Studies and profiles of radio institutions and systems

Burns, Tom (1977): *The BBC: Public Institution and Private World*. Macmillan.

Carpenter, Humphrey (1996): *The Envy of the World: 50 Years of the BBC Third Programme and Radio 3*. Phoenix Giant.

Cousins, Peter and Pam (1978): *The Power of the Air: The Achievement and Future of Missionary Radio*. Hodder & Stoughton.

Crisell, Andrew (1986, 1994): *Understanding Radio*. Methuen (first edn), Routledge (second 2dn).

Curran, James, and Seaton, Jane (1985): *Power Without Responsibility: The Press and Broadcasting in Britain*. Methuen.

Euromedia Research Group (1997): *The Media in Western Europe*. Sage.

Frith, Simon (1988): *Music for Pleasure*. Polity Press.

Garfield, Simon (1998): *The Nation's Favourite: The True Adventures of Radio 1*. Faber & Faber.

Gillett, Charlie (1971): *The Sound of the City*. Sphere.

Hale, Julian (1972): *Radio Power: Propaganda and International Broadcasting*. Paul Elek.

Hetherington, Alastair (1989): *News in the Regions*. Macmillan.

Hind, John, and Mosco, Stephen (1985): *Rebel Radio: The Full Story of British Pirate Radio*. Pluto Press.

Lanza, Joseph (1995): *Elevator Music*. Quartet.

Lewis, Peter M. and Booth, Jerry (1989): *The Invisible Medium: Public, Commercial and Community Radio*. Macmillan.

Local Radio Workshop (1982): *Nothing Local About It: London's Local Radio*. Comedia.

Local Radio Workshop (1983): *Capital: Local Radio and Private Profit*. Comedia.

Nichols, Richard (1983): *Radio Luxembourg: Station of the Stars*. Comet.

O'Malley, Tom (1994): *Closedown? The BBC and Government Broadcasting Policy, 1979–92*. Pluto Press.

Partridge, Simon (1982): *Not the BBC/IBA: The Case for Community Radio*. Comedia.

Sakolsky, Ron, and Dunifer, Stephen (eds) (1998): *Seizing the Airwaves: A Free Radio Handbook*. AK Press.

Shingler, Martin, and Wieringa, Cindy (1998): *On Air: Methods and Meanings of Radio*. Arnold.

Skues, Keith (1968): *Radio Onederland*. Landmark Press.

Walker, Andrew (1992): *A Skyful of Freedom: 60 Years of the BBC World Service*. Broadside Books.

Wilson, H.H. (1961): *Pressure Group: The Campaign for Commercial Television*. Secker & Warburg.

3. Genres and programmes

Bailey, K.V. (1957): *The Listening Schools*. BBC.

Barnard, Stephen (1989): *On the Radio: Music Radio in Britain*. Open University Press.

Bates, Simon (1990): *Our Tune*. Arrow.

Cloonan, Martin (1996): *Banned! Censorship of Popular Music in Britain*. Arena.

Cohen, Stanley, and Young, Jock (eds) (1973): *The Manufacture of News: Deviance, Social Problems and the Mass Media*. Constable.

Cohen, Stanley (1980): *Folk Devils and Moral Panics*. Martin Robertson.

Donovan, Paul (1995, 1998): *All Our Todays: 40 Years of the Today Programme*. Grafton (first edn), Arrow (second edn).

Duncan, Peter (1951): *In Town Tonight*. Werner Laurie.

Foster, Andy, and Furst, Steve (1996): *Radio Comedy 1938–1968*. Virgin.

Franklin, Bob (1997): *Newszak and News Media*. Arnold.

Gielgud, Val (1946): *Radio Theatre*. Macdonald.

Hetherington, Alastair (1989): *News in the Regions: Plymouth Sound to Moray Firth*. Methuen.

Higgins, C.S., and Moss, P.D. (1982): *Sounds Real: Radio in Everyday Life*. University of Queensland Press.

Howlett, Kevin (1996): *The Beatles at the Beeb*. BBC Books.

Lazar, Roger (ed.) (1980): *From Our Own Correspondent: 25 Years of Foreign Reports*. BBC.

Leapman, Michael (1986): *The Last Days of the Beeb*. Coronet.

Limbaugh, Rush (1992): *The Way Things Ought To Be*. Pocket Books.

Manoff, Robert Karl, and Schudson, Michael (1987): *Reading the News*. Pantheon.

Milligan, Spike (1973): *The Goon Show Scripts*. Sphere.

Scannell, Paddy (ed.) (1991): *Broadcast Talk*. Sage.

Scott, Gini Graham (1996): *Can We Talk? The Power and Influence of Talk Shows*. Insight.

4. Audiences and representations

Baehr, Helen (ed.) (1980): *Women and Media*. Pergamon Press.

Baehr, Helen, and Ryan, Michele (1984): *Shut Up and Listen! Women and Local Radio*. Comedia.

Coward, Rosalind (1984): *Female Desire: Women's Sexuality Today*. Paladin.

Frith, Simon (1978): *The Sociology of Rock*. Constable.

Frith, Simon (ed.) (1988): *Facing the Music: Essays on Pop, Rock and Culture*. Mandarin.

Gibian, Peter (ed.) (1997): *Mass Culture and Everyday Life*. Routledge.

Hargrave, Andrea Millwood (1994): *Radio and Audience Attitudes*. Broadcasting Standards Council/John Libbey.

Katz, Elihu, and Lazarsfeld, Paul (1955): *Personal Influence: The Part Played by People in the Flow of Mass Communications*. New York Free Press.

Katz, E., Blumler, J.G., and Gurevitch, M. (1974): *The Uses of Mass Communication*. Sage.

Katz, E., Gurevitch, M., and Haas, H. (1973): *On the Use of Mass Media for Important Things*. American Sociological Review 38.

McQuail, Denis (1997): *Audience Analysis*. Sage.

Mitchell, Caroline (ed.) (forthcoming): *Women and Radio*. Routledge.

Silvey, Robert (1974): *Who's Listening? The Story of BBC Audience Research*. Allen & Unwin.

5. Approaches to media – essays and commentaries

Adorno, T.W. (1991): *The Culture Industry: Selected Essays on Mass Culture*. Routledge.

Benjamin, Walter (1970): *Illuminations: Essays and Reflections*. Jonathan Cape.

Bennett, Tony, et al. (eds) (1986): *Popular Culture and Social Relations*. Open University Press.

Boyd-Barrett, Oliver, and Newbold, Chris (1995): *Approaches to Media: A Reader*. Arnold.

Branston, Gill (1995): *The Media Student's Book*. Routledge.

Corner, John, and Harvey, Sylvia (1996): *Television Times: A Reader*. Arnold.

Curran, James, et al. (eds) (1977): *Mass Communication and Society*. Arnold.

Dimbleby, Richard, and Burton, Graeme (1985): *More Than Words*. Methuen.

Gurevitch, Michael, et al. (eds) (1982): *Culture, Society and the Media*. Methuen.

Hall, Stuart et al (eds) (1980): *Culture, Media, Language*. Hutchinson.

Hood, Stuart, and O'Leary, Garret (1990): *Questions of Broadcasting*. Methuen.
Ionescu, Ghita, and de Madariaga, Isabel (1968): *Opposition*. Watts.
O'Sullivan, Tim, and Jewkes, Yvonne (eds) (1997): *The Media Studies Reader*. Arnold.
Radical Science Collective (1985): *Making Waves: The Politics of Communication*. Free Association Books.
Scannell, Paddy (1996): *Radio, Television and Modern Life*. Blackwell.
Tunstall, Jeremy (ed.) (1970): *Media Sociology: A Reader*. Constable.
Waites, Bernard, et al. (1982): *Popular Culture Past and Present*. Croom Helm.
Whale, John (1977): *The Politics of the Media*. Fontana.
Williams, Raymond (1966): *Communications*. Chatto & Windus.
Williams, Raymond (1974): *Television, Technology and Cultural Form*. Fontana.

6. Biographies and memoirs

Berryman, Gwen (1981): *The Life and Death of Doris Archer*. Eyre Methuen.
Eckersley, Myles (1997): *Prospero's Wireless: A Biography of P.P. Eckersley*. Myles Books.
Gielgud, Val (1965): *Years in a Mirror*. Bodley Head.
Gorham, Maurice (1948): *Sound and Fury: 21 Years in the BBC*. Percival Marshall.
Handley, Tommy (1945): *Handley's Pages*. Stanley Paul.
Jameson, Derek (1989): *Touched by Angels*. Penguin.
McIntyre, Ian (1993): *The Expense of Glory: A Life of John Reith*. HarperCollins.
Michelmore, Cliff, and Metcalfe, Jean (1986): *Two-Way Story*. Futura.
Milne, Alasdair (1988): *DG: The Memoirs of a British Broadcaster*. Coronet.
Pickles, Wilfred (1949): *Between You and Me*. Werner Laurie.
Priestley, J.B. (1962): *Margin Released*. World Books.
Raeburn, Anna (1984): *Talking to Myself*. Sphere.
Reith, J.C.W. (1949): *Into the Wind*. Hodder & Stoughton.
Stuart, Charles (ed.) (1975): *The Reith Diaries*. Collins.
Thomas, Howard (1977): *With an Independent Air*. Weidenfeld & Nicolson.
Young, Jimmy (1973): *J.Y. Star*.

7. Media practice

Dickinson, Sarah (1990): *How to take on the Media*. Weidenfeld & Nicolson.
Gage, Linda (1999): *A Guide to Commercial Radio Journalism*. Focal Press.
Gielgud, Val (1949): *The Right Way to Radio Playwriting*. Right Way.
Halper, Donna L. (1991): *Radio Music Directing*. Focal Press.
Horstmann, Rosemary (1988): *Writing for Radio*. A & C Black.
Kaye, Michael, and Popperwell, Andrew (1992): *Making Radio: A Guide to Basic Radio Techniques*. Broadside Books.
Keith, Michael C. (1987): *Radio Programming: Consultancy and Formatics*. Focal Press.
Longmate, Norman (1988): *Writing for the BBC*. BBC.
Mather, Diana (1995): *Surviving the Media*. Thorsons.
O'Sullivan, Tim (1994): *Key Concepts in Communication and Cultural Studies*. Routledge.
Redfern, Bernie (1978): *Local Radio*. Focal Press.
Sheppard, Roy (1986): *The DJ's Handbook*. Everest.
Wilby, Pete, and Conroy, Andy (1994): *The Radio Handbook*. Routledge.

8. Miscellaneous

Donovan, Paul (1992): *The Radio Companion*. Grafton.
Hannan, Patrick (1999): *The Welsh Illusion*. Seren.
Nobbs, George (1972): *The Wireless Stars*. Wensum.
Orwell, George (ed. W.J. West) (1987): *The War Commentaries*. Penguin.
Peak, Steve, and Fisher, Paul (1999): *The Media Guide*. Fourth Estate.
Strauss, Neil (ed.) (1993): *Radiotext(e)*. Semiotext(e).
Tracy, Sheila (1983): *Who's Who on Radio*. World's Work.
Wear, Alison (ed.) (1993): *The Radio Times Yearbook*. Ravette.
Woodyear, Clive (1999): *Radio Listener's Guide*. PAQ Publishing.

Contact addresses

1. BBC radio

Web site: www.bbc.co.uk

BBC Broadcast
Broadcasting House
London W1A 1AA
Tel: 020 7580 4458

BBC Local Radio
BBC Broadcasting Centre
Pebble Mill Road
Birmingham B5 7QQ
Tel: 0121 432 8888

BBC Production
BBC Television Centre
Wood Lane
London W12 7RJ
Tel: 020 8743 8000

BBC World Service
Bush House
The Strand
London WC2B 4PH
Tel: 020 7240 3456
E-mail: worldservice.letters@bbc.co.uk

BBC Radio 1
Yalding House
London W1A 1AA
Tel: 020 7765 4575
Web site: www.bbc.co.uk/radio1/

BBC Radio 2
Western House
London W1A 1AA
Tel: 020 7765 4330
Web site: www.bbc.co.uk/radio2/

BBC Radio 3
Broadcasting House
London W1A 1AA
Tel: 020 7765 2722
Web site: www.bbc.co.uk/radio3/

BBC Radio 4
Broadcasting House
London W1A 1AA
Tel: 020 7765 5337
Web site: www.bbc.co.uk/radio4/

BBC Radio 5 Live
Room 4094
Broadcasting House
London W1A 1AA
Tel: 020 8225 8761
Web site: www.bbc.co.uk/radio5live/

2. Commercial radio groups, UK

Border Radio Holdings Ltd
Border Television plc
The Television Centre
Carlisle CA1 3NT
Tel: 01228 525101

Capital Radio plc
29–30 Leicester Square
London WC2H 7LE
Tel: 020 7766 6000
Web site: www.capitalradio.co.uk

Chrysalis Group plc
The Chrysalis Building
Bramley Road
London W10 6SP
Tel: 020 7221 2213

EMAP Radio
97 Tottenham Court Road
London W1P 9HF
Tel: 020 7504 6200
Web site: www.emap.co.uk

Essex Radio Group
Radio House
Clifftown Road
Southend-on-Sea SS1 1SX
Tel: 01702 333711
E-mail: general@essexradio.co.uk

GWR Radio plc
PO Box 2345
Westlea
Swindon SN5 7HF
Tel: 0118 928 4300
E-mail: reception@essexradio.co.uk

Independent Radio Group plc
The Lodge
Orrell Road
Wigan WN5 8HJ
Tel: 01942 777 7666

The Local Radio Company Ltd
Close Gate House
47 High Street
Salisbury SP1 2QF
Tel: 01722 41588

Marcher Radio Group
The Studios
Mold Road
Wrexham LL11 4AF
Tel: 01978 752202
Web site: www.mfmradio.co.uk
E-mail: sales@mfmradio.co.uk

Orchard Media Ltd
Hawthorn House
Exeter Business Park
Exeter EX1 3QS
Tel: 01392 444444

The Radio Partnership Ltd
7 Diamond Court
Kenton
Newcastle upon Tyne NE3 2EN
Tel: 0191 286 0000
E-mail: trp@onyxnet.co.uk

Scottish Radio Holdings plc
Clydebank Business Park
Clydebank
Glasgow G81 2RX
Tel: 0141 565 2202
E-mail: radio@srh.co.uk

UKRD Group Ltd
Dolphin House
North Street
Guildford GU1 4AA
Tel: 01483 306156
E-mail: enquiries@ukrd.com

3. National commercial radio stations, UK

Atlantic 252
74 Newman St
London W1P 3LA
Tel: 020 7436 4012
E-mail: programming@atlantic252.com

Classic FM
Classic FM House
7 Swallow Place
London W1R 7AA
Web site: www.classicfm.co.uk
E-mail: enquiries@classicfm.co.uk

Talk Radio
76 Oxford Street
London W1N OTR
Web site: www.talk-radio.co.uk

Virgin
1 Golden Square
London W1R 4DJ
Tel: 020 7434 1215
Web site: www.virginradio.co.uk
E-mail: virgin@vradio.co.uk

4. Radio industry and related organizations

Advertising Association
Abford House
15 Wilton Road
London SW1V 1NJ
Tel: 020 7826 2771
Web site: www.adassoc.org.uk/

Advertising Standards Authority
2 Torrington Place
London WC1E 7HN
Tel: 020 7580 5555
Web site: www.asa.org.uk/

British Library National Sound Archive
96 Euston Road
London NW1 2DB
Tel: 020 7412 7440
Web site: www.bl.uk/collections/sound-archive/service.html

Broadcasters Audience Research Board (BARB)
Glenthorne House
Hammersmith Grove
London W6 0ND
Tel: 020 8741 9110

Broadcasting, Entertainment, Cinematograph and Theatre Union (BECTU)
111 Wardour Street
London W1V 4AY
Tel: 020 7437 8506
Web site: www.bectu.org.uk/info/about.html
E-mail: bectu@geo2.poptel.org.uk

Broadcasting Standards Commission
5–8 The Sanctuary
London SW1P 3JS
Tel: 020 7233 0544
Web site: www.bsc.org.uk

Campaign for Press and Broadcasting Freedom
8 Cynthia Street
London N1 9JF
Tel: 020 7278 4430
Web site: www.cpbf.demon.co.uk/
E-mail: freepress@cpbf.demon.co.uk

Commercial Radio Companies Association
77 Shaftesbury Avenue
London W1V 7AD
Web site: www.crca.co.uk
E-mail: info@crca.co.uk

Community Media Association
15 Paternoster Row
Sheffield S1 2BX
Tel: 0114 2795219
Web site: www.commedia.org.uk
E-mail: cma@commedia.org.uk

European Broadcasting Union
17a Ancienne Route
PO Box 67
CH-1218 Grand Saconnex
Switzerland
Tel: +41 22 717 2111
Web site: www.ebu.ch/welcome.html

Mechanical Copyright Protection Society (MCPS)
Broadcast Scheme Dept
Copyright House
29–33 Berners Street
London W1P 4AA
Tel: 020 7306 4050
Web site: www.mcps.co.uk/

Musicians Union
60 Clapham Road
London SW9 OJJ
Tel: 020 7582 5566
Web site: www.musiciansunion.org.uk/

National Association of Hospital Broadcasting
PO Box 2481
London W2 1JR
Tel: 020 7402 8815
Web site: www.nahbo.demon.co.uk/

National Union of Journalists
314 Grays Inn Road
London WC1X 8DP
Tel: 020 7278 7916
Web site: www.gn.apc.org/media/nuj

Performing Right Society
(address/telephone as MCPS)
Web site: www.prs.co.uk

Phonographic Performance Ltd
1 Upper James Street
London W1R 3HG
Web site: www.webkraft.org/Ppl/

The Radio Academy
5 Market Place
London W1N 7AH
Tel: 020 7255 2010
Web site: www.radioacademy.org

Radio Advertising Bureau
77 Shaftesbury Avenue
London W1V 7AD
Tel: 020 7306 2500
Web site: www.rab.co.uk
E-mail: rab@rab.co.uk

The Radio Authority
Holbrook House
14 Great Queen Street
London WC2B 5DG
Tel: 020 7430 2724
Web site: www.radioauthority.org.uk

Radio Communications Agency
Wyndham House
189 Marsh Wall
London E14 9SX
Tel: 020 7211 0211
Web site: www.radio.gov.uk
E-mail: library@rad.gtnet.gov.uk

Radio Independents Organisation
PO Box 14880
London NW1 9ZD
Tel: 020 7485 0873

Radio Joint Audience Research (RAJAR)
Collier House
163–169 Brompton Road
London SW3 1PY
Tel: 020 7584 3003
Web site: www.rajar.co.uk
E-mail: rajar@dial.pipex.com

Radio Studies Network
c/o Peter Lewis
London School of Economics and Political Science
Houghton Street
London WC2A 2AE
Web site: www.mailbase.ac.uk/lists/radio-studies

Scottish Association of Smallscale Broadcasters
Struan House
The Square
Aberfeldy
Perthshire PH15 2DD
Tel: 0131 332 8270
E-mail: wwright@sol.co.uk

Student Radio Association
(address/telephone as Radio Academy)
Web site: www.studentradio.orguk/8080/
E-mail: sra-exec@studentradio.org.uk

UK Digital Radio Forum
Fourth Floor
Landseer House
19 Charing Cross Road
London W1V 7AD
Tel: 020 7753 0348
Web site: www.digital-radio.org

Voice of the Listener and Viewer
101 King's Drive
Gravesend DA12 5BQ
Tel: 01474 352835
E-mail: vlv@btinternet.com

5. Training organizations

BBC Centre for Broadcast Skills Training
Wood Norton
Evesham WR11 4YB
Tel: 01386 420216
Web site: www.bbc.co.uk/woodnorton

Broadcast Journalism Training Council
39 Westbourne Gardens
London W2 5NR
Tel: 020 7727 9522
Web site: www.bjtc.org.uk

National Training Organisation for Broadcast, Film, Video and Multimedia
(Skillset)
91–101 Oxford Street
London W1R 1RA
Tel: 020 7306 8585
Web site: www.skillset.org
E-mail: info@skillset.org

The Radio School
7–9 The Broadway
Newbury RG14 1AS
Tel: 01635 232800
Web site: www.radioschool.co.uk

Women's Radio Group
90 de Beauvoir Road
London N1 4EN
Tel: 020 7241 3729
Web site: www.twiza.demon.co.uk.org
E-mail: wrg@twiza.demon.co.uk

6. Publications

Broadcast
33–39 Bowling Green Lane
London EC1R ODA
Tel: 020 7505 8014
E-mail: bcast@media.emap.co.uk

Media, Culture and Society
6 Bonhill Street
London EC2A 4PU
Tel: 020 7374 0645
Web site: www.sagepb.co.uk
E-mail: market@sagepub.co.uk

Media Education Journal
74 Victoria Crescent Road
Glasgow G12 9JN
Tel: 0141 334 4445

On Air
Room 227 NW
Bush House
The Strand
London WC2B 4PH
Web site: www.bbc.co.uk/worldservice/onair
E-mail: on.air.magazine@bbc.co.uk

The Radio Magazine
Crown House
25 High Street
Rothwell NN14 6AD
Tel: 01536 418558
Web site: www.theradiomagazine.co.uk
E-mail: radiomagazine.goldcrestbroadcasting@btinternet.com

Index